1992

The Political Aesthetic of Yeats, Eliot, and Pound

The politics of Yeats, Eliot, and Pound have long been a source of discomfort and difficulty for literary critics and cultural historians. In *The Political Aesthetic of Yeats, Eliot, and Pound,* Michael North offers a subtle reading of these issues by linking aesthetic modernism with an attempt in all these writers to resolve basic contradictions in modern liberalism. The many contradictions of modernism, which is seen as inwardly personal and yet impersonal, subjective and yet beholden to tradition, fragmented and yet whole, mark the reappearance in art of these political contradictions. Though Yeats, Eliot, and Pound certainly attempted to resolve in art problems that could not be resolved in actuality, their very attempt resulted in a politicized aesthetic, one that confessed their inability to do so. Yet this aesthetic retained an element of critical power, precisely because it could not cover up the political contradictions that concerned it; the poetry remains a valid criticism of the status quo and even in its failure suggests the beginnings of an alternative. The book includes accounts of the political activities of the three writers, reinterpretations of their critical theories in light of their politics, and a rereading of some of their major works, including *The Tower, The Waste Land,* and the *Pisan Cantos.*

The Political Aesthetic of Yeats, Eliot, and Pound

MICHAEL NORTH
University of California, Los Angeles

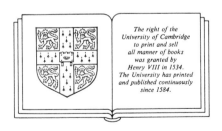

The right of the
University of Cambridge
to print and sell
all manner of books
was granted by
Henry VIII in 1534.
The University has printed
and published continuously
since 1584.

CAMBRIDGE UNIVERSITY PRESS

Cambridge

New York   Port Chester   Melbourne   Sydney

Published by the Press Syndicate of the University of Cambridge
The Pitt Building, Trumpington Street, Cambridge CB2 1RP
40 West 20th Street, New York, NY 10011, USA
10 Stamford Road, Oakleigh, Melbourne 3166, Australia

First published 1991

Printed in Canada

Library of Congress Cataloging-in-Publication Data
North, Michael, 1951–
    The political aesthetic of Yeats, Eliot, and Pound / Michael
North.
        p.   cm.
    Includes bibliographical references and index.
    ISBN 0-521-41432-6
    1. Political poetry, American – History and criticism.   2. Politics
and literature – United States – History – 20th century.   3. Politics
and literature – Ireland – History – 20th century.   4. Political
poetry, English – History and criticism.   5. Yeats, W.B. (William
Butler), 1865–1939 – Political and social views.   6. Eliot, T.S.
(Thomas Stearns), 1888–1965 – Political and social views.   7. Pound,
Ezra, 1885–1972 – Political and social views.   I. Title.
PS310.P6N6   1992
821'.91209358 – dc20   91-27277
                                                              CIP

A catalog record for this book is available from the British Library.

ISBN 0-521-41432-6 hardback

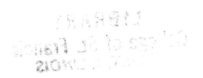

Contents

143,045

Preface and Acknowledgments

Readers of Walter Benjamin will recognize a polemical assertion in the title of this book. Benjamin defines fascism as the aestheticization of politics, and it is now quite common to suggest that Yeats, Eliot, and Pound are fascists in this general sense even if they were not all card-carrying members of a fascist party. If the aestheticization of politics is the attempt to resolve in art contradictions that are really economic or political, then the charge against these three is a just one. But it is my contention that the very attempt to resolve economic or political contradictions, instead of just leaving them out of art altogether, inevitably politicizes the aesthetic. That is to say, the smooth workings of art are disrupted by what it cannot resolve. This is the case, I think, with Yeats, Eliot, and Pound, who, precisely because of their failure, are more faithful to the real conflicts of our century than many writers whose politics we now find easier to accept.

I am interested, therefore, in what these three poets have to say *about* political issues, but I am even more interested in the presence of politics as a disruptive force in the formal organization of their works. I think it is necessary to be quite specific about the particular political allegiances of the three, which were actually quite different from one another, but it is not my purpose to offer extended biographical accounts. Rather, I want to concentrate on the way specific political choices, such as Yeats's allegiance to the Anglo-Irish Ascendancy or Pound's to Mussolini, entail difficult poetic choices as well. The relationship of the individual to the community, of literature to practical action, of the individual parts of a work of art to its overall structure – these are problems the poets tried to solve simultaneously and by the same means, so that practical conflicts and theoretical difficulties emerge as formal problems in the poetry.

It is my hope that what I have to say here will affect current opinion about literary modernism in general. A movement like modernism can survive and even thrive as long as it is hated and despised, but it may not be able to outlive the indifference that follows acceptance. Nowadays, modernism, which tried so hard to shock, is simply taken for granted, dismissed before it has a chance to be disliked. Those critics who think it important to show that modernism makes good sense unwittingly conspire with their opponents, who need a bland caricature to set up as a straw man. I feel that modernism still has a claim on our interest precisely because it does not make good sense, because we find in it more of the unfinished business of our time than in any other literature. This is one explanation for my choice of examples. It is not possible to argue that the politics of Yeats, Eliot, and Pound are typical of a movement that also includes Joyce and Woolf, but I hope that more can be learned from the most extreme cases or, to instance Pound alone, the most extreme failures.

If modernism has become something of a dead issue in literary discussions, modernity is a very live one wherever the Frankfurt School and Jürgen Habermas have any influence. I think that these debates have great relevance for the study of literary modernism, not least because of the very strong resemblances between the founders of the Frankfurt School, who operated overtly on the left, and the right-wing poets who are my subjects. Theorists like Lukács and Adorno figure very largely in my analysis, but this does not seem to me an "application" of a critical theory to an inert body of texts. German theorists and American and Irish poets share a common meditation on the problem of modernity, so much so that I think that Eliot can tell us as much about Lukács as Lukács tells us about Eliot. If, as Habermas has famously suggested, modernity is an unfinished project, then literary modernism is both a spectacular example of modernity's unrealized promise and a theoretical investigation of the causes of that failure.

I was aided in the writing of this book by a series of grants from the UCLA Academic Senate Committee on Research. I would like to thank Kristin Leuschner and Rob Sproul for their help as research assistants.

A number of colleagues and friends have read portions of the book in manuscript. I would especially like to thank Ronald Bush for his helpful advice at several different stages. Calvin Bedient and Stephen Yenser also offered a number of suggestions without which this would have been a far less successful work. Finally, I owe a general debt of gratitude to Marjorie Perloff and Edward Mendelson for their help and encouragement over a number of years.

Introduction

The politics of Yeats, Eliot, and Pound have long been an embarrassment and a scandal. Yeats's authoritarianism, Eliot's prejudices, and Pound's fascist anti-Semitism have presented sympathetic critics with insuperable problems of explanation.[1] The poetry is often saved from contamination by being placed in quarantine, while the growing number of critics hostile to the poetry can easily condemn it by association. Arguments about whether Yeats and Eliot were or were not fascists – about Pound there is little room for doubt – continue as if under a similar obligation to the either-or, simply because the question seems too serious to permit any vacillation.[2] The hope behind this book is that both the politics of these three poets and the relationship of politics to their poetry can be understood better if the either-or can be avoided, not just where fascism is concerned, but also where aesthetic modernism touches modern politics in general.

Faith in a coherent and unified modernity – one in which enlightenment brings material progress, political freedom, and cultural renaissance – is now so quaint as to seem pre-modern. The most that is now claimed for modernity, even by its strongest remaining supporters, is that it is "an incomplete project."[3] Even the ironic hopefulness of Schiller and Hegel is outmoded, as is the dialectical faith of Marx that the evils of modernity would call up their own solution. The only real quarrel is over where to lay the blame for the failure of modernity: on technology, on liberal democracy, on cultural modernism, or on enlightenment itself.[4]

The aesthetic modernism of the late nineteenth and early twentieth centuries is part of this quarrel. Aesthetic modernism is at once part of the larger modern project of enlightenment, emancipation, and progress and a reaction against that project. E.J. Hobsbawm claims that until the twentieth century "there was no general rift between political and artistic 'modernity.' "[5] By the beginning of the century, however, the rift visible at least as early as Baudelaire had become "general," so that aesthetic

·modernism could be defined by its antagonism to the other elements of modernity: rationalism, material progress, liberal democracy.[6] Even artists and writers who seemed most enthusiastically modern – boosters of technology such as Marinetti – were in fact using one aspect of the modern to declare war on all the rest.

By 1939, W.H. Auden could summarize in one paragraph what had become a familiar indictment:

> The most obvious social fact of the last forty years is the failure of liberal capitalist democracy, based on the premises that every individual is born free and equal, each an absolute entity independent of all others; and that a formal political equality, the right to vote, the right to a fair trial, the right of free speech, is enough to guarantee his freedom of action in his relations with his fellow men. The results are only too familiar to us all. By denying the social nature of personality, and by ignoring the social power of money, it has created the most impersonal, the most mechanical and the most unequal civilisation the world has ever seen, a civilisation in which the only emotion common to all classes is a feeling of individual isolation from everyone else, a civilisation torn apart by the opposing emotions born of economic injustice, the just envy of the poor and the selfish terror of the rich.[7]

The promise of modern political movements to win individual freedom and self-fulfillment for all had come to seem a hollow form; the rights and freedoms guaranteed by liberalism seemed mere abstractions, blank checks that could never be filled in or cashed.[8] One source of the power of aesthetic modernism was its implicit claim to effect the liberation that liberal democracy had promised but failed to deliver.[9] Even a reactionary modernism could seem vital in contrast to the ossified remnants of a failed system, and it was reactionaries like Marinetti who promised the most thorough and the most thrilling revolutions. When Ezra Pound called liberalism "a running sore," or when T.S. Eliot complained that his society was "worm-eaten with Liberalism," they joined the attack on a system that had come to epitomize the failure of modernity.[10]

Reactionary critics like Eliot and Pound identified in liberalism the same weakness that Auden had found: the misconception that the individual is "an absolute entity independent of all others." In classical political theory, freedom was a social concept, the freedom to participate in the community. Modern, liberal conceptions of freedom are in contrast subjective and personal. Freedom means the absence of external constraint.[11] This difference in the concept of freedom, of the proper relationship between individual and society, implies a new definition of the two terms of the relationship. But this new definition is in a sense no definition at all, because the individual who is to be free of constraint must also be independent of all influence and prior to all purpose. This theoretical individual has no particular character, no goals, no inclinations except the fulfillment of a self that seems to lack anything specific to fulfill. Like this individual, the community defined by liberal theory is a neutral arena in which different goods contend according to certain rules. Separating the individual from the community thus results in the removal of particular social or moral values from the realm of politics. Therefore, the formalism that Auden criticizes is not part of the decline of liberalism but is in fact the very essence and origin of a system that specifies forms but not ends, procedures but not particular values.[12]

The paradoxical result of such abstract, formal notions of individual freedom is, as Auden argues, "a civilisation in which the only emotion common to all classes is a feeling of individual isolation from everyone else." Hegel argued, at the very birth of modern politics, that liberal formalism is inherently oppressive, that the promise of individual freedom is shadowed by its opposite. If the community embodies no particular good except the freedom of the individuals within it, then the state is internally inconsistent and oppressive by definition, because it can only enforce its laws by abridging the freedom that is its end. If the only means of influencing individuals is by force or appeal to self-interest, then authority can only be coercive or manipulative.[13] As Jürgen Habermas puts it, the law of freedom "is *also* a law of coercion. The inverse of private autonomy, to which this law secures the right, is the psychological motivation of coercion, of obedience."[14]

Hegel felt that the modern state mitigated this contradiction by including a number of agencies that rightly mediated between the individual and society as a whole, but Marx argued that these agencies merely confessed the very split they were supposed to mediate. For Marx, in his early critique of Hegel, the liberal attempt to guarantee freedom by investing rights in an abstract individual thwarts itself by allowing only an abstract collective: "The abstraction of the state as such belongs only to modern times because the abstraction of private life belongs only to modern times." Thus Marx begins his attack on bourgeois society by complaining that "allness remains merely an external plurality or totality of individuals. Allness is no essential spiritual, actual quality of the individual [but] merely the sum total of individuality."[15] Bourgeois society is characterized by a gap between the concrete individual and his or her theoretical counterpart and thus by a similar gap between a collective that depends on real, concrete beliefs or interests and a purely formal, abstract collective.

Thus the complaint, especially common among Marxists, that despite its promise of individual freedom, modern society is less open to variation and change than more traditional societies. Individualism itself becomes a principle of conformity, as Horkheimer and Adorno charge: "Men were given their individuality as unique in each case, different to all others, so that it might all the more surely be made the same as any other."[16] What looks like the promise of individual freedom becomes, because of its abstract nature, a means of eliminating differences and even of enforcing conformity. At the same time, the purely formal equivalence of individuals within the system destroys old associations without replacing them with anything meaningful. Thus it is also argued that if liberalism frees the individual at all it is only to integrate him or her more completely into the machine of industrial capitalism where workers, like the parts they manipulate, must be interchangeable. In short, a political theory based on the formal opposition of individual and community devalues both and mocks its own promise by destroying community without truly setting the individual free.[17]

The anti-liberal reaction of such as Yeats, Eliot, and Pound can be characterized best by the inconsistencies it suffers in trying to oppose this contradictory system. The three seem allies in a program of anti-individualism, a critique of a philosophical and political theory that, in Yeats's words, "separates us from one another because it makes us always more unlike. . . . " Here is the condition that calls forth Yeats's Irish nationalism, Eliot's concept of tradition, and Pound's celebrations of "the whole people" against critics and schismatics. And yet, within a few years of his complaint against excessive differentiation, Yeats criticized the same system for making human beings "as like one another as the dots and lozenges in . . . mechanical engraving." Eliot and Pound could also speak as committed individualists, proclaiming, against standardization, that "the truth is the individual."[18] Confusion persists about modernism, which can seem both impersonal and idiosyncratic, because the major modernists themselves held contradictory opinions.

Behind this contradiction lie the contradictions of liberalism and the consequent necessity to attack it from two sides at once, to defend both the individual and community. The three poets share an aspiration to disentangle actual individuals from theoretical individualism, "the variety and uniqueness of persons," as Eliot put it, from the "purely material individuation" of liberal democracy. They argue for what Pound called individualism "without any theoretical and ideological bulwarks." This would also disentangle the individual from the "artificial, mechanised or brutalised control" that Eliot saw as a reflex of the liberal system.[19] At the same time, the connection that all three saw between "liberal individualism" and "inhuman capitalism" would be broken, and society returned to a time before the French Revolution had "left the French peasant at the mercy of the capitalist," as Yeats said, quoting Kropotkin.[20] Instead of capitalism, with its merely mechanical organization, and liberalism, with its formal guarantees, the three hoped to achieve a community based on shared values. Finally, they attempted to reverse the specious separation of individual and community with which all the other contradictions began. If liberalism had devalued both individual and community, anti-liberals like Yeats, Eliot, and Pound hoped for a system in which "the wholly personal" would be connected to a "multitude now and in past time."[21]

According to Russell Berman, "Modernist anti-liberalism was regularly directed at the failures of a progressivist liberal project, leading in turn either to a rejection of that project (fascist modernism) or its radicalization on the left."[22] Yeats, Eliot, and Pound certainly seem to belong in Berman's first group, and yet anti-liberalism cannot be divided so neatly into left and right. The theoretical distribution that puts Marxism on one side and fascism on the other, with liberalism as a mean between them, ignores certain historical facts. From the time of Hegel, left and right have shared a common antagonist in liberalism. Karl Mannheim asserts that the critique of capitalism and liberal democracy was "initiated by the 'right-wing opposition' and that it was only subsequently transferred from here to the designs of the 'left-wing' opposition."[23] In other words, the liberal system first antagonized an entrenched status quo, which developed in conservative terms a critique later adapted to more radical uses. The attack on industrial capitalism and liberal democracy as atomizing, demeaning, and dehumanizing, and the corresponding search for an organic system of social relations are, as Raymond Williams has shown, common "both in this kind of conservative thinking and in Marxist thinking. The common enemy (or, if it is preferred, the common defender of the true faith) is Liberalism."[24]

Fascism cannot be placed securely on one side of the spectrum because it is the explosive coalescence of the left and right wings of anti-liberal thought. In France, according to Zeev Sternhell, fascism was the result of "the shift to the right of elements that were socially advanced but fundamentally opposed to liberal democracy."[25] In Italy, fascism emerged from a socialist labor movement, and it was invented and named by the former socialist Benito Mussolini. The foremost English fascist, Sir Oswald Mosley, had been a member of Ramsay MacDonald's Labour cabinet. Even in Germany, certain proto-Nazis took quite seriously the coalition of nationalism and socialism that gave the party its name. Spengler, for example, was capable of identifying the "old style Prussian spirit and socialist values."[26] Fascism appealed to European intellectuals in part because it seemed to resolve into one doctrine all the available modes of opposition to the liberal status quo and in this way to rise above politics and merely political disagreements.

There are, of course, obvious differences between left-wing and right-wing critiques of liberalism. Conservatives attack liberalism in the name of the past and long to return to it, whereas Marxists base their critique on the hope of a better future. And yet, in the years between the two world wars, it was often the right that seized the future for its slogans, especially the far right in Germany and Italy, where fascism posed as a "young" movement against a moribund left.[27] The radical right also proved adept at using the sort of egalitarian language usually considered more proper to the left. And both wings were inspired by sociological arguments that human beings are not primarily motivated by reason or even by self-interest but rather by ideology.[28] Conservatives defend something called culture, whereas the left speaks in terms of class or totality, but both groups diverge from liberalism, as Williams says, in being "unable to think of society as a merely neutral area, or as an abstract regulating mechanism. The stress has fallen on the positive function of society, on the fact that the values of individual men are rooted in society, and on the need to think and feel in these common terms."[29] Here the left and the right converge, in skepticism about the neutral, freely choosing individual of liberalism, in homage to the idea that individuals are inescapably members of a given society.

In the various movements that make up aesthetic modernism, the left and the right are similarly mixed. In England, the arts and crafts movement housed both socialists like Crane and Ashbee and conservatives like Voysey and Lutyens.[30] In Germany, the same ambiguity persisted into the 1920s, when the Deutsche Werkbund planned an exhibition to celebrate the *Neue Zeit* that was to include socialist, National Socialist, and *Völkisch* sympathizers.[31] There were similar cases in France, where the architectural projects of Le Corbusier and Walter Gropius and the art of Fernand Léger were featured in the proto-fascist journal *Plans* along with the writings of Drieu La Rochelle.[32] The crusading zeal of aesthetic modernism, its promise to overcome a stultified society and make with the tools of art a new future, was equally available to the left and the right.

Much of this ambiguity survives in the political beliefs of the great Irish, English, and American modernists. Yeats began his active political career as a socialist under the influence of Morris, whose anti-capitalism, Elizabeth Cullingford suggests, may have created Yeats's later interest in the anti-capitalism of the fascists.[33] Eliot, whose version of tradition is often cited by left-wing critics as definitive of modernist totalitarianism, said as late as 1936 that "the traditional poet will be submissive, reactionary or revolutionary according to his perception of the need of his time and place."[34] Before throwing in his lot with Mussolini, Pound flirted with the thought of Lenin, and submitted himself to the tutelage of Mike Gold and *The Masses*.[35] Perhaps the most spectacular expression of this ambiguity comes from Wyndham Lewis, who defined his position in 1928 as "partly communist and partly fascist, with a distinct streak of monarchism in my marxism, but at bottom anarchist with a healthy passion for order."[36] Lewis is no doubt posing for effect, but there was enough radical criticism even in the most authoritarian modernists to lead the next generation, Auden's generation, into the Communist Party. As Stephen Spender says, "the younger generation, in coming to their revolutionary conclusions, owed their view that we were in a revolutionary situation to the insights of the reactionaries."[37]

Young Englishmen might be led into the Communist Party by their reading of *The Waste Land,* as Spender insists they were, because the portrayal of modern society contained in that poem strongly resembled one being developed at the same time by European Marxists. Ten days after Eliot's poem was first published, Georg Lukács wrote the introduction to a group of essays called *History and Class Consciousness.* These essays were perhaps the most thorough exposition ever written of the crisis of liberalism, the contradictions in its philosophy, and its implication in the development of capitalism. Lukács argued that once bourgeois thought takes "the purely inward freedom of individual moral practice" as its basic value a whole series of oppositions opens up within it: "between subject and object, freedom and necessity, individual and society, form and content, etc." If the general can only be considered in opposition to the particular, the social in opposition to the individual, then "reality disintegrates into a multitude of irrational facts and over these a network of purely formal 'laws' emptied of content is then cast." Whatever commonality there is in such a system appears only as an alien imposition, an abstract and seemingly impersonal law, that can only rule over but not truly unify the individuals within it. Liberal individualism, that is, comes accompanied by an iron control: "The atomisation of the individual is, then, only the reflex in consciousness of the fact that 'natural laws' of capitalist production have been extended to cover every manifestation of life in society. . . . " With this basically Hegelian analysis, Lukács uncannily recreated the early philosophical writings of Marx, with which he could not have been familiar at the time.[38]

History and Class Consciousness began a new movement within European Marxism, which had duplicated within itself the crisis of modernity. As Eugene Lunn says, the failure of working class solidarity during the First World War, the defeat of the European working class revolutions that followed it, and the subsequent rise of fascism presented European Marxism with a critical challenge. The "rationalist and confident assumptions about the course of history" that Marx had shared with bourgeois liberals were called into question. The mechanistic philosophy of the Second International seemed as defunct as liberalism, and for many of the same reasons. The twin emphases represented in Lukács's title, history and consciousness, restored to Marxism elements removed by a materialistic, scientistic, and determinist dogma. Lukács's was in this sense perhaps a conservative revolution within Marxism, as he felt himself in later years, a turn away from objective modes of analysis and prediction, away from the side of Marx that welcomed capitalist development as a prelude to communism, and toward an anti-capitalism that was romantic and idealist. Yet the Marxism of the Second International suffered in its own way from the same rigidities and bifurcations as liberal democracy, the Lukács's work represented the Marxist version of the revolt against its contradictions.[39]

The philosophical ambition to overcome the oppositions Lukács identifies was, of course, a general one. It is not pure coincidence, therefore, that Eliot's years as an academic philosopher were spent worrying out this relationship. The conclusion of his dissertation, that there is no absolute point of view from which to distinguish between subjective and objective, is the result of an epistemological skepticism, but it also sketches the beginnings of a value judgment on which Eliot would base a political position. In 1916, the same year in which he finished the dissertation that declared his inability to distinguish between individual minds and the objective world, Eliot delivered a series of lectures that castigated ·Romanticism for attempting to do just this. Romanticism led its devotees into two contradictory extremes, "escape from the world of fact, and devotion to brute fact," or, in other words, solipsistic idealism and utter realism. The classicism Eliot was just beginning to promote at this time was an attempt to overcome this dichotomy, and Eliot was well aware that his solution bore a strong resemblance to other solutions chosen by the left.[40]

Though Pound and Yeats were much less sophisticated philosophers, they worked in their own ways to resolve the same dichotomies. About the time Eliot delivered his lectures, Pound denounced "state education" for turning its students into mere compilers of data, of details that can only be unified by massive abstract generalizations. The state behind such education, Pound suggests, treats its citizens in the same way, reducing them to mere ants but also herding them together into ant heaps, rationalizing their lives but removing all "human value" from its "rationalistic explanations."[41] In the same year Yeats began the occult investigations that were to arrange in interpenetrating cones beauty and truth, value and fact, particular and universal, quality and quantity, abstract and concrete. From its very beginnings in the automatic script of Yeats's wife, this project was also a political one because Yeats tended to see democracy as the ultimate fall into contradiction of individual and race, and the aristocracy as the fruitful balance of these as contraries. Years later, Yeats was to trace both communism and fascism to Hegel's attempt to reconcile these contraries, bequeathed to him by Kant. Yeats plotted out modern politics on what he called the "Genealogical Tree of Revolution," on which he hung communism and fascism as the fruits of Hegel's philosophy. In this way, Yeats's "Genealogical Tree of Revolution" duplicates Lukács, even as it arranges Lukács's communism as a parallel movement to the fascism then engaging Yeats himself.[42]

Despite Lukács's antagonism toward aesthetic modernism, an antagonism that obscured his own early enthusiasm for certain of the modern movements, there was, therefore, a strong similarity between the Western Marxism that followed *History and Class Consciousness* and even the sort of modernism practiced by Yeats, Eliot, and Pound.[43] This unexpected convergence might be explained in a number of ways. There may be no coincidence in the fact that Lukács and the three poets made their concurrent analyses of the contradictions of modern politics in the years around 1917, for modern politics had by then spectacularly collapsed and a whole host of theories, which had yet to be securely divided into left and right, rose up in explanation. Lukács had come to Marxism from a much more conservative anti-capitalism, which deplored modern society for the mortal wounds it had dealt to culture. This kind of romantic anti-capitalism is also strong in Yeats, who hoped that Ireland might avoid the capitalist phase altogether, in Pound, with his vehement hatred of unproductive, mercantile capitalism, and even in Eliot, whose work, according to F. O. Matthiessen, grew out of "his revulsion against the lawless exploitation by which late nineteenth-century American individuals made any coherent society impossible."[44] *History and Class Consciousness* marked a return to Marxism of this romantic strain, present in Marx himself but purged from the movement by the Second International.[45] Its return made possible an unacknowledged anti-modern convergence, in which both left and right decried the effects of liberal theory and capitalist practice.

The elements of a common aspiration, if not a common project, can be made fairly clear. Lukács hoped to counteract empiricism and abstraction through history, through a context in which "the opposition of the individual case and historical law is dissolved." In political terms, this meant rejoining the individual and the community, separated by definition in liberal theory. If, as Lukács asserts, "historical knowledge is an act of self-knowledge," then the purely contemplative relationship of individual to history is broken and "the 'contingent' relation of the parts to the whole" is dissolved. History becomes an act of self-consciousness that is simultaneously the awareness of solidarity with a community.[46]

This aspiration is shared even by the most reactionary of the modernists. Eliot's criticism rests, as Richard Shusterman has recently shown, on a belief in "the historicity of human knowledge," a belief so close to that of Lukács in spirit that Lee Congdon takes a passage from "Tradition and the Individual Talent" to gloss his discussion of *History and Class Consciousness*.[47] In the same year in which Lukács published this work, Yeats declared his own "substitution of the historical sense for logic." He was raising the reactionary banner against democracy, but his terms and his values echoed Lukács's nonetheless. When Pound attacked what he called *Kultur* because it separated particular facts from general principles, and when he attempted to heal this split with a revived sense of history, he also participated in this politically ambidextrous attack on the "antinomies of bourgeois thought."[48]

Yeats, Eliot, and Pound incorporate history in their work as part of this attack. They deploy history, as Lukács did, as a militant value against liberal democracy and capitalism. History, in this sense, is at once the alternative to discrete facts and to empty generalizations, to scientism, positivism, and the liberal version of natural law. It disputes the existence of a theoretical individual separable from the human community and makes community life dependent on specific values instead of timeless laws.

The modern turn to history as an antidote to liberalism recapitulates an antagonism older than liberalism itself, one that extends back to Winckelmann, Vico, and Herder.[49] Vico's attack on the doctrine of natural law, in which he called into question "the existence of a fixed, unchanging human nature, common to all men, everywhere, at all times," became the basis for a whole tradition.[50] The tradition was developed by Hegel, especially in the essay *Natural Law,* in which he challenges the liberal concept of "man in the image of the bare state of nature" as an artificial separation of the individual from a particular history and community.[51] Hegel's influence is clear in Marx, who attacks capitalism for presenting itself as an ahistorical system operating on the basis of timeless laws, in Croce, who sets history against the "abstract rationalism of the Enlightenment," and finally in Lukács and his successors in Western Marxism.[52]

As this list of names may indicate, the historicism that begins with Vico is adaptable to a variety of political uses. Dependent as it is on a notion of cultural unity, this kind of historicism can be attacked as conformist and even authoritarian.[53] Originally, however, it was part of the assertion of "national individuality," of regional and even local difference against a uniform definition of humankind.[54] Georg Iggers says of eighteenth-century historicism that it was bound up with the "attempts of political theorists to defend local rights and privileges against the encroachment of the centralizing Enlightenment state."[55] In this sense and at this time, historicism is a conservative protest against progressive amalgamation of region into nation and nation into an undifferentiated humankind.

An emphasis on historical particularity is conservative and even anti-modern insofar as it opposes liberal derivations of right from nature with rights based on custom. In this sense, according to Mannheim, "historical thinking" itself is anti-revolutionary, born as it is in opposition to the realization of natural law in the French Revolution.[56] In vesting rights not in the individual but in the family, the region, or even the state, historicism is fundamentally anti-democratic.[57] Even historicist opposition to the state can have repressive implications if it seeks to replace the state with a restrictively defined culture or a mystically determined collectivity, a people or *Volk*.[58] In all these ways, historicism seems committed to the past, to a defense of tradition, or, in the worst case, to a simple reinforcement of the status quo.

If historicism is conservative and even repressive in one sense, it is, however, radically liberating in another, in that it establishes the right of different places and times to their own standards. For Abdallah Laroui, revolutionary praxis is "historicism in action" because historicism asserts the value of the particular against an "abstract universalism."[59] At least from the time of the Young Hegelians, historicism has been current in the form Karl Löwith calls "historical futurism," a form that sanctions and even demands change on the grounds that each period must have its own character.[60] History, in this sense, becomes a principle of pure difference, one that can be phrased in quasi-revolutionary terms.[61] Thus it is no wonder that at virtually the same time, history was made a revolutionary value by Lukács and part of a reactionary program by Eliot, Yeats, and Pound. It was also possible for these individuals to switch places, with Lukács sliding into Stalinism and into a repressive aesthetic anti-modernism while the poets fomented revolution against the very literary authorities to whom he appealed. Yet the very fungibility of history in serving both left and right – progress and reaction – reveals its dangers for both sides.

History functions for both left and right as a source of critical power against their common antagonist, but it also entangles left and right in the very system they hope to challenge. For the assertion, voiced most stirringly by Hegel, that human beings are historical creatures, that each individual "exists in a particular society with a particular religion, and in a particular constellation of knowledge and attitudes concerning what is right and acceptable," confesses the tie that binds the historical critic to his or her society, the society formed by liberal democracy, rationalism, and the capitalist system. If, as Hegel says, it is as impossible to escape one's own context as it is to "jump over Rhodes," then how can historical values ever be reintroduced into the liberal society from which they have disappeared?[62] How is the dissatisfied conservative or radical socialist even to imagine such values? Where are new norms and values to come from, and even if they could be derived from a system opposed to value as such, how could they be prevented from solidifying into another repressive tradition? Finally, and most importantly, how can any value be imposed on a liberal society without tyranny, without tearing up liberal democracy by the roots and removing from it even the emancipation won from the Middle Ages? What happens in the case of *competing* values? How are these to be balanced in the absence of liberal political mechanisms?

Historicism may thus exacerbate the very problems it was meant to solve.[63] The very longing for community, for common values, separates the individual who suffers from it even further from the society of the moment. Thus Roger Scruton's rueful confession that "in becoming self conscious" the modern conservative "has set himself apart from things. The reasons that he observes for sustaining the myths of society are reasons which he cannot propagate; to propagate his reasons is to instil the world with doubt. Having struggled for articulacy, he must recommend silence."[64] Critics of liberalism unwittingly confirm its disunity and moral pluralism by taking on the role of critic. To attempt to break out of the liberal consensus is to confirm it by setting up the anti-liberal as merely another personal choice or opinion.

Behind such difficulties lies the fact that historicist emphasis on context, on the power of the historical moment over individual opinion, has the ironic effect of legitimizing the very present that critics of liberalism want to change. By historicizing value, historicism seems to make it impossible to judge any society's values, and thus leads to relativism. To know a distant culture may be difficult enough, but to evaluate that culture seems impossible if each time and place has its own individual standards of value. Though most historicists made their peace with this limitation when it concerned the past, many were made uncomfortable by its implications for the present. If there are no extrinsic standards of value, then how can any activity that is self-consistent be reprehended? These social and political implications disturbed the very thinkers who had introduced historicism.[65] Finally, historicism seems weak precisely where it challenges the liberal order – on the issue of value. For it begins to seem nothing more than an authoritarian caricature of the liberal marketplace, where everyone can pick and choose because none of the choices really matter.

Hegel solved this problem by subsuming all relative values within a unified history, making humanity one spirit with one project. Other historical solutions to the problem of relativism have generally rested on similar foundations. These would include Herder's belief in human diversity itself as a stable ideal whole and Dilthey's assumption of a "substratum of general human nature."[66] The hermeneutic value of such solutions has been questioned by many.[67] Their weaknesses as standards of value have also been attacked, particularly by Leszek Kolakowski, who asks, apropos of Hegel's infinite spirit, how "an infinite being" could be "other than *one* being?"[68] In other words, can there be deviation and even conflict within this single huge human organism? Doesn't the very structure of unity suppress individual moments that might not fit? In short, doesn't historicism resolve the problem of relativism by ceasing to be historical?

Ahistorical conceptions of human nature such as these are commonly thought to be conservative by implication. Kolakowski also argues, however, that covert definitions of an ideal humanity very similar to these survive in Marx. Alienation as a concept implies "a non-historical or prehistorical norm of humanity" and requires "a preliminary value-judgement and an idea of what 'humanity' means."[69] This is certainly true of the early Marx, who speaks quite easily of "the human essence."[70] Marxists themselves are apt to argue that humanity is not a prehistorical norm but a goal to be realized in the future, not a lost actuality but a regulative ideal.[71] In either case, its status as a norm remains unargued. Why should any particular goal be identified with the species as a whole? Doesn't this theory of history as the unfolding of a single being compromise "human plurality," as Seyla Benhabib charges?[72] If a purely descriptive historicism is relativistic and therefore weak in critical power, prescriptive ideals like these that are openly or covertly normative rest on beliefs that have great capacity for authoritarian misuse.[73]

Finally, it seems that the opposition to liberalism ends in recreating its dichotomies, because the opposition is no more able to link disparate particulars without ahistorical, a priori generalities than liberalism itself, nor can it imagine a community that comes out of historical experience instead of arbitrary philosophical conceptions. Surely Lukács's notorious solution to the gap between Marxist theory and actuality – "imputed class consciousness" – reveals by the gesture with which it "imputes" what does not exist its own bifurcation of fact and value. In a similar fashion, conservative nostalgia for bygone values confronts the facts of the present with ideals that appeal precisely because they do not fit the facts. In both cases, tyranny exposes the failure of historicism to extract its norms dialectically from history, as mere acquiescence in the conditions of the present exposes the same failure in a different way.[74]

These are the difficulties faced in the politics of Yeats, Eliot, and Pound, difficulties they share with a broad range of anti-liberal critics. Their common critique of the bifurcations and contradictions of liberalism leads to quite different proposed solutions, and yet each solution seems forced to confess its inability to overcome the liberal system, a failure that is expressed when the solution recreates the division it was supposed to heal. History, which is to be the alternative to liberal separation of individual from context, particular from generality, and fact from value, displays in their works both extremes. What begins as a plea for difference, for the basic modernist right of each period to its own standards, ends, especially in Pound's work, with an atemporal standard that erases all historical difference. Pound could move in almost no time at all from "Make it New" to the utter historical stasis of "man, earth: two halves of the tally," and in so doing he exposes an ambivalence that seems a philosophical necessity and not just a mixture of moods.[75]

The practical political projects of the three face the same contradiction. Yeats railed against England, against its politics, its economic system, its lack of historical values, and the cultural nationalism for which he was such a strong spokesman was supposed to counteract English influence by holding the Irish together without sacrificing their individuality. As Elizabeth Cullingford says, Yeats hoped to achieve unity "not by a narrowing of vision, but through acceptance of diversity." Yet the whole drama of Yeats's political career consists of the teetering balance of these opposites, a balance Yeats himself brought down many times, advocating free divorce laws, for example, to protect individual freedom, while almost simultaneously portraying the family as the source of all social strength. Eliot, too, hoped to achieve a balance of unity and diversity, to bring out of the Second World War "a common world culture which yet will not diminish the particularity of the constituent parts." This balance would have been a political version of the intellectual compromise suggested in "Tradition and the Individual Talent," but Eliot is finally forced to confess that the sort of balance he seeks is "ineffable."[76] If the reconciliation he seeks cannot even be conceived, how much more difficult to realize it in practice?

Pound's case is perhaps the most revealing because it is the most extreme. Fascism offered total reconciliation of the nagging contradictions of modern society. It posed as a fulfillment of individual ambition and of social justice, as a fusion of theory and praxis, a dissolution of the liberal split between fact and value, particular and precept. It appealed to Pound because it seemed to make hard choices unnecessary, because it proclaimed, as Goebbels did in Germany, that it had overcome the crisis of culture.[77] Of course, it simply reinstated this crisis in far more extreme terms, glorifying the pure will of the free individual over all social goods while simultaneously repressing actual individual differences, unleashing economic competition in theory while rigorously controlling the economic lives of its citizens in fact. Fascism was the most powerful movement between the wars because it seemed the most comprehensive resolution of the contradictions of modernity, and Pound's fascism similarly represents the most extreme version of the sort of compromise sought by his friends and fellow poets, as it led to the most spectacular collapse.

Pound's case thus illustrates an important fact about the politics of anti-liberalism. Cullingford praises Yeats for trying to reconcile unity and diversity, as Sanford Schwartz has praised Eliot and Pound for trying to establish "unity without uniformity, identity without suppression of differences." Michael Levenson makes a similar claim, arguing that Eliot's vision "was not one of individuals versus authority, but of an authority composed of individuals."[78] Such critical formulations rightly expose a side of the three poets not often acknowledged, a desire to respect difference as well as uniformity, individuality as well as community. But these three poets became most politically threatening when, like Lukács, they imagined that such reconciliations had been accomplished, at least in theory if not in fact. Only when they were forced to acknowledge their failure to reconcile, when they phrased the claims of individual and community in such an uncompromising way as to reveal their radical incompatibility, when these opposites obstinately refused to be synthesized, then and only then did their politics retain a promise of openness and freedom. When the contradictions of liberal democracy refused solution, there remained some hope for a real solution.

Political questions such as these are directly related to the poetics of Yeats, Eliot, and Pound. The reconciliations they hoped to effect had been, since the late eighteenth century, the special province of the aesthetic. As liberal society developed its contradictions, the aesthetic was called upon more and more to resolve them. As Terry Eagleton puts it, the aesthetic serves society "as a dream of reconciliation – of individuals woven into intimate unity with no detriment to their specificity, of an abstract totality suffused with all the flesh-and-blood reality of the individual being."[79] At least since Schiller, the aesthetic object has enjoyed the peculiar privilege of being "a whole in itself," which gives it the power to harmonize faculties that are in conflict outside it.[80] The attempt to rejoin subject and object, individual and community, fact and value is therefore inevitably aesthetic.

From I.A. Richards on, twentieth-century criticism has taken the reconciliation of such opposites as the preeminent task of literature.[81] Overcoming the bifurcations and contradictions of modern life is, according to M.H. Abrams, the task of all post-Romantic poetry. In "Structure and Style in the Greater Romantic Lyric," Abrams defines a genre of poetry in which the epistemological opposition of subject and object and the modern estrangement of humans from nature are resolved in a poetic structure whose organic form perfectly mingles part and whole. According to the theory, philosophical and social conflicts are resolved aesthetically in a form whose harmony is guaranteed by its autonomy. The founding and still most typical poet of this tradition is Coleridge, for whom the goal of all poetry was "to convert a *series* into a *Whole*," to manifest "Unity or Revelation of the *One* in and by the *Many*." The synthesis of part and whole is the poetic basis of a philosophical reconciliation of "intellect with emotion, and of thought with object. . . . " According to Abrams, this is "the central enterprise common to many post-Kantian German philosophers and poets, as well as to Coleridge and Wordsworth." Abrams also inducts modern poets and novelists such as Eliot, Yeats, and Lawrence into this post-Romantic company, a company dedicated to resolving in literature the philosophical contradictions of modernity.[82]

Though Abrams's theory has been attacked from several sides, it remains influential, if only implicitly, in the criticism of modern poetry.[83] Accounts of the poetics of modernism have had to confront a whole series of opposites: personality and impersonality, individual talent and tradition, concrete image and mythic construct, montage and spatial form. To prevent these opposites from seeming mere contradictions, critics sometimes propose two or more different modernisms or follow Abrams's lead and define modern poetry as a poetry of synthesis. Schwartz, for example, argues that the apparent contradictions in the poetics of Eliot and Pound, their equal insistence on concrete experience and abstract conception, on fact and myth, on individual perception and impersonal distance can all be resolved by supposing a continuum linking extremes. These conflicts can be converted into "a coherent dialectical relationship between personal and impersonal aspects of poetry."[84] Though Schwartz links Eliot and Pound to quite a different philosophical tradition than the one deployed by Abrams, the conclusion is the same – a Coleridgean reconciliation of multiplicity with unity.

Schwartz's argument is essentially a philosophically informed version of a common account of modernist poetics, one represented particularly well by Michael Levenson, who proposes a method of reading *The Waste Land* that will reconcile the "radical individualism" with the search for "objective principles" that he sees as the two sides of modernism. Eliot is the hero of Levenson's book because he takes the "history of oppositions, disproportions and asymmetries, a history of distinctions drawn then dramatized, a doctrinal struggle waged often between mutually excluding extremes" and brings equilibrium to it.[85] In this way, Levenson and the others extend the traditional claims made for the aesthetic. Claims that modernists like Yeats, Eliot, and Pound offer aesthetic resolutions of the tension between part and whole, fact and myth, personality and impersonality are inseparable from the claim that they also offer social reconciliations of unity and difference.

In fact, it is just those poetic devices that seem to represent reconciliation that instead reveal its impossibility. Yeats's Major Robert Gregory, for example, serves as the epitome of the perfect aristocratic life, which

Yeats sees as a harmonious reconciliation of disparate talents into a unity. Thus he seems the finest example of the resolution of one and many that Cullingford says Yeats yearned to accomplish, because he is an intensely private individual who is yet a compact of all the virtues of his race and sect. He also seems to be, especially in poems like "An Irish Airman Foresees His Death," a perfect representative of Yeats's belief in an aesthetic form that would be independent of actuality precisely because of its inner balance. Yet the poems surrounding Gregory are full of doubt and qualification, hesitations that reveal Yeats's sense of the incompatibility of intense individuality and representative amplitude. These doubts surface when Yeats is forced to contemplate the conflict between Gregory's self-absorption, which can seem so beautiful, and the social demands of his position. In a sense, Gregory betrays his society by his death, by the very turning inward Yeats celebrates, because that death cuts off the Gregory line and abandons his countrymen to the British occupiers. The manifest inutility of Gregory's gesture strikes even Yeats, who must then contemplate and defend his own self-absorption, and, implicitly, the autonomy of the very work that portrays this conflict.

"In Memory of Major Robert Gregory" makes visible a conflict between Yeats's sense of political obligation and the value of formal autonomy. This basic conflict unsettles all the other poetic relationships that autonomy is supposed to resolve, which then reveal the true rivalries within modern politics. Thus, for example, the conflict between personal experience and impersonal form in *The Waste Land*. As Levenson suggests, this is the most basic problem posed by the poem: "How can one finite experience be related to any other? Put otherwise, how can difference be compatible with unity?"[86]

For many critics, these questions are answered by the figure of Tiresias, who sweeps individual experiences up and gathers them into his own multilayered consciousness, where they are related if not unified. But there are really two Tiresiases in *The Waste Land* – one in the notes, who represents Eliot's rather belated fear of his own poem, and one in the poem itself. The first of these, by making all men one man and all women one woman, brings all the individuals in the poem into relation, and thus creates harmony out of discord. Tiresias is, in this sense, a representation of poetic autonomy, of the resolution of social conflict through aesthetic harmony. In the poem itself, however, Tiresias represents something quite different. Here he is identical to all men and all women only because the conditions of modern capitalism have standardized men and women to such an extent that individual experience has ceased to exist. Eliot links him syntactically to the "human engine," the machine within which the "young man carbuncular" and his typist lover become automatic parts. In this role, Tiresias betrays Eliot's deep fear of the contradictory process whereby modern society both divides and forcibly integrates its members. The poem thus recoils from the very process that appears as an aesthetic resolution in the notes. Because Tiresias is a vehicle for this political concern, he cannot also consistently function as a purely aesthetic device to achieve artistic harmony.

Similar conflicts govern the relationship of part to whole within the organizational architecture of the poem. Without autonomy, the poem cannot resolve its parts into an organic whole because some of those parts will always have ties and implications elsewhere. A poet like Pound does not shirk this necessity but rather provokes it. Pound's involvement with current events was so passionate that it violated the bounds of aesthetic form and made a poem that, as Pound admitted, does not cohere. Instead of using aesthetic resolutions to smooth over political conflicts, Pound allowed political conflict to disrupt the aesthetic surface of the poetry. The conflict of part and whole in the architecture of a poem or sequence, the tendency of all these poets to embed lyrics in larger forms that tug against lyric unity, is a direct result of an interest in materials that cannot be made smoothly coherent with a lyric surface.[87]

In these various ways, then, the poetry of Yeats, Eliot, and Pound proves the relevance of Abrams's paradigm only by failing to meet its terms. If Yeats, Eliot, and Pound had been content with the conventional autonomy of art they could perhaps have achieved at the aesthetic level a sort of reconciliation, but they were in fact utterly inconsistent on the question of autonomy. Yeats certainly advocated organic form and autonomous art, yet he also declared himself against "the solitary book," against the aestheticization that separates art from life. No one advocated the freedom of the artist and the autonomy of art as violently as did Ezra Pound, but he also followed a rigorously sociological approach to literature that tied it irrevocably to economics. Eliot, too, seems a prophet of the autotelic, yet his criticism is also sociological, and he too believed that "the great poet, writing himself, writes his time." On this most basic aesthetic level, the modernists are resolutely irresolute.[88] Having disrupted the Romantic autonomy of art through their political ambitions and desires, they cannot rely on it to resolve the contradictions between particular and general or part and whole. Rather, their involvement in politics, by making true autonomy impossible, forces these contradictions out into the open.

It was for reasons somewhat like these that Lukács turned against the aesthetic modernism that had once intrigued him. As Adorno says, Lukács came to demand of literature "a reality which must be depicted as an unbroken continuum joining subject and object." For Lukács, modernism failed at this reconciliation, producing mere subjectivism amounting to solipsism or realistically reporting inert facts without hoping to affect them.[89] Instead of helping to heal the epistemological split of modernity, aesthetic modernism merely advertised it. But Lukács's opposition shows how much more promising this failure is than the enforced success he dictated to a specious modern "realism."

Adorno's answer to Lukács's charge shows how the earlier Lukács can be used to challenge both this crude demand for reconciliation and the more subtle suggestions of it in much recent American criticism. In *Theory of the Novel,* Lukács developed a theory of irony, a kind of negative mysticism in which fragmentation was to be itself a common fate and thus the promise of a better future. As he said in *History and Class Consciousness,* "the intellectual restoration of man has consciously to take its path through the realm of disintegration and fragmentation." In his rejoinder to Lukács's attack on modernism, Adorno deploys this idea ironically against Lukács himself. For Adorno, the isolation of the modern writer, the inability of the modern to universalize, is a valid reflection of the fact that "the monadological condition persists universally." In other words, the very split between subject and object is so pervasive as to be the unifying factor that modern art seems to lack. Modern poetry transcends the opposition between individual and community not through harmony but rather through discord, because that discord is a common condition suffered by all. Thus the greatest works of literary modernism – *The Tower, The Waste Land,* the *Pisan Cantos* – are not those that display some triumphant resolution of social or aesthetic discord, but those that make discord itself into an organizational principle. Individuals are related in such works not by similarity but by their lack of similarity, by the suffering they endure in the absence of genuine community.

As Pound's case shows more clearly than any, the writers of the right shared with Lukács the temptation to believe that the antagonisms of modernity had been overcome by an actual political system. This temptation is evident as well in the dream of a form that would balance fragment and totality, immediate experience and abstract form, personal voice and impersonal construct. But the insistence of these poets on *both* sides in each of these dichotomies, and the intensity with which they referred their work to politics, meant that their poetry could never be composed, that it would continue to proclaim an inescapable problematic. Thus it retained some measure of critical power. To quote Adorno and Horkheimer: "That factor in a work of art which enables it to transcend reality certainly cannot be detached from style; but it does not consist of the harmony actually realized, of any doubtful unity of form and content, within and without, of individual and society; it is to be found in those features in which discrepancy appears: in the necessary failure of the passionate striving for identity."[90]

Sympathetic critics of Yeats, Eliot, and Pound now commonly regret their involvement in politics. Because their allegiances generally lay with the most repressive forces of the twentieth century, it is hard to disagree. Unsympathetic critics, a category that would include proponents of virtually all of the brands of post-structuralism, commonly denounce any "striving for identity," and it is quite easy to see a connection between an aesthetic drive for reconciliation and authoritarian politics. Yet this connection, which Yeats, Eliot, and Pound did abundantly illustrate, is not sufficient reason to reject either politics or the aesthetic project of reconciliation. The critical power that Adorno and Horkheimer find in the aesthetic comes from the frustration of a passionate desire to resolve the contradictions of modern politics. The desire and a sense of its failure are in a way necessary to one another; together they prevent mere complacency.

The real value of the political activities of these poets lies in the way they exhibit this connection. How else to explain the fact that only the most truly totalitarian of the three, Ezra Pound, has been rehabilitated by post-structuralism and adopted as forebear by post-modernism? Yet this is not really a contradiction at all. The "de-centered" aspects of Pound's work cannot be lifted free of its "passionate striving for identity" because there is a symbiotic connection between the two. Pound would not have been radically disruptive of the reigning aesthetic order if he had not also been avid for a more cohesive social order. Thus the seeming contradiction between the revolutionary aesthetics of Pound's modernism and his reactionary politics, a contradiction now just as commonly seen as an identity, is actually neither a contradiction nor an identity but rather a painful symbiosis of the two. The difficult truth about all three of these poets is that there remain bits and shards of freedom even in their most totalitarian fantasies, but we cannot separate these fragments from the totality that contains them. It thus becomes impossible to uncritically accept or to utterly dismiss these poets, so that their value is finally to keep painfully in view the problems they tried so hard to solve.

1

W.B. Yeats: Cultural Nationalism

1. THE ISLE OF FREEDOM

W.B. Yeats is the most universally admired poet of the modern period, but he is not often considered a true modernist.[1] Being modern was not part of Yeats's program in poetry or in politics. As early as 1886, he used "modern" as a natural term of opprobrium, and fifty years later he distinguished himself and his contemporaries from "revolutionists" like Eliot by saying, "we wrote as men had always written" (EI, p. 499).[2] As a young man and as an aged poet, Yeats recoiled from the modern world built by technology, a world that had created the urban masses and was in turn sustained by them, and he felt a distaste for poetry that spoke of this world. Thus Yeats can seem an anomaly in the modern period, his long life in the twentieth century the accidental survival of a poet who might well have succumbed, as Johnson and Dowson did, to a more timely end.

Yet it may be unreasonable to refuse the term "modern" to any poet not entirely positive about the modern world, a world that has been uncomfortable with itself from the beginning. W.J. McCormack suggests instead that "Yeats is more revealing of the values of Modernism than Eliot is, precisely because he is less 'pure' a Modernist."[3] Yeats's life and work show as well as those of any poet how aesthetic modernism emerges from modernity's quarrel with itself. Because he was a Victorian and still something of the nineteenth-century liberal he affected to hate, Yeats suffered these conflicts as a personal quarrel, an internal contest between individualism and nationalism, right and duty, freedom and history. Being modern was not part of Yeats's program, but serving these conflicting values was, and in that sense he is a truly modern poet.

Yeats became a great modernist in part because Ireland suffered these conflicts with him. In McCormack's opinion, "The Anglo-Irish Literary Revival . . . is the first sign of English-language Modernism. . . . "[4] The Revival, with Yeats always very near its head, pushed Ireland on its way toward modern statehood while simultaneously pulling it back toward its primitive past. Ireland demanded from England both equality, which could have been granted within the Empire by economic and political concessions, and recognition of its distinct nationality, which could only come with a total break.[5] Within its own society, Ireland had to decide between being a liberal state, with a citizenship based on abstract natural right, and a nation, with a citizenship based on historical and cultural identity. A good deal of its political turmoil has occurred because of its inability to combine these two ideals.

Yeats's politics are inextricable from this tension in Irish nationalism. Late in his life, Yeats was to trace both fascism and communism back to Hegel's attempts to resolve the liberal contradiction between right and duty, individual and community. To understand his own place as an individual in any community, English or Irish, to understand the position of his hereditary class, the Anglo-Irish, in Ireland, to understand the relationship between poetry as an aesthetic act and politics as a series of practical acts, Yeats had to puzzle out the philosophical questions both fascism and communism tried to answer. Elizabeth Cullingford claims that Yeats aimed to achieve his much-desired unity not "by a narrowing of vision, but through acceptance of diversity."[6] But how was Yeats to achieve what his society could not? How, even at the abstract level of poetic statement, could Yeats resolve a conflict much deeper than any political contest of his time and yet at the heart of them all? The reconciliation of difference with unity, of individual right and public duty, which Hegel imagined as the work of the modern state, remained a dream.[7]

Yeats's most popular early poem, "The Lake Isle of Innisfree," is about a utopia where right and duty do not conflict. At first, two obvious literary references seem to pull the poem apart along the line between these two ideals. In his autobiography, Yeats regrets taking for the first line of his poem the "conventional archaism – 'Arise and go'" (A, p. 103). But Yeats could not have altered this phrase without substantially changing the character of his poem. Jeffares identifies the most famous example of the convention, Luke 15:18, the climax of the story of the Prodigal Son: "I will arise and go to my father."[8] Clearly, Yeats borrows more from this parable than the verbal formula. He tells in his autobiography how the poem was composed "when walking through Fleet Street very homesick," and how he was called back to Sligo by a jet of water seen in a shop window. Though Yeats was poor and far from prodigal, he did nonetheless feel the contrast between London with its crowded streets and shops and the simpler Sligo. Like the Prodigal Son, he is called back to his home, to the house of his fathers.

Though the poem does not mention Ireland or England, this call is

implicitly patriotic. The name Innisfree, heather island, may have re-
minded some readers of Innisfail, island of the stone, one of the many
poetic appellations attached to Ireland. Innisfree's wattled cottage belongs
in just such a poetic Ireland. When Oisin breaks away from Niamh,
longing to rejoin his Fenian brotherhood if only for a day, it is "the
Fenian's dwellings of wattle" (VP, p. 55, l. 115) that figure the whole
ancient way of life. These dwellings appear in *The Wanderings of Oisin* as
being "of wattles and woodwork made" (VP, p. 58, l. 162), phrasing that
clearly anticipates that of "Innisfree": "of clay and wattles made" (VP, p.
117, l. 2). In a sense, the later poem also represents the call of the Fenian
brotherhood, a call not just to a particular place but also to a particular
time. For his *Selected Poems* of 1921, Yeats altered "And a small cabin
build there" to read "And a small cabin built there" (VP, p. 117), imply-
ing a return to a cabin long since built, to a past life still in existence.

The other obvious literary echo draws the poem back to a different
cabin. As Yeats makes clear in his autobiography, the "nine bean-rows"
of the first stanza come from Thoreau: "My father had read to me some
passage out of *Walden,* and I planned to live some day in a cottage on a
little island called Innisfree . . . " (A, p. 47). Thoreau, something of a
Prodigal Son himself, remarks that "the greater part of what my neigh-
bors call good I believe in my soul to be bad. . . . "[9] When Yeats recoils
from the "roadway" and the "pavements grey" and resolves to "live
alone," he may not anticipate an experiment in Thoreauvian self-reliance,
but neither does he seem anxious to join a group in exile. The references
pull the poem in two different directions, toward two different ideals,
toward community with the past on one hand and toward individual
difference on the other.

Though Yeats was never a sophisticated political thinker, he seems
viscerally aware even in the early days that these need not be stark opposites. "Innisfree," even with all its references attached, would make
perfect sense if Ireland were seen as a place where individuals can be
different precisely because of their community, whereas England represents the sort of disunity made by a jumble of identical elements. A
passage of Yeats's short novel, *John Sherman,* written at about the same
time as "Innisfree" and containing the same brief incident from his life,
suggests that Yeats saw Ireland in just this way: "In your big towns a
man . . . knows only the people like himself. But here one chats with the
whole world in a day's walk, for every man one meets is a class."[10] As
Yeats told Katharine Tynan in a letter written in 1889, "Down at Sligo
one sees the whole world in a days walk, every man is a class. It is too
small there for minorities" (CL, p. 153). Where London is large enough
to break up into classes, each one isolated from the rest, Sligo is too small

to allow for the existence of classes except insofar as each individual constitutes his own. The small town is therefore more unified than the large city and yet its citizens possess a greater distinction.

Yeats sees Sligo through the prism of a sophisticated primitivism akin to that of Simmel or Weber. For Weber, the unity of primitive societies is not attributable to conformity but, in fact, to the uniqueness of each activity. As Fredric Jameson puts it, "each activity is symbolically unique, so that the level of abstraction upon which they could be compared with one another is never attained: there is no least-common-denominator. . . . "[11] Yeats sees England as a place where people are both isolated and forcibly associated, and he imagines Ireland as a paradise of Hegelian resolution, where personal uniqueness and social harmony will coincide.

At the same time, however, Yeats defines his own freedom in a way that implicitly reinforces the very ethics that led to the atomized crowd in the first place. To inhabit a place like Sligo is apparently to be free, to find "some peace" (l. 5). But just how does this poem define freedom? The title itself contains a seeming contradiction, matching "Innis," Irish for island, with "free." The poem wraps its promise of freedom in layers of insulation: It is to be found only in the "deep heart's core," at the very center of the person, who is alone on an island, encircled by a lake, which is itself on another island, isolated by a sea from the starting point of the poem. However Yeats may define freedom, he certainly does not associate it with ease of movement. The association of peace with veils, with twilight, suggests that for Yeats freedom means being covered up.

In other words, freedom in "The Lake Isle of Innisfree" is negative freedom, freedom *from*. Isaiah Berlin says in his classic essay, "Two Concepts of Liberty," "By being free in this sense I mean not being interfered with by others."[12] This concept of freedom, of course, lies at the very basis of English liberalism; Berlin cites Hobbes and Bentham.[13] It draws a circle around the individual and forbids entry to others, making government an ethically neutral medium designed to keep the various circles from impinging as much as possible. Concerned with right rather than with good, such governments dedicate themselves to managing the contest of various goods, without favoring one or the other. Liberal theory imagines a self that is similarly neutral, "prior to its ends," as Michael Sandel puts it.[14] The ethical freedom of the self, its right to choose any activity or goal, is prior to any of the activities or goals it might choose. The self does not exist to enjoy or accomplish anything in particular, but primarily to be free. As the poet of negative freedom, in "The Lake Isle of Innisfree" at any rate, Yeats imagines a state that is blissful primarily because it is free of characteristics; the self comes into its own only when all impetus, all direction, even all feeling is removed.[15]

The antithetical structure of the poem also reflects its conception of freedom, because individual freedom in this analysis can be defined only against the exterior forces that threaten it. Innisfree represents freedom from London, a "peace" that is nothing more specific than the cessation of London life. Consequently, that social life is also imagined in ethically neutral terms. As Hegel complains against Rousseau, once the individual is defined by opposition to the social, that general life can only be seen as "an external abstract universal."[16] But such an abstract opposition can only impoverish the patriotic element of the poem. Seamus Deane complains that in Yeats "freedom is almost always realized as interior freedom, with no political repercussions whatsoever."[17] This freedom is no less "interior" with respect to Ireland than it is with respect to England. If Yeats imagines Ireland as a spiritual and ethical island, as well as a geographical island, he also imagines the self as islanded within Ireland. Deane is also upset with the political quietism of Yeats's concept of freedom, its difference from a freedom *to* identified with some particular good. His political quarrel with Yeats is to decide whether Home Rule is an ethically negative or positive concept.[18]

The conflict is also specifically linguistic, embedded in the very name Yeats has made so famous. Innisfree, Jeffares tells us, means "heather island," and should be spelled Inis Fraoigh.[19] But Yeats avails himself of the convenience that the Anglicized place name contains a common English word. How more compactly could the divided allegiance of the poet be expressed than in this necessity to bring into a different language a place name from his home country in order to express its freedom? The place name occupies the exact divide, the hyphen, between the two halves of the Anglo-Irish experience. The only remnant of Irish in the otherwise thoroughly English speech of the poem, the place name acts to connect the poem linguistically to its subject, but just by virtue of its difference, the name also advertises the distance of that subject. McCormack warns his readers not to "mistake the accessibility of those place-names on the map for the integration of a poet in a known and comprehensive culture." Quite the contrary, the "place-names radiated meaning for the very reason that their language was no longer an acknowledged vernacular."[20] The exoticism imported into the poem by the place-name depends on its oddity, on the very fact that it does not belong in the English verse of the poet. Thus the very name that Yeats gives to his longing for community also betrays his individual isolation in England.

The poem turns structurally on a similar paradox. Hugh Kenner suggests that "the 'Celtic' measure of 'Innisfree' followed the six-beat iambic of [Yeats's] English friend Ernest Dowson." Kenner points out that if you simply drop the word "now" from the first line, the result is indistinguishable from "a Rhymer's Club measure to which Yeats has been faithful in his fashion."[21] The pattern is even more pervasive in "Innisfree" than Kenner allows. The first three lines of each stanza have thirteen syllables, and of these nine lines seven have the medial caesura preceded by the extra unaccented syllable. Scanned in this way, the poem reads as if a six-beat iambic line were simply stretched by the imposition of one syllable in the middle of the line. In three of these seven lines the "imposed" syllable is the word *there* and in two more it is the word *now*. Thus there runs down the middle of the poem a kind of core utterance, which is in fact a faithful summary of the central aspiration of the poet: "there now." The rhythm of each line contains a sigh, a lapse in the scansion, at which point the poet breathes pure longing.

This is perhaps what Yeats means when he says in his autobiography that "Innisfree" was his first poem "with anything in its rhythm of my own music. I had begun to loosen rhythm as an escape from rhetoric and from that emotion of the crowd that rhetoric brings . . . " (A, p. 103). The escape from rhetoric through the loosening of common rhythms becomes in "Innisfree" a geographical escape: "there now." By virtue of the same process, a prosodic variation acquires political significance. The poet expresses his freedom, his difference, by a strategically placed sigh. In its very rhythms, then, the poem celebrates the concept of negative freedom by carving out a space in the middle of convention and filling it with a caesura and a lapse in accent. To be free simply means to evacuate a space still to be defined by the surrounding unfreedom. Or, in Kenner's terms, the poem is Celtic insofar as it can open a tiny hole in the English fabric.

If we remember how Yeats places himself on an island in order to be free, it might not seem too paradoxical to suggest that he is imprisoned by an idea of freedom. His classically liberal conception of freedom as the absence of exterior influence can hardly be compromised with his nostalgia for a communal past. "The Lake Isle of Innisfree" remains such an alluring poem because it allows its readers to participate as Yeats takes both sides, enjoying both the Prodigal's return and Thoreau's rugged self-reliance, rejecting modernity while reasserting the concept of freedom on which modern politics and modern industry depend.

It makes little sense, perhaps, to suggest that "The Lake Isle of Innisfree" is a modern poem, and yet it may be most modern where it seems least so. One can hardly return to Innisfree without having left it, just as one cannot regret the past without having lost it. The nostalgia of this poem is therefore perfectly modern, which may account for its continuing popularity. But "The Lake Isle of Innisfree" is also modern in a more specifically political sense, in that it attempts to reconcile individual and community, right and duty, by means that widen instead the distance

between them. In this sense, it is not only typically modern, it is also an epitome of Yeats's life in politics.

2. THE SUCCESS AND FAILURE OF THE IRISH REVIVAL

Ireland's independence was delayed so long that it accumulated a number of different, even incompatible, justifications. Prior to the Union, the only politicized class, the Protestant landowners, approached England with "a mere demand for the individual rights and constitutional arrangements which the counterparts of the Ascendancy enjoyed in England."[22] From the beginning of its resurgence after the Famine, Irish nationalism made its plea in a different way as well. Thomas Davis, spokesman for Young Ireland, "left Trinity College a materialist, a utilitarian, a believer in progress through universal education – that is to say, a Benthamite."[23] Like other Protestants before him, Davis concentrated first on winning for the Irish the basic individual rights and economic benefits of English citizenship. His approach changed, however, after a trip to Germany in 1839–40, when he discovered the historical theories of the German Romantics.[24]

According to Malcolm Brown, Davis never abandoned his dream of a modernized Ireland, but simply attached it to a cultural nationalism based on a plea to history.[25] But this potent combination concealed an inconsistency. Irish claims were made to rest on two incompatible bases: natural right and historical right. Ireland could either claim its share of the material progress made by the industrial state and demand its rights on the abstract principle of equality, or it could assert its right of separation on the grounds of its historical uniqueness as a culture, worthy of self-rule precisely insofar as it rejected the model of material progress invented by its powerful and successful neighbor. The great Italian nationalist Giuseppe Mazzini, to whom so many in Ireland looked as a moral example, rejected the claims of Irish nationalism because the Irish "did not plead for any distinct principle of life or system of legislation. . . ."[26] For Mazzini, in other words, there was a vast difference between a demand for better government and nationalist self-assertion. In his eyes, Irish nationalism meant nothing more than the desire to become more like England. The taint of Davis's Benthamism remained.

This ideological conflict amounts to a good deal more than a clash of definitions, for Ireland's partition came about in part because of an inability on the part of its politicians to resolve the difference between cultural nationalism and the liberal state. On a much smaller scale, the conflict replicated itself within the mind and life of Yeats.[27] That his early career would be dominated by Davis's cultural nationalism and not by his liberalism was determined in part by the influence of John O'Leary, who began that career by introducing Yeats to Davis's poetry. O'Leary retained right up to the fall of Parnell the traditional Fenian disdain for the parliamentary option. Based on years of disappointment, on the conviction that Irish independence would only come as the result of force, this disdain shaded off into a contempt for democracy itself. Yeats's own accents can be heard in O'Leary's description of an election campaign as "all that was blatant and insincere expanding itself in addresses over the advertising columns of the newspapers, and the foolish and self-seeking all the country over open-mouthed (in every sense of the word) and otherwise active in the strife."[28] As Yeats later claimed, O'Leary "hated democracy . . . with more than feudal hatred" (A, p. 141). A nationalist but not a republican, O'Leary nourished what Yeats called an "aristocratic dream" (EI, p. 510) that Ireland would one day have its own king.

O'Leary introduced Yeats to a version of Davis's Young Irelandism that severely deemphasized its liberal element. Instead, O'Leary offered what his modern biographer calls "cultural Home Rule."[29] Compatible with the Ruskin and Morris Yeats had been reading, this sort of nationalism turned away from traditional liberal questions of franchise and representation toward the task of repairing Ireland's indigenous culture. According to Yeats, in his autobiography, "Young Ireland had sought a nation unified by political doctrine alone . . . " (A, p. 136). Yeats himself intended to move beyond "the ideal of the good citizen, and of a politics and a philosophy and a literature which would help him upon his way" (UP, 2:185). As he put it in 1907, he wanted to move from "a purely political nationalism . . . to a partly intellectual and historical nationalism . . . " (UP, 2:237). The defeat and death of Parnell, which, by virtually removing parliamentary progress as an option, had "freed imagination from practical politics, agrarian grievance and political enmity, and turned it to imaginative nationalism" (EX, p. 343) seemed to offer the cultural movement its moment.[30]

Thus began what Yeats called in a letter to O'Leary "the revolt of the soul against the intellect" (CL, p. 303). The immediate expression of this revolt was of course the struggle of the Irish against the British Empire. Because "the intellect of Ireland is romantic and spiritual rather than scientific and analytical" (UP, 2:159) it was being systematically violated by the imposition of alien forms of thought: "An imitation of the habits of thought, the character, the manners, the opinions – and these never at their best – of an alien people was preventing the national character taking its own natural form . . . " (M, p. 84). But the conflict was in fact much larger than the immediate political contest. It was instead "part of the ritual of that revolt of Celtic Ireland which is, according to one's point of view, the Celt's futile revolt against the despotism of fact or his necessary revolt against a political and moral materialism" (UP, 2:91).

Yeats's revolt involves a double repudiation of liberalism, first as the system that ruined England and threatens Ireland, and second as an inherently weak basis for attacks on that system. Instead, Yeats enlists himself in the movement Davis had discovered in Germany. The revolt of the soul against intellect, of the German Romantics against the Enlightenment, appears here as the revolt of individual historical nations against a doctrine that would make all nations the same by making all individuals equal. Nationalism of this kind bases its claims on the belief that humanity is naturally divided into unique communities, all of whose distinguishing characteristics are ultimately derived from a common essence.[31]

Yeats first learned to think in such terms from Ruskin and Morris, from the indigenous English reaction against the social system built by the Enlightenment. He dated his intellectual life from his reading of Ruskin, and he dramatized his political beginnings as a conflict between his own belief in Ruskin and his father's faith in Mill (M, p. 19; OTB, p. 14). The nationalism he practiced had at its source the dream of "enlarging Irish hate, till we had come to hate with a passion of patriotism what Morris and Ruskin hated" (E, p. 307). Though cultural nationalism is potentially conservative and anti-democratic, it is not necessarily at odds with the sort of socialism Yeats discovered at Morris's evening gatherings. In his survey of nineteenth-century politics, Berlin says that "Conservatives and socialists believed in the power and influence of institutions and regarded them as a necessary safeguard against the chaos, injustice, and cruelty caused by uncontrolled individualism. . . . " Socialists, like conservatives, "accused the liberals of legislating 'unhistorically' for timeless abstractions. . . . "[32] The common aim is the reconciliation of individual and community, freedom and history, set apart by liberal theory.

Ideally, cultural nationalism should foster both unity and diversity, because it opposes a liberal system in which "uncontrolled individualism" divides individuals from one another while simultaneously removing local and national characteristics as a source of meaningful differentiation. In actual practice in Ireland, however, cultural nationalism proved both coercive and divisive. It led Yeats himself to two seemingly incompatible ends. He formulated cultural definitions of Irish nationality that proved, quite ironically in his own case, to be restrictive and arbitrary, so that he was forced, for sheer self-preservation, to fall back on liberal guarantees of individual rights. Yeats thus demonstrated as a personal contradiction the seemingly inevitable recreation of liberal dichotomies by the system that was supposed to overcome them.

Cullingford traces Yeats's cultural politics back to Davis's "conviction that Ireland's demand for political separation from England depended on her existence as a separate cultural unit. . . . "[33] If Ireland was to base its claims to independence on national uniqueness, it had somehow to define the culture that set it apart. Young Ireland had fostered the idea of the "Irish note," a concept whose power derived from its vagueness. Yet that vagueness became embarrassing in descriptions like this one from Yeats's friend Katharine Tynan:

> By the Irish note I mean that distinctive quality in Celtic poetry the charm of which is so much easier to feel than to explain. . . . Some of the parts which go to make up its whole are a simplicity which is *naive* – a freshness, an archness, a light touching of the cords as with fairy-finger tips; a shade of underlying melancholy as delicately evanescent as a breath upon glass, which yet gives its undertone and its shadow to all; fatalism side by side with buoyant hopefulness; laughter with tears; love with hatred; a rainbow of all colours where none conflict; a gamut of all notes which join to make perfect harmony.[34]

All this inept attempt makes clear is that the "Irish note" is called upon to unify a whole range of elements not naturally in union. In 1900, Yeats claimed, in response to an attack by D.P. Moran, that he had "avoided 'Celtic note' and 'Celtic renaissance' partly because both are vague and one is grandiloquent . . . " (UP, 2:241). But he certainly believed in "certain ardent ideas and high attitudes of mind which were the nation to itself . . . " (E, p. 306). By means of these ideas and attitudes, Yeats felt he could distinguish "eternal and ancient Ireland" from "that passing and modern Ireland of prosaic cynicism and prosaic rivalries . . . " (UP, 2:141). Culture, in this analysis, serves as the "Irish note" does, to unify what seems superficially to be in rivalry or opposition.

In his early optimism, Yeats ignored a truth expressed best by F.S.L. Lyons. In Ireland, Lyons says, culture "has been a force that has worked against the evolution of a homogeneous society and in so doing has been an agent of anarchy rather than of unity."[35] The Irish cultural revival proved almost exactly the opposite of what Yeats set out to prove. Whatever it touched in its attempt to define Irish culture turned out to be a cause of division instead of unity. Most basic for an Anglo-Irish writer was, of course, the language question. In response to Douglas Hyde's famous address, "The Necessity for De-Anglicising Ireland," Yeats asked plaintively: "Can we not build up a national tradition, a national literature, which shall be none the less Irish in spirit from being English in language? Can we not keep the continuity of the nation's life, not by trying to do what Dr. Hyde has practically pronounced impossible, but by translating or retelling in English, which shall have an indefinable Irish quality of rythm [sic] and style, all that is best of the ancient literature?" (CL, p. 338) Here, despite his denial, Yeats falls back on the "Irish note," that indefinable something that makes an alien language Irish after all. In groping for some common ground between English and Ireland, however, Yeats violated the principles of his own movement, which came to rely more and more on Irish "as the symbol of cultural difference."[36]

Race, of course, divides almost as surely as language. All his life, Yeats attempted to subordinate race to history, to argue that "certain native traditions" are passed on from father to son and "mould the foreign settler after the national type in a few years" (UP, 2:202). Of course, he had to flout history itself to argue that the Anglo-Irish Ascendancy had been assimilated into the indigenous culture it invaded. And though most scholars would agree that the word *Celtic* has virtually no meaning as a racial designation, Yeats created an even greater ambiguity in attempting to define a Celticism that is unified and yet not exclusive, pure even though it results from a mixture of races. Yeats argues that there is something peculiarly Irish that remains after the addition of Norman, Scottish, and English elements. The fact that "cosmopolitanism" became a common term of abuse during the Revival signifies his failure to convince many others.[37] It became increasingly difficult for Yeats himself to argue on one hand that Ireland was spiritually distinct, most especially from England, and to argue on the other that it could accommodate English elements without substantial alteration.

Religion would not even bear mention as an element of a unified Irish culture if Yeats had not insisted so strongly on a kind of folk religion, on a body of myth and superstition antedating and, he hoped, post-dating Christianity. The tremendous energy Yeats poured into projects associated with Irish folklore seems in proportion to the divisive power of the Christian sects within his country. Defining Irish spirituality in terms of folklore meant, as George Watson says, "that he did not have to consider the (for him) awkward fact of the peasant's devout Catholicism."[38] But there is another weakness in this project as well, for all of Yeats's attempts to connect the Irish folk tales and habits to a worldwide mystical tradition serve only to *lessen* the national character of Irish folklore.[39]

A good deal of Yeats's own patriotic feeling derived from his native geography, from his love for Sligo. But he apparently felt little sympathy for the desires of the landless to own what they had worked over generation after generation. Geography, in any case, could hardly unify when more than one group wanted the same plots of land. The most general cultural appeal of all is usually to history, but Ireland's is a history of discontinuity, of revolts and defeats. Commemoration in Ireland is the commemoration of strife and often its reenactment, as Yeats well knew when he planned the centennial of 1798 as a separatist coup. As Watson puts it, Ireland is such a deeply divided country there is "a total lack of a relatively steady tradition, like that of the English or French."[40]

This is precisely what the revival proved, that any conceivable definition of Irish culture led not to unity but to greater division. According to

Denis Donoghue, "If there is a distinctive Irish experience, it is one of division, exacerbated by the fact that division in a country so small seems perverse."[41] Even more perverse, perhaps, is the fact that the very attempts to conceive of a unified Irish culture exacerbated the divisions that made such a culture impossible. In a relatively homogeneous society, according to Nicholas Mansergh, the concept of a nation is apt to be unifying, but "in a plural society the more explicitly that concept is formulated, the more likely it is to be divisive."[42] That Yeats's schemes for the Irish Literary Society almost immediately broke up in controversy and that his dreams of an Irish national theater brought riots instead of unity should not seem accidental. These conflicts are instead the logical products of Yeats's own plans. "Davis's ideal of a nationalism transcending differences of religion, class and ancestry, and appealing to Irishmen of all traditions, did not die with him," says J.C. Beckett. "But those who have professed to support this ideal have failed to recognize . . . that its realization would involve the negation, not the fulfilment, of the past history of Ireland."[43]

Conflicts within the Irish Literary Revival dramatized the fact that culture cannot be confected. In the absence of common conceptions of culture, cultural arguments are both ahistorical, based as they must be on artificial, arbitrary notions, and coercive, because cultural unity is not an assumption but an imposition. Cultural nationalism failed to unify Ireland, but it did give one side the weapons it needed to coerce its opponents. Ironically for Yeats, that side was not his own. Yeats soon found himself being beaten with a stick he had been among the first to shake. In an 1898 letter to Lady Gregory, Yeats reports very proudly an incident at a "Masonic concert" to which he was taken by his uncle: "Somebody sang a stage Irishman song – the usual whiskey shallelagh kind of thing – and I hissed him and lest my hiss might be lost in the general applause waited till the applause was done and hissed again. This gave somebody else courage and we both hissed" (L, p. 304). Nine years later, when the audience hissed and booed what it thought were stage Irishmen, Yeats was on the other side. The crowds arrayed against him were crowds he helped to bring into being, using ideas and even tactics he helped to make popular. The *Playboy* riots might be seen, then, not as Yeats's failure to make an audience for Irish national drama, but as the irony of his success.

Philip Marcus notices that Yeats's arguments for a purely national subject matter were "a potential threat to his own work."[44] To defuse this threat, according to Marcus, Yeats went back to Irish antiquity, where it seemed he could find Irish subject matter congruent with his other literary and mystical interests. This solution, however, was self-defeating. It was the self-defeat, as Beckett has it, of the Anglo-Irish intelligentsia in general:

> But this study of Gaelic antiquity proved more potent and more divisive than those who encouraged it could have foreseen. The popular imagination was caught by the picture of a glorious past, of an Ireland with a distinctive culture of its own, untouched by English influence; and the very vagueness of the outline left the imagination free to shape the picture as it would. From this cloudy but exciting concept of a golden and heroic age sprang the idea of a Gaelic nationality, of an Ireland that would reject not only English power but English culture and express its independence not only in its own government but its own language.
>
> In preparing the way for this development Anglo-Irish writers played a major part. Though they had no political purpose, they could neither restrain nor control the force they had released; and they contributed, unwittingly, to the downfall of their own tradition.[45]

Yeats was one of these Anglo-Irish writers who tried to create a concept of cultural nationalism that would include their own tradition, only to see that nationalism taken over by an opposition that used it against the Anglo-Irish themselves.

The prudery Yeats confronted in the *Playboy* riots seems the very essence of small-mindedness. Yet this puritanism can hardly be separated from the myth of Irish moral superiority that Yeats himself helped to create. John Hutchinson describes the growth of this puritanism through the 1880s: "Gaelic Ireland gradually became the Catholic *insula sacra:* a unique spiritual haven of traditional folk simplicity, free from all the evils of modernity – a secular literature, alcoholism, sexual immorality, socialist agitations and materialist ideals."[46] Yeats, of course, had no desire to combat sexual immorality or alcoholism, or to make Ireland a *Catholic* sacred island, but he had celebrated "the Celt's futile revolt against the despotism of fact" and "against a political and moral materialism" (UP, 2:91).[47] Seamus Deane contends that Yeats's anti-materialism was easily turned against his own class, because the Anglo-Irish Ascendancy had been seen for so many years as holding its position of superiority through a purely material power, whereas its tenants and underlings had created in compensation a myth of their own moral superiority.[48]

On the other hand, Watson suggests that the rioters objected just as much to those characteristics Synge chose to idealize: "What the Anglo-Irishman chooses to celebrate – 'wildness', 'savagery' – is so close to what the Englishman had for centuries chosen as the major denigratory feature in his image of the Irish – violence, and another kind of savagery."[49] Dublin Catholics who were by no means crude and unlettered – Conor Cruise O'Brien lists his uncles Richard Sheehy and Francis Skeffington, the latter considered by James Joyce the second cleverest man at the Royal University, after Joyce himself – objected to the play because it idealized qualities the English had made a mockery.[50] In this respect, Yeats and Synge remain imprisoned in the Anglo-Irish predicament, their reaction against English stereotype nothing more than a reflex of English prejudice. Even in their love for the Irish they remained English, having simply reversed the emphasis of English stereotypes.

To Yeats, however, the riots proved just the opposite. The split he had seen between Ireland and England now became in his mind an internal split within Ireland itself. Resistance to Synge's plays and to his own, with the exception of *Cathleen ni Houlihan,* foot-dragging on the part of those who should have jumped at Hugh Lane's art collection, all seemed to reveal the penetration of English influence. The important word in Yeats's accounts of these controversies is *new,* suggesting both that something different has entered Irish life and that it is to be associated with the modern age that Ireland had successfully avoided until then. As early as 1902, he deplored the "new commonness / Upon the throne and crying about the streets . . . " (VP, p. 198). In a journal passage of 1909, Yeats speaks of "the new class which is rising in Ireland" with its "thought made in some manufactory" (M, p. 139). In his speech at the *Playboy* debate in 1907, he decried the national movement for making the mistakes of "the newly enfranchised everywhere . . . " (EX, p. 227). Here Yeats charges democratic liberalism with the conflicts brought about by his own cultural nationalism; his opposition is not the democratic middle class but other cultural nationalists who see him as dangerously liberal and individualistic himself.

Consciously or not, Yeats turns against his antagonists exactly the weapons they used against him, and the fact that the same charges were hurled in both directions shows how close Yeats remains to his opposition. Though he had been under attack as dangerously cosmopolitan, he accused his opposition of being a "cosmopolitan and denationalised class" (UP, 2:155). Though he was himself suspect as more English than Irish, he attacks his opponents as bringing into Ireland modes of argument and behavior associated previously only with the English. In other words, the purity established as an ideal by cultural nationalism is used by both sides in the debate. The real conflict is about the terms by which that purity shall be defined. Though Yeats had done as much as anyone to promote the ideal, he stood to lose most from its implementation because of his Anglo-Irish background.

Though Yeats attempted to remain consistent by using his old cultural arguments against the new foe, the conflict brought out in him a different argument as well. John Kelly maintains that attacks on Yeats's Anglo-Irish background made him "more wary of claiming a racial sanction for his ideas than he had been hitherto."[51] But such attacks also forced Yeats to find a new sanction in a different theory, that of individual civil rights. In these years, Yeats begins to defend the prerogatives of the individual with classically liberal arguments. He asserts "intellectual freedom" against "the hatred of ideas" (UP, 2:306–307). He decries the attack on the *Playboy* as "the annihilation of civil rights" (UP, 2:351). He defends over and over "the right of the individual mind to see the world in its own way, to cherish the thoughts which separate men from one another, and that are the creators of distinguished life, instead of those thoughts that had made one man like another . . . " (UP, 2:353). In 1905, he wrote John Quinn, "We will have a hard fight in Ireland before we get the right for every man to see the world in his own way admitted" (L, p. 447).

Yeats exposes the weakness of his cultural nationalism by implicitly admitting that liberalism provides the only model that can settle controversy without oppressing the losers. Yet this weakness propels Yeats into a major contradiction. On one hand, he bases his defense of himself and Synge on the doctrine of individual rights. His language makes clear the dependence of this doctrine on an opposition between individuals and the mass. The "thoughts which separate men from one another" are authentic, sincere, whereas those thoughts entertained by many alike are specious propaganda. The very notion of rights thus arises from the necessity to defend the individual from the rest of the world. On the other hand, Yeats attacks democracy and the "newly enfranchised," who are apparently unjust in asserting *their* rights. His cultural arguments depend on a notion of the Irish race radically incompatible with his individualism, because authenticity comes, in this analysis, from a common stock of memories, customs, and stories. Indeed, Yeats had based his arguments for the moral superiority of the Irish precisely on their cultural cohesiveness, on their difference from the atomized mass of the English, which was, of course, the product of the very individualism to which he now turned.

If cultural nationalism had simply recreated the tensions it was supposed to dissolve, if it had become both divisive and coercive, then Yeats needed a new alternative to give him hope for reconciliation. This he found in the aristocracy. Though Yeats had always felt that poets are "the most aristocratic of men" (UP, 2:131), he had begun his theater work by accepting what he called "the baptism of the gutter" (L, p. 339). He made common cause with "poverty against wealth," even with "the intellectual movement which has raised the cry that was heard in Russia in the seventies, the cry 'To the people' " (EX, p. 83). Here he chose sides, and he challenged other writers to choose "whether they will write as the upper classes have done, not to express but to exploit this country."

Yeats's dedication to the people did not survive the controversies over the Abbey Theater and Hugh Lane's pictures, and his antipathy to the upper classes began noticeably to fade. "Every day," he said in 1909, "I notice some new analogy between [the] long-established life of the well-born and the artist's life" (M, p. 156). Despite his friendship with Lady Gregory, this aristocracy was less an actual class than the resolution of a logical problem. For Yeats to continue voicing his cultural theories, based as they were on the spiritual unity of the Irish, while also standing on his rights as an individual, based as they were on a negation of public uniformity, he had to invent a minority that could serve to represent the whole. In 1904, Yeats speaks of "those few scattered people who have the right to call themselves the Irish race." Most Irish, apparently, are not really Irish. Yeats goes beyond this to assert a general rule: "It is only in the exceptions, in the few minds where the flame was burnt, as it were, that one can see the permanent character of a race" (EX, p. 147). This very odd brand of racialism, in which the race is epitomized precisely by those who do not fit comfortably into it, clearly comes from Yeats's immediate political situation. The aristocracy represents the conjuncture of two different political theories: the cultural nationalism of the 1890s and the liberal individualism that emerges as Yeats confronts his own nationalism rampant against him.

At the end of "J.M. Synge and the Ireland of His Time," published in 1910, Yeats meditates over the monastic brilliance of Mont Saint-Michel and longs for some such order for Ireland. Only from such an order "can we come upon those agreements, those separations from all else, that fasten men together lastingly . . . " (E, pp. 422–423). Unity, this formula suggests, comes from difference; only separation can truly fasten things together. Surely the aristocracy is the necessary social expression of this paradox, incarnating as it does for Yeats a national being out of its very difference from the common ruck. Thus Protestant landowners became the true Irish despite the growing claims of the Catholic masses to that status, precisely *because of* their difference from the mass. The Ascendancy becomes, in Hegelian terms, a universal class, a part that because of its very independence from the whole comes to represent it.

This is nothing more than the ancient claim of the aristocracy to be a general class. According to Guido de Ruggiero, the "aristocracy was the 'general class' *par excellence,* exempt from the cares of daily life precisely in order that it might turn all its activities to the service of the common weal."[52] As Yeats himself puts it in 1931, "the Few are those who through the possession of hereditary wealth, or great personal gifts, have come to identify their lives with the life of the State, whereas the lives and ambitions of the Many are private" (EX, p. 351). But how can this part represent that which is its very antithesis, and what is to happen to the majority, which has to be removed somehow from "the whole"? Paul de Man points out that there is something logically unstable about "an ideal which is persistently referred to as Unity of Being, but most frequently expressed . . . by such terms as 'to reject' or 'to limit.' "[53] More dangerously, there is something politically unstable about a whole that exists in contradistinction to elements somehow outside the whole. Yeats's decision at this time that "the people are conquered by an ideal of life upheld by authority" (M, p. 180) shows in what direction that instability might lead.

3. MAJOR GREGORY'S RESPONSIBILITIES

By its own lights, the aristocracy can rightfully represent the whole of which it is only a tiny part because of its freedom from material need, which translates into an independence from immediate interests. Yeats's association of the aristocracy with the arts makes a certain kind of historical sense, therefore, as long as art is put in the autonomous realm to which the aristocracy laid first claim.[54] In his many battles against what he saw as middle class mobs, Yeats often put his art in this defensive position. He called, in one of his theatrical pamphlets, for young men who would value "fine things for their own sake" and not for "momentary use" (EX, p. 123). Though Yeats seems to be gallantly choosing sides with art that transcends mere use, the real purpose of his argument is to break down the very distinction between what seems useful and what refuses to be used: "One can serve one's country alone out of the abundance of one's own heart, and it is labour enough to be certain one is right, without having to be certain that one's thought is expedient also" (EX, p. 123). In other words, a writer can be of service only by refusing the peremptory claims that he serve obvious, immediate interests; he works hard to be sure that what he makes is not merely useful.[55]

In such passages, Yeats picks apart and remakes the common notion of the writer's responsibility. By redefining service and labor, he armors himself against accusations of escapism, elitism, and social irrelevance. He argues, in fact, that a writer discharges his patriotic duty precisely by refusing the most immediate claims of patriotism. At times, this argument takes the liberal form in which the writer serves all by keeping open a free space for disinterested debate. More often, Yeats goes back behind liberalism to a kind of autonomy that is not even potentially open to all because its independence is inseparable from its peculiarity. Yeats's first explicitly political book of poems, *Responsibilities* (1916), defines its title by portraying an aristocracy that is exemplary because of its peculiar independence from ordinary ideas of useful service. The autonomy of this class then sanctions the autonomy of the poems about it, which become responsible precisely by defying the conventional demands of public duty.

Yeats opens his campaign with the poem usually called "Pardon, Old

Fathers" after the plea contained in its first line. Yeats asks pardon for an irresponsibility of his own: He has broken the family line. "I have no child, I have nothing but a book / Nothing but that to prove your blood and mine" (VP, p. 270, ll. 21–22). Yeats's ancestors, on the other hand, proved their blood again and again, accumulating a tradition that "has not passed through any huckster's loin" (l. 8). Yeats does, he admits, have merchants as forebears, and the line between merchant and "huckster" may seem a very subjective one, but Yeats's merchant ancestors prove their blood by doing something useless and a little crazy such as leaping overboard after a hat (ll. 13–14). The family defines itself in such moments, in the soldiers "that gave" (l. 9), and not in hucksters that grasp.

The family Yeats describes embodies a kind of freedom that comes from its willingness to ignore ordinary measures, ordinary values. The hat derives its value from the merchant's willingness to jump overboard after it and not from its cost in pounds, shillings, and pence. Yet the motto of the poem seems to be "Only the wasteful virtues earn the sun" (l. 18). Yeats certainly intends by his language to overturn ordinary concepts of value, to suggest that what seems waste in fact accrues something far more important than gold. He had used the phrase "high wasteful virtues" in his introduction to Lady Gregory's *Gods and Fighting Men,* which returned to the era of the rakes and duelists, men who "fight duels over pocket handkerchiefs, and set out to play ball against the gates of Jerusalem for a wager, and scatter money before the public eye" (EX, p. 27). To be wasteful and immoderate in this fashion, even to be irresponsible, the poem argues, is to "earn" nonetheless.

The economic language conceals the poem's implicit argument about family and tradition. The Yeats line distinguishes itself from all other merchants by refusing to grasp, to hold on, to accumulate. In the strictest etymological sense, it is no tradition at all because it does not hand on but instead relinquishes what it might hold. But the poem paradoxically argues that *only* waste earns, or, in other words, that only the ungrasping, free-spending can accumulate anything worth having. Though the poem begins by indicting Yeats himself and ends by calling him "barren," it turns out that his barrenness is exactly in the family line. As T.R. Whitaker notes, Yeats's "barren passion" is itself a "wasteful virtue."[56] Thus *not* having a child is a perfectly good way to continue the tradition. Though Yeats seems to be accusing himself of failing in his responsibilities, he in fact remains responsible to the history of his family precisely in that failure.

Yeats places his book, the one introduced by this poem, at the exact intersection of these paradoxes. The rhetoric of the poem is remarkable in the way it identifies and defines by antithesis. The Yeats blood, for example, "has not passed through any huckster's loin." This line defines purity and continuity by negation, bringing to mind the possibility that blood can avoid huckster's loins by expiring altogether. In fact, the family line seems often to distinguish itself by opposition, by mustering with those "that withstood." This pattern of opposition and antithesis turns on the word "only" in line 18. For the antitheses become more and more exclusive as the poem goes on, until it ends in a crescendo of negatives:

> Pardon that for a barren passion's sake,
> Although I have come close on forty-nine,
> I have no child, I have nothing but a book,
> Nothing but that to prove your blood and mine.

In the economy of the world, a book amounts to very little, but in the economy of the poem, a book is the only real value, because "only the wasteful virtues earn the sun." The book, in fact, acquires value precisely insofar as the world's economy values it at nothing. As the ultimate antithesis, the negative version of everything else, it is the ultimate scale of value.

In "September 1913" Yeats elaborates further the counter-economy behind this tradition. In the counter-economy, the apparent antithesis between giving and saving disappears. The first stanza fills the word *save* with a heavy irony by approaching it through a double accounting: "add the halfpence to the pence / And prayer to shivering prayer" (VP, p. 289, ll. 3–4). Denigration of the mercantile spills over into denigration of religion, based on the common Protestant prejudice against the temporal power of the Catholic church. Yeats distills centuries of Irish sectarian hatred into this single image, in which a Catholic using a rosary becomes a kind of spiritual accountant. "For men were born to pray and save" thus becomes a sourly ironic equation of prayer and banking, with "save" losing all its spiritual significance in the mercantile metaphor.

The irony modulates in the second stanza, which turns on the question, "And what, God help us, could they save?" (l. 14). Yeats returns to the term *save* its spiritual significance in order to praise the different religion practiced by the Irish martyrs, who had little time to pray (l. 13). They could not save themselves, being hung by the British, nor could they save the savers, whose close-fisted self-interest betrays them. In both stanzas, "save" fatefully rhymes with "grave," for to attempt to save is to lose. To throw everything away, on the other hand, is to approach salvation. The third stanza names certain Irish heroes, all distinguished by their patriotic profligacy:

> Was it for this the wild geese spread
> The grey wing upon every tide;
> For this that all that blood was shed,

> For this Edward Fitzgerald died,
> And Robert Emmet and Wolfe Tone,
> All that delirium of the brave?

The true Irish hero gives his blood freely, lavishing it "all." The expansiveness of the rhetoric has a characteristic ring: "every," "all," "all." To give is somehow to enlarge oneself, to become great, to encompass all. Thus this stanza places "brave" where the other had "save," in very pointed contrast. The cycle reaches conclusion in the next and last stanza, in which "gave" occupies the crucial spot: "They weighed so lightly what they gave" (l. 30). These heroes, though they lie in the grave, are Ireland's hope for salvation, which can only come from giving.

A good deal of Yeats's propaganda in the poems of *Responsibilities* has to do with actual donations, especially those forthcoming and not forthcoming with respect to Hugh Lane. As donor, Lane fits easily into Yeats's tradition of free-handed men, as the unnamed "Wealthy Man who promised a Second Subscription to the Dublin Municipal Gallery if it were proved the People wanted Pictures" fits into the opposite tradition of mercantile meanness. This poem shows how easily such economic matters shade off into historical ones for Yeats. In it, he charges the wealthy man:

> Look up in the sun's eye and give
> What the exultant heart calls good
> That some new day may breed the best
> Because you gave, not what they would,
> But the right twigs for an eagle's nest!
> (VP, p. 288, ll. 32–36)

The image of the nest recalls that in "Upon a House shaken by the Land Agitation," a poem published two years before the one in question. There, Yeats asks what good will come if Coole Park should be unable

> To breed the lidless eye that loves the sun?
> And the sweet laughing eagle thoughts that grow
> Where wings have memory of wings, and all
> That comes of the best knit to the best?
> (VP, p. 264, ll. 4–7)

In these poems, the nest stands for a particular kind of historical accumulation. Fostering and fostered by "the memory of wings," the nest represents race memory, faultlessly preserved in the animal world but imperiled in the world of humankind. In this human world, the poems suggest, memory depends on social cohesion, where all is "knit" together like the twigs of the nest. Social structures of this kind are not made, but are instead the result of the "gifts that govern men" (l. 10). When a wealthy man gives, then, he is not just adding to the pile of twigs but is also reenacting the bountiful graciousness of nature that made the nest in the first place. He demonstrates his gifts by giving. This is the most positive version of giving as saving in these tendentious poems. For the gift is the article beyond economy, and giving is the life built up by aversion to mere use. Paradoxically, all accumulation, all tradition, and all history come only from this indifference to saving.

The final gift, "gradual Time's last gift," according to "Upon a House," is language, "a written speech / Wrought of high laughter, loveliness and ease" (ll. 11–12). Here Yeats is so wrought up into his own mood of aristocratic spontaneity he forgets how well he has argued elsewhere – in "Adam's Curse," for example – that "ease" is a mere effect of the poet's labor. But ease of language is troubled even in these poems. As Whitaker puts it, "In each poem celebrating Yeats's family tradition, the very mode of utterance – apology, question, challenge, elegy – embodies a recognition of the counterforces of isolation and fragmentation within the self, within society, and within the cosmos as a whole."[57] But these rhetorical stances confess more than the fragility of the aristocratic tradition. They show as well that traditional continuity is inseparable from opposition and contradiction. For the very ease and spontaneity that Yeats calls a gift is in fact defined by opposition to the ordinary economy. Only the "best" is knit together to make the nest, so that the metaphor places an image of coherence in implicit opposition to the disorder around it. The gift, we might say, is only given after having first been withdrawn, removed from the crass economy of exchange.

Even as Yeats lays claim to the traditional independence of the aristocracy, even as he appropriates for himself and his art the peculiar privilege of the general class, he exposes the contradiction on which it is based. What the aristocracy gives had first to be taken, and the material independence of the class is not in fact the basis of its service to the community but rather a result of its exploitation. That Yeats himself was well aware of this emerges in a work in which he handles these contradictions much less smoothly. His earliest work on the Protestant aristocracy appeared in 1891 and was entitled something close to *Irresponsibilities:* "A Reckless Century." This article on the Hellfire Club, a group of eighteenth-century Irish "rakes," returns again and again, with ever-differing emphasis, to the concept of responsibility. The Hellfire Club, Yeats tells his readers, ran its riots in a political vacuum, when "the nation had little or no sense of national duty and public responsibility," when the gentry "held allegiance only to England, and were responsible to no man" (UP, 1:201). Without any national feeling, the gentry revealed its essentially mercantile and sensual nature, unlike the poor. Yeats draws a pointed contrast between "the irresponsible turbulence of the gentry" and the "popular indignation when the mob attacked the Parliament House and made the members swear truth to Ireland . . . " (UP, 1:201). This must be the only time in the entire corpus that Yeats uses the word *mob* in a positive sense. Here all patriotic feeling belongs to the people and none to the upper classes, who must be brought to patriotic responsibility by force.

Yet when Yeats comes to that point in the essay when he must draw conclusions, he muffles this political distinction. The eighteenth-century gentry, he says, needed "only the responsibility of self-government and the restraint of a trained public opinion to have laboured devotedly for the public weal" (UP, 2:202). Even in 1891, Yeats does not really believe in so conventional a definition of responsibility and useful labor. Before another sentence is out, his real sympathies emerge: "It is better to be violent and irresponsible than full of body-worship and money-grubbing" (UP, 2:202). It is not really responsibility and hard work at all that make a nation, but exactly their opposites: "If a man or a people have energy all is well with them, and if they use it for ill to-day they will turn it to good to-morrow" (UP, 2:202). In the last paragraph, Yeats puts a twist in the tail of his own argument, for it now appears clearly that the rakes and duelists of the eighteenth century, in all their wasteful independence, have more true Irish spirit than the mob that stormed Parliament to force on its members an Irish oath. Somehow violent self-indulgence becomes patriotism.

This essay arrays against one another the forces Yeats portrays again in *Responsibilities,* the overtly patriotic mob and the seemingly detached aristocracy. Though Yeats concludes by throwing in his lot with the aristocracy, the exposition shows how difficult it is to square his own patriotic feelings with the traditional detachment of that class. The synthesis of individual right and common duty, of difference and unity, a synthesis that autonomy was to accomplish in both politics and art, simply comes apart. Though Yeats tries to show that irresponsibility and responsibility are essentially the same, his argument demonstrates despite him their necessary conflict.

Yeats's most concerted attempt to put right and duty, difference and unity, back together again is "In Memory of Major Robert Gregory." Though it was written four years after most of the poems in *Responsibilities,* Yeats's poem for Robert Gregory is in fact the culmination of his attempt to redefine responsibility and with it the relationship between individual and community, art and politics. Gregory seems the finest example of the free-handed aristocrat, having given his very life. "An Irish Airman Foresees his Death" makes it clear that this sacrifice was not offered for any utilitarian purpose or to a political cause: "Nor law, nor duty bade me fight, / Nor public men, nor cheering crowds . . . " (VP, p. 328, ll. 9–10). The final lines of the poem seem to recall Yeats's celebration of "the wasteful virtues":

> The years to come seemed waste of breath,
> A waste of breath the years behind
> In balance with this life, this death.

To the ordinary observer, Gregory seems to have wasted his life, throwing it away on a cause not even his own. At the end of the poem, however, Yeats takes care to upset this ordinary calculation by calling the long stretch of ordinary life a waste. It is part of Gregory's splendor that he sees life in such terms, that, as the last line implies, his scale of values is so different from the common. What seems a waste thus acquires all its value precisely from the way it evades common measure.

Once Yeats saw Gregory primarily as an artist, Frank Kermode argues, "it follows that he was to have been *different,* isolated, cut off from life and action."[58] In this reading, Gregory's death is necessary, because his difference from the common makes life an indignity: "What made us dream that he could comb grey hair?" (VP, p. 327, 1. 88). As Yeats asks through his mouthpiece *Ille* in "Ego Dominus Tuus":

> What portion in the world can the artist have
> Who has awakened from the common dream
> But dissipation and despair?
> (VP, p. 369, ll. 49–51)

In this reading, Gregory's death represents an apotheosis, the single possible moment of perfect balance, perfect unity, which can never be known in the long drawn-out compromise of daily life. The death represents the utter independence from all material claims that distinguishes both art and aristocracy.

Persuasive as it is, Kermode's reading has been criticized for underestimating the feelings of loss and disappointment also present in "In Memory of Major Robert Gregory."[59] The most puzzling such reservation appears in "Shepherd and Goatherd," the first poem Yeats wrote to commemorate Gregory's death. There, the shepherd describes the dead hero not as the master of every kind of work, as Yeats describes him in "In Memory of Major Robert Gregory," but as alone in his aversion to work:

> You cannot but have seen
> That he alone had gathered up no gear,
> Set carpenters to work on no wide table,
> On no long bench nor lofty milking-shed
> As others will, when first they take possession. . .
> (VP, p. 341–342, ll. 48–52)

These lines sort oddly with the more famous ones in "In Memory of Major Robert Gregory":

> What other could so well have counselled us
> In all lovely intricacies of a house

As he that practiced or that understood
All work in metal or in wood,
In moulded plaster or in carven stone?
(VP, p. 327, ll. 73–77)

The rhetorical difference, all those *nos* balanced against those repeated *alls*, underscores a real tension in Yeats's presentation of his hero. For Gregory is celebrated on one hand for avoiding all human endeavor and on the other for mastering it all. The perfection of the aristocratic life appears in its independence from ordinary service but also in its mastery of all forms of it.

In these specific lines, Yeats confronts as well the great unspoken topic of the elegies for Gregory, the break he represents in the continuity of the house, for Gregory's talents about the physical house obviously represent his role in the temporal house of his family. "Shepherd and Goatherd" very obliquely exposes this topic when the shepherd says that Gregory conducted himself "As though he knew himself, as it were, a cuckoo, / No settled man" (VP, p. 341, ll. 54–55). Gregory does not settle into the house because he senses somehow his difference from the settled life of daily continuity. Again, Gregory seems to receive praise for his difference, but the cuckoo metaphor carries a complex negative charge, because the cuckoo does not build a nest but invades those of other birds. Yeats had revealed the latent political content of the metaphor in 1903, when he criticized a Catholic bishop for failing to realize "that his new puritanism is but an English cuckoo" (EX, p. 113). Yeats draws here for his own propagandistic purposes on the common Irish sense of English usurpation, but he must not realize how vulnerable his own class is to this very charge. To call Gregory a "cuckoo" might seem a criticism of his English background. In any case, the cuckoo metaphor in "Shepherd and Goatherd" carries with it disquieting echoes from *Responsibilities*. There, the nest was Yeats's preferred metaphor of historical continuity and tradition. When he lavishes so much praise in "In Memory of Major Robert Gregory" on Gregory's skills as decorator, his concern is surely more than aesthetic, for the house represents the complex of customs and memories that keeps a family alive. When he represents Gregory in "Shepherd and Goatherd" as only lightly settled in the house, perhaps even an interloper in it, Yeats exposes the real cost of his adventure in the First World War, the break in continuity caused by his death. At the same time, he opens a gap in his own value system, because the autonomy of the aristocracy now begins to look at least a bit like irresponsibility.

The last poem written on Gregory's death, "Reprisals," which was never published in Yeats's lifetime, exposes this cost quite bitterly. In this poem, Yeats contrasts Gregory's death in the English cause with English attacks on his home by the Black and Tans during the Anglo-Irish war.

As is almost always the case when Yeats contrasts England and Ireland, the result of their conflict is a break in Irish tradition:

> Men that revere your father yet
> Are shot at on the open plain.
> Where may new-married women sit
> And suckle their children now?
>
> (VP, p. 791, ll. 17–20)

The memories of men and the children suckled by women come under attack by the English. The fault is, of course, that of the invading English, but the crucial break in the continuity of the Gregory estate came with Robert's death. In "Reprisals," Yeats asks Gregory to set aside the "battle joy" of his "last exciting year" and return somehow to his estate.

That estate appears many years later in "Stories of Michael Robartes and His Friends," one of the many layers of front matter prefaced to the second version of *A Vision*. Bernard Krimm suggests that the Bell estate in "Stories" strongly resembles Coole.[60] Old Mr. Bell, whose line had almost died out, devoted his retirement to the reduction of strife in the animal world, which he intended to achieve by teaching the cuckoo to build a nest. As he dies, his wife, Mary Bell, brings into the sickroom a nest she claims was made by one of their cuckoos, but which in fact she had made herself. The false nest represents the cuckoo in Bell's own house, his son, fathered in fact by John Bond. The whole episode, only part of a much more elaborate fiction, seems a joke, and yet the connection to the nest metaphor in *Responsibilities* cannot be missed,[61] nor can the ironic relationship to the Gregory elegies. Yeats seems to have taken the cuckoo metaphor from "Shepherd and Goatherd" for elaboration into a much more complex historical meditation. In doing so, he reflects back very ironically on the empty nest left by Gregory at Coole.

Much of this irony is visible in "In Memory of Major Robert Gregory" itself. The poem begins as a formal housewarming, a ceremony that knits "new friend" to old within the confines of the house. In this ceremony, Yeats seeks to reenact the welcome he received from Lady Gregory at Coole, where he found "New welcome and old wisdom at her fire" (VP, p. 340, l. 32). But, as Daniel Harris points out, the desired continuity of ceremony is constantly disrupted and qualified.[62] The very introduction of the ceremony into the poem is immediately qualified: "Always we'd have the new friend meet the old . . . " (VP, p. 324, l. 9). "Always" implies continuity, habit, and yet this continuity is syntactically displaced into the past by the use of the modal auxiliary in its past form, as if it were no longer continuing.[63] This second stanza dwells on the possibility of quarrel and hurt, on a possible discourtesy that might disrupt the ceremony, and it seems to end with ironic satisfaction:

> But not a friend that I would bring
> This night can set us quarrelling,
> For all that come into my mind are dead.

Death seems to solve the problem of discourtesy, but Yeats points his irony three stanzas later with the phrase "that discourtesy of death" (l. 48). Death, in the immediate context, mars the courtly life, but it also commits the ultimate discourtesy of breaking the continuity of ceremony. It is the ultimate quarrel, the ultimate misunderstanding, that prevents new and old from settling into the same quarters. "He might have been your heartiest welcomer," Yeats says to his new wife, and the conditional emphasizes how the ceremony of welcome has been disrupted.

The praise lavished in the rest of the poem on Gregory's accomplishments is constantly qualified by similar conditionals. Gregory's prowess as a painter is potential, not actual: "He had the intensity / To have published all to be a world's delight."[64] He "could . . . have counselled us" (l. 73) in the decoration of the house. These conditions emphasize loss the more they inflate Gregory's talents. In so doing, they illustrate a basic conflict in the values exposed by Yeats's reaction to Gregory's death. The "wasteful virtues" seem the epitome of the aristocratic life. In balancing his entire life on a pinpoint of time, Gregory seems the paragon of that system of value. And yet his very wastefulness makes continuation of the aristocratic life impossible. Yeats's inconsistencies about Gregory merely expose inconsistencies latent in the poems of *Responsibilities,* inconsistencies that arose out of the political disappointments of the years between 1890 and 1907. The contradiction between the individual irresponsibility of the aristocrat, which Yeats idealizes, and responsibility to the family as a historical constant, does not appear until Yeats confronts an actual case close to his own home.

Gregory is, on one hand, an example of the kind of careless life Yeats criticizes in "A Reckless Century." His individual indulgence makes patriotic commitment and public service impossible. In the *Responsibilities* poems, Yeats had attempted to transform such carelessness into civic responsibility, for rather obvious political reasons. He had been forced to argue in the course of his struggles in the Irish Revival that individuals have a right to these differences, yet this argument from natural right clashed with the cultural nationalism Yeats himself still believed in, and with his personal sense of responsibility to Ireland. The poems of *Responsibilities* are examples of his attempt to resolve this conflict by arguing that even one's most idiosyncratic acts might serve a patriotic purpose if patriotism is properly understood. The inconsistencies in his poetic responses to Gregory's death mark the reappearance of the conflict between individual right and public duty.

In a sense, this inconsistency had been implicit even in the earliest Romantic attempts to propose autonomy as an aesthetic and political value. Two recent editors of Schiller's letters *On the Aesthetic Education of Man* find their author defining personal wholeness in two different ways – as something "achieved in the brief moment of aesthetic contemplation" and "as a changing pattern in time, a constantly shifting hierarchy of interests and values and powers. . . . "[65] For them, Schiller's success as a political philosopher lies in his ability to mediate between these two definitions, "to accommodate to his ideal of a Whole Man, not only specialization of vocation or skill, but also that retrenchment of 'wholeness' involved in civic responsibilities."[66] This is precisely the mediation Yeats tried to effect in the poems of *Responsibilities*. In his elegy for Robert Gregory, he seems to make personal wholeness an effect of momentary intensity. Thus D.J. Gordon and Ian Fletcher can say with perfect justice: "For a moment Gregory had been what he was. His triumph was alien and impossible to the modern world."[67] But "In Memory of Major Robert Gregory" also represents wholeness as achieved through the accumulation of all the different roles of public life. Gregory was not "soldier, scholar, horseman" all at once but one at a time, and the very intensity with which he attacked each different discipline made achievement in some other for that time impossible. As Harris insists, "the unity of Gregory's entire life is evident throughout."[68] To achieve this kind of unity, however, the hero must accept the "retrenchment" that specialization requires, to be a partial human being at any particular moment so as to be a complete one over the whole course of life. To be a well-rounded man, a Sidney, a paragon of civic virtue, Gregory had to accept the inevitable compromise of perfect wholeness that particular responsibilities entails. On the other hand, the one moment of utter integration enjoyed at the point of death exists only insofar as Gregory cuts all earthly ties.

The rhetorical version of this clash between two different conceptions of unity is Kenneth Burke's paradox of the absolute. The general can be seen either as the fulfillment, the highest version, of the particular, or as its antithesis.[69] In Yeats's elegy, Gregory is related to the rest of the world in these two quite different ways. "All" is, as Richard Ellmann observes, the most important word in the poem.[70] Gregory loved "all things"; he would have "published all"; he knew "all lovely intricacies" because he practiced "all work"; he was, in short, "all life's epitome." The word represents Yeats's tendency to see Gregory as a compendium, summing up the various virtues observed singly in the other friends, Johnson, Synge, and Pollexfen.[71] The refrain, "Soldier, scholar, horseman" represents the same process of accumulation, as does the trope "our Sidney," because Sidney lived at the very pinnacle of his society, reflecting its various glories brightly in public life. By extending "all" into his adverbs of time such as "always," Yeats associates this sort of wholeness with habit and ritual.[72]

Precisely because he sums up so much of human life, however, Gregory differs from every other living human. Thus Yeats puts him in an antithetical relationship to the rest of the world, especially in stanzas X and XI. "What other could so well have counselled us," he asks at the beginning of stanza X. The next stanza is elaborately antithetical: "Some burn damp faggots, others may consume. . . . " The fine concluding line of this stanza establishes an implied antithesis with a rhetorical question: "What made us dream that he could comb grey hair?" "Nothing" is the implied answer, because nothing in Gregory's life resembled the common run, so that the antithesis between the hero and the life around him seems absolute. Peter Sacks suggests that Yeats constructs Gregory self-consciously as a rhetorical figure – synecdoche. But this is a synecdoche constructed out of antitheses and oppositions, a seemingly impossible, if very effective, rhetorical figure.[73]

The impossibility underlines de Man's charge that Unity of Being can hardly be unified when it is defined by such terms as "to reject" and "to limit."[74] If Gregory is, in a sense, a figure for figuration itself, his unstable position in Yeats's poem exposes a more general figurative instability, a strategy of metaphorical identification constantly qualified by ironic contrast. The aristocratic hero is the figure upon which these two modes converge. The convergence also expresses the political dilemma of Yeats's poetry, which is to make an alien aristocracy into a patriotic representative of the Irish people and to make Yeats himself patriotic in his very disagreement with the course of his country. Homi Bhabha describes a common colonialist strategy that resembles Yeats's: "The 'part' (which must be the colonialist foreign body) must be representative of the 'whole' (conquered country), but the right of representation is based on its radical difference."[75] The intersection of Yeats's individualism and his cultural nationalism, his politics of right and his politics of duty, Gregory is also an attempted philosophical synthesis in which the general would be both antithesis and fulfillment of the particular. "In Memory of Major Robert Gregory" is one of Yeats's most courageous attempts to solve this political and philosophical problem, which Hegel had solved with the concept of sublation. Yeats's attempt is not nearly so elegant, nor so philosophically powerful, as Hegel's, but it remains closer to actual practice. For this very reason, his poems expose despite themselves the radical incompatibility of the divergent values within them. The very issue he raises to prominence – responsibility – wrecks the compromise the aristocracy seems to offer.[76]

4. THE LEANING TOWER

In an essay published in 1919, at the beginning of the troubles that were to bring out his greatest political poems, Yeats climbed down from his aristocratic perch for a moment to praise "all that cleanness and neatness that the countryman's ownership of his farm has brought with it to Ireland." It may seem odd to hear Yeats commending such tidy middle-class virtues, but his deepest sympathies are more truly engaged by a less mundane effect of ownership: "the spiritualisation of the soil" (EX, p. 273). For Yeats, the family can only exist through some such spiritualization: "No family has the full condition of perfection that cannot share in . . . 'the spiritualisation of the soil'. . . . I understand by 'soil' all the matter in which the soul works, the walls of our houses, the serving-up of our meals, and the chairs and tables of our rooms, and the instincts of our bodies; and by 'family' all institutions, classes, orders, nations, that arise out of the family and are held together, not by a logical process, but by historical association . . . " (EX, pp. 273–274). For Yeats, all true political institutions arise out of the family, the historical kindred, and all such families depend on some connection to significant soil for their spiritual health. Family property therefore becomes the basis of a metaphorical relationship linking necessarily all aspects of human life. On the other hand, a politics of mere ownership, of titles bought and sold, would be, as de Man suggests in his discussion of Rousseau's *Social Contract,* metonymic.[77] The difference between this life of historical association and the more modern life of logic therefore runs parallel to a poetic difference, "derivable perhaps from the truth that all emotional unities find their definition through the image, unlike those of the intellect, which are defined in the logical process" (EX, p. 273). Yeats thus associates the family and all its institutions with the poetic image, which unifies, as against logic, separation, and the threat they pose to the metaphorical extension of the family.

In *A Vision* and elsewhere more and more as he aged, Yeats gave this historical and aesthetic construct the name "kindred."[78] Perhaps the most celebrated use of this term in nineteenth-century political discourse occurred in Henry Sumner Maine's *Ancient Law,* a landmark of the historical school of law published in 1864. Writing as a conservative determined to undermine the liberal foundation of law on the free consent of equal citizens, Maine derived all primitive law from the "association of kindred." Like Yeats in his later years, Maine based civil rights on membership in a family and not on an abstract definition of the individual. Because no nation can exist without some movement in and out of families, Maine suggested that kinship groups could enlarge themselves legitimately by a metaphorical process: "The incoming population should *feign themselves* to be descended from the same stock as the people on whom they were engrafted." This is, of course, just what Yeats does when he maintains that even the Anglo-Irish are truly Irish, even perhaps Celtic.[79] Because a true nation can only be organized on terms of similarity, the different must, in what Maine calls the original legal fiction, metaphorically transform itself into more of the same.[80]

In his most famous contribution to political terminology, Maine contrasts the association of kindred to that achieved by contract: "The movement of the progressive societies has hitherto been a movement *from Status to Contract.*" From true kindred to feigned kindred the society grows and expands until it is no longer held together by resemblance at all but merely by "local contiguity."[81] Maine thus led the way for later generations of conservatives who would lament the advent of liberal democracy with its political structures based on the consent of free individuals and with the corresponding replacement of history by abstract principles. He also suggests how such political changes might reflect themselves in poetry by describing the decline of metaphor, or what he calls the legal fiction of kindred, to the level of metonymy.

The great sequences of *The Tower,* based as they are on metaphors of building, concerned with the continuity of families, take up these political and poetic questions. But the very example Yeats uses to praise the continuity of families on their own soil shows his own problematic position. For, in order to own their land, the Irish farmers had to take it from Protestant landlords of the very kind so often praised in Yeats's poetry. Thus, according to McCormack, Anglo-Irish literature is unified by the common metaphor of endangered property: "Anglo-Irish literature *is* Protestant to the extent that the land *was* Protestant."[82] The sequences of *The Tower* are Anglo-Irish in this sense, in that they celebrate a myth of historical continuity from which Yeats was himself to be excluded because of his Protestant background.

The conflict in these poems over property runs even deeper, however, because the issue is not that of mere ownership. Oliver MacDonagh contends that Maine's theory of political change accurately describes a shift in Irish ideas about property during the nineteenth century from communal equity to individual right. The chief beneficiaries of this change were, according to MacDonagh, the Anglo-Irish Ascendancy, the members of which "began as natural supporters of the absolutist and individualist concepts of property."[83] Demands based on a "communal concept of Irish land" were voiced by Catholic challengers of the Protestant hegemony, and finally by Great Britain itself, which gradually chipped away at the absolute right to property by way of settling Ireland's political disagreements.[84] In other words, Yeats suffers from a deep conflict between political principle and practical politics. The interests of his own class lie with the change from communal to individual rights that he so deplores. In politics and in economy, Yeats finds himself in the painful position of relying on the very principles he opposes.

Metaphor therefore has a complex political status in Yeats's work. In terms of race, property, and politics, metaphor is the term for what Yeats values, a homogeneous people rooted to its ancestral ground, acting on timeless traditions and not contemporary impulse. But Yeats's own particular political position was at odds with these conditions. His own status in the predominantly Catholic state that was coming into being as he wrote the poems in *The Tower* depended on toleration of distinct minorities. His own ancestral class, it was becoming painfully clear, had achieved its prominence by breaking the ancestral hold of families over their land. Yeats thus finds himself caught between status and contract, kinship and pluralism, metaphor and metonymy.

The great sequences of *The Tower* are shaped, perhaps even motivated, by Yeats's search for "befitting emblems of adversity," a search he mounts not just for particular images but rather for a kind of image, one that would fulfill all the political demands once satisfied by metaphor but also including within it "adversity." On one level, Yeats asks himself in these poems of civil war for a new concept of the house that would apply even to a house divided. On another level, he hopes to define the Irish house in such a way as to include elements clearly at odds with its historical character, Protestant elements at odds with a Catholic majority, English elements at odds with a Celtic tradition. In so doing, Yeats poses for himself the most serious questions facing cultural nationalism in particular and anti-liberal politics in general. How are rival historical traditions to make their peace with one another and survive on the same ground? How are individuals to retain their right to differ if citizenship implies membership in a community of mind? Ireland's experience, from the time of *The Tower* until the present, dramatizes the failure of all possible answers to these questions. If the sequences in that book are "a quintessentially modernist achievement," as Ronald Bush suggests, they are so because they make this failure itself into a poetic principle, so that it is not the discovery but the frustrated search for befitting emblems that links the poems together.[85]

"The Tower" seems to be about personal matters, the "troubled heart" Yeats complains of at the beginning, and poetic ones, the imagination he immediately calls on to quell his own complaint. Yet the poem was first published in an issue of the *Criterion* that began with Eliot's somewhat wry assertion that "every 'literary' review worth its salt has a political interest." Eliot proves his own point by setting himself against mass singing, mass praying, and even mass voting, and by facing his own commentary with Yeats's poem.[86] The poetic problem with which that poem begins, the decline of imagination to the level of argument and abstraction, is almost immediately rewritten in cultural and historical terms. Yeats had long since identified the poetic imagination, as distinct from "the logical process," with family property, both material and spiritual. The transition from Part I of "The Tower," concerned with the bitter choice of argument over imagination, to Part II, which begins on the foundations of Yeats's own house, thus makes perfect sense. When Yeats sends "imagination forth" to call images and memories "From ruin or from ancient trees," he is sending his poetry back to its source in the spiritualized soil of a familial past. Even at this early stage, however, the poem contains a fearful concession, for Yeats sends imagination out to wrest images from a "ruin," not from a thriving house. When the word "ruin" returns some lines later, it signifies a significant break in imaginative continuity; the bankruptcy of the "ancient . . . master of this house" is a financial, physical, and poetic ruination, for it separates the present from the time "Before," a time touched directly by the "Great Memory."

The house therefore comes on the scene already in ruins, which is why Yeats must interrogate the scene, drawing forth its memories, before he can complete the task of the poem, which is to link again past, present, and future on the scene of familial constancy. Before he can complete Part III, the making of his will, he must have something to bequeath, which he hopes to draw by pure imaginative force from the soil itself: "Beyond that ridge . . . "; "upon that rocky place." This feat would be a dual accomplishment in that it would restore imaginative continuity after its interruption and also, by mingling folk memories with episodes from Yeats's own work, efface the fact that Yeats himself has no ancestral claim on this soil.

When Yeats declares that for his heirs "I choose upstanding men," he rather artfully obscures the fact that he has done precisely the same thing in relation to his forebears, whom he has chosen just as willfully. But this situation is not Yeats's alone. He admonished a correspondent in 1938, "Remember, that our class in Ireland has always chosen its nation."[87] The Anglo-Irish Ascendancy chooses Irishness, when it wants to. In "The Tower," Yeats tries to make this free choice, which by his own lights is surely an unhappy necessity, as the sort of association that can hardly be considered metaphorical in Maine's terms, into the very epitome of ancestral tradition.

Just as Yeats himself vociferously, even antagonistically, chooses his heirs and declares his inheritance, he defines the ascendancy as a class by its freely-given allegiance:

> Bound neither to Cause nor to State,
> Neither to slaves that were spat on,

Nor to the tyrants that spat,
The people of Burke and Grattan
That gave, though free to refuse . . .
                    (VP, p. 414)

Here Yeats adapts to the Ascendancy the traditional claims of the aristocracy as general class, repeating as he does so key terms like "gave" from
Responsibilities. In other words, the Ascendancy is bound together by the
fact that it is bound to nothing else; it is linked intimately to the Irish
landscape, its streams and hills, precisely by its freedom, which is nothing other than its ability to leave Ireland behind if necessary. What might
have seemed the weakest aspect of the Anglo-Irish claim, the relative
thinness of its tenure on the ground, now seems its greatest strength.

Another survival from the poems of *Responsibilities* occupies a crucial
place in this section of "The Tower." In the midst of his last will and
testament, Yeats returns to a favorite metaphor:

As at the loophole there
The daws chatter and scream,
And drop twigs layer upon layer.
When they have mounted up,
The mother bird will rest
On their hollow top,
And so warm her wild nest.
                    (VP, p. 415)

This brief stanza interrupts the final section of "The Tower," coming
after a forty-four line section in which Yeats begins to make his will and
preceding another twenty-two lines in which he completes it. As an
aside, it calls attention to itself, forcing the reader to attempt to fit it into
the continuity it breaks. The stanza may not be metaphorical at all; the *as*
may be a simple preposition diverting attention for a moment to the
outside world. But the resemblance is so strong between a mother bird
making her nest and Yeats making his will that a metaphorical reading
inevitably accompanies the literal one. There are, however, a number of
different possibilities contained even within the metaphorical reading.
How far back does the metaphorical equation suggested by "as" extend?
Perhaps the mother bird makes her nest as "Man makes a superhuman /
Mirror-resembling dream" (ll. 164–165). Perhaps she makes it as "man
made up the whole" of life "Out of his bitter soul" (ll. 149, 151). Or
perhaps the resemblance extends in the other direction, to the way Yeats
decides to "make my soul" (l. 181), a process that ends in "a bird's sleepy
cry" (l. 194).

Beginning as it does, so abruptly, with the word that acts as the link in
a simile, this stanza calls attention to the process of resemblance in metaphor. But the stanza only contains the second half of the metaphorical
comparison. In the same gesture, it announces and truncates a metaphor,

both advancing and impeding the process of resemblance. Because Yeats associates the repetitive, hereditary patterns of traditional family life with metaphor, with an "image" made out of historical association and not by logic, the nest might easily be his metaphor of metaphor. If so, the incompletion and the strange isolation of this stanza call into question the very process of resemblance that it represents. To make this comparison, Yeats must stop his poem in full career, so that the illustration becomes a distraction and a puzzle, a digression that leads away from the main business even as it tries to extend it. In the very process of making this metaphor, Yeats brings into his poem a formal discontinuity, dividing in one way what he links in another.

The incomplete simile of the nest implies thematically that Yeats builds up tradition as nature does, twig upon twig, but in formal terms it brings back into the poem the ruined house of the first section. Thus it epitomizes the discontinuities in the poetic argument of the whole poem. For ruin is both the problem to be solved and an indispensable part of the solution. What might seem a real weak spot in Yeats's position, the fact that he could not have occupied his tower unless the traditional inhabitants of it had been ruined, can also be seen as a strength, because it allows Yeats to exercise the virtue of free choice. What is true of Yeats follows as well for the whole Anglo-Irish Ascendancy: Its very separation from things Irish is the occasion for a stronger bond. As an interruption, the metaphor of the nest dramatizes the fact that Yeats's historical lineage depends on interruption. Thus it is one of his most perfect emblems of adversity, a metaphor of the house that includes, even insists on, the sort of discord and difference that seemed to threaten house and poet alike.

If this solution seems esoteric, it matches nonetheless a real political decision Yeats could not escape. Just after writing "The Tower," Yeats defended the mixed Anglo-Irish style of the Abbey Theater by saying, "All, at this late day, have mixed strains of blood . . . " (UP, 2:467). Thus it is impossible for anyone to attack the Abbey from the standpoint of pure Irish ethnicity, because no such thing exists. Five years later, Yeats again emphasized the ethnic pluralism of the Irish, arguing that "the newest arrivals soon inter-married with an older stock, and that older stock has inter-married again and again with Gaelic Ireland. . . . Ireland, divided in religion and politics, is as much one race as any modern country" (EX, p. 347). All modern countries, that is to say, are the result of intermarriage, so that ethnic politics have little place in them. Before long, however, Yeats would preach selective breeding in On the Boiler, in the hopes of pruning back the "gangling stocks" that threatened Irish genetic health. Politically as well as poetically, then, Yeats faces the choice between ethnic purity and pluralism, ancient continuity tied to the soil and aristocratic independence.

When Yeats makes his will in "The Tower," he forces on himself a compromise between an ethnic nation and the pluralist state he sees as bulwark against the persecution of his own stock. In "Meditations in Time of Civil War," the possibility of compromise seems more remote. The sequence seems to start where "The Tower," dated three years later, concludes. "Ancestral Houses" takes as given the interdependence of violence and sweetness, bitterness and gentleness. There seems, in fact, to be a complicated, circular pattern of frustration at work in the poem, whereby a "violent, bitter man," prompted by his pain, builds sweetness and gentleness into a house, whose very comforts cloy and cause the line to decay:

> But when the master's buried mice can play,
> And maybe the great-grandson of that house,
> For all its bronze and marble, 's but a mouse.
> (VP, p. 418)

Real familial continuity, the poem suggests, is not sustained naturally or effortlessly. In fact, it seems at best an assertion blindly but powerfully made against the facts.

In "My House," Yeats makes the resemblance between this sort of aristocracy and his own poetry explicit. His own "emblems of adversity" will sustain, he hopes, a lonely line of descendants, as the tradition of the tower's founder sustained his "dwindling score" until it utterly disappeared. Both lines include, even depend on, adversity, as a prerequisite for continuity, however diminished. The problem for the rest of the poem is to find emblems capable of representing adversity, which also means finding a kind of familial property that can guarantee continuity while still including violence and bitterness.

Kenneth Burke pointed out some time ago the relevance to these sections of a passage in *A Vision*: "An object is sensuous if I relate it to myself, '*my* file, *my* chair,' etc., but it is concrete if I say '*a* chair, *a* fire,' and abstract if I but speak of it as the representative of a class – '*the* chair, *the* fire,' etc." The middle five poems of "Meditations in Time of Civil War" use the possessive pronoun: "My Table," "My Descendants," etc. Burke says, "The motif here becomes a way of reaffirming an individual integrity, with its related properties, as against the puzzles of fragmentation."[88] As valuable as it is, Burke's reading may be too individualistic. The first of these poems, "My House," specifically dedicates itself to the family, and the succeeding sections entitled with the possessive pronoun take up questions of family continuity and safety. Property, in other words, is not defined in individual terms but in familial ones. In fact, family property stands in the sequence as the middle term between the particular and the general, between the high abstraction of "Ancestral Houses" and the embittered violence of "The Stare's Nest by My Window." As such, it may also be the metaphor Yeats demands in "My House" that could mediate between adversity and gentleness.

In "My Table," Sato's sword is offered as such an emblem. It represents a changeless tradition, passed from hand to hand over a five hundred year period:

> Our learned men have urged
> That when and where 'twas forged
> A marvellous accomplishment,
> In painting or in pottery, went
> From father unto son
> And through the centuries ran
> And seemed unchanging like the sword.
> (VP, p. 421, ll. 15–21)

Though the tradition may *seem* unchanging, it is in fact founded on a painful consciousness of change: "only an aching heart / Conceives a changeless work of art" (ll. 13–14). This consciousness of change, with all its pain, *is* the tradition passed down along with its appropriate emblem, the sword. What the "rich inheritor" inherits is "an aching heart," a tradition of pain that gives him "waking wits" and keeps the line vigorous.

Though Yeats begins the next poem, "My Descendants," as if he were the rich inheritor of Sato's tradition, this poem and the two that follow are plagued by fear. Yeats himself becomes a kind of "moor-hen," trying to guide his "feathered balls of soot," and his tower becomes a ruined nest, the "empty house of the stare" featured in the penultimate poem of the sequence. The tower is ruined, the nest empty, because there is "More substance in our enmities / Than in our love" (l. 19). That is to say, adversity and division overcome familial love: The civil war triumphs. No longer is it possible for Yeats to proclaim that "love and friendship are enough" (IV. 20). The events of the civil war, described in "The Stare's Nest" in bald detail, convince him that adversity cannot be contained within the family, that, Sato's sword notwithstanding, a tradition of conflict is a contradiction in terms.

Only the final poem of the sequence, "I See Phantoms of Hatred and of the Heart's Fullness and of the Coming Emptiness," manages to combine these seemingly incompatible qualities. It does so by means of a rather complicated set of antitheses. Yeats first pits the phantoms of hatred against the phantoms of the heart's fullness. The phantoms of hatred appear as a "rage-driven, rage-tormented, and rage-hungry troop, / Trooper belabouring trooper, biting at arm or at face . . . " (VP, p. 426, ll. 11–12). Here Yeats merges what had seemed opposites: the soldiers of "The Road at my Door" with the "daemonic rage" of "My House." The soldiers of the civil war give physical form to an intellectual hatred almost indistinguishable from the imagination itself. Thus Yeats is carried away by the spectacle of these phantoms and "all but cried" along with them "For vengeance on the murderers of Jacques Molay" (ll. 14–16).

The other phantoms seem quite different. With them returns the metaphor of the fountain:

> their minds are but a pool
> Where even longing drowns under its own excess;
> Nothing but stillness can remain when hearts are full
> Of their own sweetness, bodies of their loveliness.
> (ll. 22–24)

Thus the image of aristocracy from "The Tower" and "Ancestral· Houses" returns, along with its peculiar economy of fullness defined by antithesis. There is even a hint here, in the word *sweetness,* that these phantoms come in answer to Yeats's call to the honey-bees in the preceding poem. Together, the two sets of phantoms simply pose again the question with which this sequence began, how can violence be reconciled with aristocracy and the familial continuity on which it depends?

Yeats resolves the antithesis between the two sets of phantoms and concludes his poetic quest by means of another antithesis. The third element in the equation, the "coming emptiness," resolves the antithesis between the two sets of phantoms by opposing both. Confronted with this third phantom, the troopers and the ladies conflate themselves:

> The cloud-pale unicorns, the eyes of aquamarine,
> The quivering half-closed eyelids, the rags of cloud or of lace,
> Or eyes that rage has brightened, arms it has made lean,
> Give place to an indifferent multitude, give place
> To brazen hawks.
> (ll. 25–29)

Yeats hangs a great deal on the word *or.* By means of it he combines what had seemed antithetical. The rest of the stanza shows that this combination depends on the mutual opposition of ladies and troopers to the "multitude":

> Nor self-delighting reverie,
> Nor hate of what's to come, nor pity for what's gone,
> Nothing but grip of claw, and the eye's complacency,
> The innumerable clanging wings that have put out the moon.
> (ll. 29–32).

The "indifferent multitude" remains cold both to hate and to love, resolving the two by meeting both with complacency. Thus, love may contain hatred, family may contain disunity, the aristocracy may contain bitterness and violence, the fitting emblem may contain that which is adverse to it, insofar as all these things differ from mere complacency and indifference.

Yeats's note to this stanza shows how close he comes, even after all his revision, to the solution of "The Tower." He says, "I suppose I must have put hawks into the fourth stanza because I have a ring with a hawk and a butterfly upon it, to symbolize the straight road of logic, and so of mechanism, and the crooked road of intuition . . . " (VP, p. 827). Imagination may reconcile itself to any loss, to any violence, so long as it remains distinct from argument and logic. As in the earlier poem, the seeming antithesis between imaginative creation and destruction is dissolved by a larger antithesis between imagination and logic. But these antitheses are social as well. "Mechanism" and logic, as Yeats makes quite clear in *A Vision,* are the intellectual practices of democracy. Thus the phantoms that sweep through the end of "Meditations in Time of Civil War" are a "multitude." As the negative terminology of the stanza reveals, Yeats sees the multitude in terms of sheer otherness, as sheer negation. In the face of such utter absence, the violence of the aristocracy can seem almost a positive trait.

"Nineteen Hundred and Nineteen," also an earlier poem placed later in the sequence of sequences, seems to undermine even this tenuously balanced solution. Once again the poem begins with the problem of ruin, in this case self-inflicted ruin. Civil war means the destruction of the images that once represented and fostered community. The willingness of "Incendiary or bigot" to destroy the olive stump that signifies the Athenian polity means that polity has ceased to exist. Yeats may intend as well a criticism of Athenian democracy, of law "indifferent to blame or praise, / To bribe or threat" based on an enlightened public opinion. Faith in such a system is also imperiled, even mocked, by the cruel internecine violence of the period. When men act like "weasels fighting in a hole," the concept of neutral law seems even more fragile than ivory, more brittle than golden grasshoppers and bees.

If weasels fighting in a hole represent the discord of civil war, they also represent, later in the poem, the horrible community that replaces the one destroyed in civil war:

> We, who seven years ago
> Talked of honour and of truth
> Shriek with pleasure if we show
> The weasel's twist, the weasel's tooth.
>   (VP, p. 431)

"We" have at least one thing in common, one thing that makes it possible for us to speak with the collective pronoun, and that is our relish for violence. Thus the fifth section of the poem poses as a chorus, a patriotic song, for those who agree in mockery and violence. These singers are unified by their disdain for historical continuity and its representations, for "calendars" and "monuments." They sing as the wind shrieks, leveling everything, destroying eminence, even distinctions of "good, wise, or great" from the brutal mass.

Civil war thus has two quite different effects in this poem. On one hand, it destroys the symbols of democracy and with them the community they represent. On the other hand, civil war appears as the actual outcome of democracy, its discord just the reflex of a uniformity of mind more coercive, more complete, than that of any other system. One by one, the great, the wise, and the good are dragged down by the wind: "Wind shrieked – and where are they?" (l. 107). What is left in the final stanza in the fifth section of the poem is the mockers themselves, everything else having been leveled. The end of the section thus reveals the bitter justice of its pronoun. For there is nothing left at the end but "we," all exceptional men having been dragged down. "We" *are* the leveling wind, leveling everything so as to create the collective "we" out of the destruction of individual distinction.

In this sense, civil war appears simply as the final, quite natural, manifestation of a system that brings discord by leveling out all the differences that used to structure traditional society. The alternative, or at least the antithesis, of this system, is the swan, Yeats's old symbol of the aristocracy. In the third section of "Nineteen Hundred and Nineteen," the swan thrusts out its breast in pride, the quintessential aristocratic virtue, and rides "Those winds that clamour of approaching night." Thus it seems the antagonist of the leveling "we," a solitary aristocrat breasting the waves thrown up by a revolutionary crowd.

Beyond this political meaning, the swan also represents the soul, as Yeats says explicitly at the beginning of the section. Yeats conceives the soul as "solitary" by definition, yet this solitude is constantly marred, he suggests, by "art or politics." The soul is entangled in a labyrinth made from these worldly ambitions so that even when it longs to cast off body and "trade / The ancient habit sticks. . . . " The independence of the soul, like the traditional independence of the aristocracy, is compromised by particular activities that might tie it to earth.

Thus the swan stands for a destruction even more thorough than that threatened by the crowd, because it reaches almost beyond the grave:

> The swan has leaped into the desolate heaven:
> That image can bring wildness, bring a rage
> To end all things, to end
> What my laborious life imagined, even
> The half-imagined, the half-written page . . .
> (ll. 79–83)

The swan is therefore represented as the victim of change, breasting the wind associated with destruction, and as the agent of change. As Harold Bloom puts it, the swan represents "the solitary reverie setting itself against the apocalypse" while being itself "apocalyptic."[89]

At this point, the whole poem seems to be a mere compact of paradoxes. Yeats fears destruction, which he associates with the democratic masses, but he also makes destruction an essential part of the definition of the solitary soul. The independence of the aristocrat, of the individual per se, from all specific ties, is itself akin to destruction. Art, which appears at the beginning of "Nineteen Hundred and Nineteen" as the conservator of tradition, representative of the community to itself, also appears as just another clog at the heel of the soul, kicking itself free in the upper cosmos. It seems as if even the traditional autonomy of art is insufficient for Yeats, who must surpass art itself. Even metaphor undoes itself in this poem. The swan is both a specific metaphor, standing explicitly for the soul and implicitly for the aristocracy, and a metaphor of metaphor, riding as it does on the "troubled mirror" that doubles and reflects. Yet the swan is also an "image that can bring wildness, bring a rage / To end all things. . . . " It is, in other words, an image that destroys images, that ends "What my laborious life imagined, even / The half-imagined, the half-written page. . . . " In this sense, the swan is Yeats's most complex "emblem of adversity," a complex made up of the poet, his class, and his poetry that puts discord and even destruction at the heart of all three.

The poem ends with an even more perfect emblem, one that serves as the most fitting conclusion to the sequence of three great political sequences in *The Tower* because it shirks none of the responsibilities Yeats has incurred in writing it. The last section of "Nineteen Hundred and Nineteen" begins with another version of the tumult of violence that ended "Meditations in Time of Civil War." Horses, riders, garlands, wind, whirl in a vortex of evil, until the wind drops and dust settles as if a curtain has parted for the final attraction: the "insolent fiend Robert Artisson." On one level, Artisson represents an upheaval of the classes, having brought Lady Kyteler low by his occult powers. For this reason he is called that "insolent fiend." He seems an earlier, more lurid version of the democratic masses that appear at the end of "Meditations in Time of Civil War." "His great eyes without thought" resemble the "eye's complacency" of those horrible beings. Like them, he seems to exist as an antithesis to the whirling daughters of Herodias and to the aristocracy they represent. But isn't Artisson also a repetition of Raftery, the blind poet of "The Tower," who also works by enchantment? And wouldn't he therefore represent, by extension, Yeats himself, another master of the occult, who says in that poem "For if I triumph I must make men mad"? In this sense, Artisson would represent a truer version of the complicity suggested in "Meditations in Time of Civil War" when Yeats is caught up in violence and cries for an occult revenge.

Yeats's decision to represent the crowd in the form of a single individual thus betrays a deep ambivalence, which is nonetheless the source of the strength of these sequences. For the destruction caused by the mindlessness of the masses is indistinguishable from that the poet demands himself, "a rage / To end all things." In fact, Yeats has represented the aristocracy so well in all its blind violence that he can hardly portray it here as the innocent victim of a violent underclass. The very exclusiveness of the aristocracy is a kind of violence, yet the leveling of the underclass seems to mean violence as well. Robert Artisson is such a discomfortingly uncanny figure because he conflates these disparate impulses. He is at once common and occult, public and private, destructive of the aristocracy and yet, as the epitome of violence, constitutive of it as well. Finally he seems the antithesis of poetry, stupid and blindly material, yet this "Son of Art" bears certain marks of resemblance to the very poet who created him.

In one sense, Robert Artisson marks a failure, Yeats's failure to clearly distinguish himself, his poetry, and his class from the democratic violence of the civil war. "Nineteen Hundred and Nineteen" is therefore both strategically ironic and quite sincere when it uses the collective pronoun to confess an Irish rage for violence, because Yeats's "rage to end all things," a rage constitutive of the solitary soul and the class it represents, is just as threatening to the Athenian ivories as the most mindless physical violence. The very exclusiveness with which the soul is defined as solitary imperils the community symbols by defying community as an imposition. The real community to which Yeats inescapably belongs is therefore the community of violence, the community represented by Robert Artisson. In this sense, Artisson is one of Yeats's greatest images, for he confesses what the Civil War and the Troubles also proved, that the Irish do not hold in common any ideals, belief, or practices, but only the violence caused by the lack of these. Despite what Yeats suggested in 1919, it is not historical association or logic, neither culture nor abstract principles of right, that unite the Irish, but rather the violence caused by the contest between them.

5. SENATOR AND BLUESHIRT

In 1812, Sir Samuel Romilly listed these principles as the defining characteristics of a Whig:

> He should justly appreciate and be ready at all times to maintain the liberty of the press and the trial by jury which are the great securities for all our other liberties. He should be a sincere friend of peace. . . . He should be a constant advocate for economy in the public expenditure and a determined enemy to corruption and peculation. He should be ready, when he sees abuses arising from any of our present institutions, to enquire into the causes of them, and to suggest a remedy, notwithstanding the reproach of being an innovator. Above all he should be a man incapable of being severed from his duty by the threats of power, the allurements of the great, the temptations of private interest or even the seduction of popular favour.[90]

In his service as a Senator of the Irish Free State, Yeats fit perfectly this rather old-fashioned definition of a Whig. Though he professed to hate Whiggery,[91] Yeats represented almost single-handedly the principles of disinterested inquiry, independence, and individual rights that Romilly associates with the Whig.

As a Senator, Yeats opposed the tendency of the new state to censor books and newspapers on moral grounds. He broke with the party whose general principles he most favored on the issue of independent inspection of prisons and the independence of the judiciary (SS, pp. 60–61).[92] He spoke in favor of religious freedom on the grounds that the individual conscience should be left free (SS, p. 93) and on the basis of a political modernism: "The living, changing, advancing human mind, sooner or later refuses to accept this legislation from men who base their ideas on the interpretation of doubtful texts in the Gospels" (SS, p. 96). Later in life, Yeats was to regret his service in the Senate, which he believed had betrayed him into the work of abstraction (EI, p. 400). But it is difficult to agree, because his practical politics in the Senate approach more closely than his abstract opinions at any time in his life the sort of liberal tolerance now associated with political virtue. As Cullingford puts it, "He pleaded for a modern, tolerant, and liberal nation. He based his argument on the satisfaction of the individual. . . . "[93]

Yet, even in advancing the liberal pieties, Yeats could turn them inside out. The best example is his famous speech on the bill to outlaw divorce. Much of this speech represents a defense of individual rights of self-determination, along with a defense of the right of a minority to differ with the stronger majority: "I think it is tragic that within three years of this country gaining its independence we should be discussing a measure which a minority of this nation considers to be grossly oppressive" (SS, p. 99). But in the very course of defending individual rights, Yeats drifts into an almost primitive tribal bitterness:

> We against whom you have done this thing are no petty people. We are one of the great stocks of Europe. We are the people of Burke; we are the people of Grattan; we are the people of Swift, the people of Emmet, the people of Parnell. We have created most of the modern literature of this country. We have created the best of its political intelligence. Yet I do not altogether regret what has happened. I shall be able to find out, if not I, my children will be able to find out whether we have lost our stamina or not. You have defined our position and given us a popular following. If we have not lost our stamina then your victory will be brief, and your defeat final, and when it comes this nation may be transformed.

(SS, p. 99)

According to Harris, "What begins in noble opposition to religious intolerance, tragic consciousness that one of Ireland's chief disasters may be repeated, ends in a vituperative war-cry as sectarian as the bigotry Yeats sought to denounce."[94]

The puzzle of Yeats's later politics is to discover how he might combine in a single paragraph liberalism and bigotry, individualism and tribal jealousy. This puzzle is in one sense simply the final version of an Irish quarrel Yeats had participated in all his life, one he felt acutely because of his background and class position. But the quarrel takes another turn in the last decade of Yeats's life, as Irish politics brought forth what looked like an indigenous fascist movement.

Even as a Senator, Yeats had little faith in democracy. In his last speech as a member of the Senate, he cautioned his fellow members, "I think we should not lose sight of the simple fact that it is more desirable and more important to have able men in this House than to get representative men into this House" (SS, pp. 151–152). While a Senator, he faced one last controversy over the Abbey Theater, in the course of which he claimed that "at no time, neither in the beginning nor in its final maturity, does an intellectual movement express a whole people, or anybody but those who are built into it" (UP, 2:470). In politics and art, Yeats favored the leadership of a self-appointed elite over the people, even while he was speaking in favor of individual rights on the Senate floor. By the end of his life, of course, this elitism had become almost fanatical, so that he could say, in *On the Boiler,* "The whole State should be so constructed that the people should think it their duty to grow popular with King and Lord Mayor instead of King and Lord Mayor growing popular with them" (OTB, p. 10). Little trace of any kind of liberalism survives in Yeats's work at this time, but during his Senate service he managed to combine ringing defenses of individual rights with disdain for the democratic system founded on those rights.

The contradiction expresses the uncomfortable position of Yeats's hereditary class in the new state. As he entered the Senate, he also began to transform himself into a spokesman for the Anglo-Irish Ascendancy and to construct a pantheon out of the Irish writers of the eighteenth century, for whom he had previously felt little sympathy.[95] According to Harris, Yeats told Lady Gregory that he "had refrained from vaunting the intellectual and ethical superiority of Protestant Ireland while the Anglo-Irish remained an oppressive power; with Catholic Ireland now in control, he felt free to assert that greatness."[96] This seems at least half true. Yeats's defense of the individual in the Senate is often merely defense of his class, as the divorce speech makes clear. Because that class has been rendered a powerless minority by extension of the franchise and the settlement of Irish independence, Yeats becomes a passionate defender of minority rights. As such, he faces the essential political question that had baffled the creators of the Free State: How to contain within a fervently nationalist state a minority historically inimical to that nationalism? That Yeats allowed himself to advance liberal arguments with which he had little real sympathy shows how few political solutions there are to this problem. But the real oddity of Yeats's later politics is how close he came to the ideology of the new state even while grimly opposing its policies.

Yeats's politics of this period depend on two figurative extensions. Though he seems to advocate individual rights, he identifies those rights with a particular class, the Anglo-Irish Ascendancy. This identification is possible because he sees his class in terms of the figure of the heroic individual. The class is always expressed by an honor roll of names: Burke, Grattan, Berkeley, Swift, Goldsmith, Parnell. These men form a class only in that Yeats sees them all as solitary and heroic individuals. Born, Yeats says in his essay on Berkeley, "in communities where solitaries flourish" (EI, p. 401), these men constitute the class of the classless, the group made of those who belong to no group. As McCormack puts it, "the common identity which the Irish Augustans possess is the paradoxical sharing of isolation."[97] Thus Yeats uses over and over again in his later years the phrase "Anglo-Irish solitude" (EX, pp. 308, 325). Conceiving this class as if it were in fact a solitary individual, Yeats can advance its interests under the banner of individual rights. Because Irish Protestants were in fact in some need of legal protection as the Free State became more closely identified with Catholicism and the Irish language, Yeats's paradoxical definition of his class has a certain practical merit.[98]

Yeats also speaks, however, of "Irish solitude" (EI, p. 400), revealing how easy it was for him to assume that his own class composed the entire nation. This is the second figurative extension, by means of which an isolated and newly powerless class comes to represent the whole from which it is excluded. In the divorce speech, for example, Yeats makes the Ascendancy synonymous with Irish literature and politics, leaving to the Catholics music and perhaps sports. He declares in *On the Boiler*, "Berkeley, Swift, Burke, Grattan, Parnell, Augusta Gregory, Synge, Kevin O'Higgins, are the true Irish people . . . " (OTB, p. 30). The addition of Kevin O'Higgins cannot diminish the Protestant nature of this list, nor the audacity of asserting, just as Ireland was becoming overtly Catholic in faith and theoretically Irish in language, that it is instead English and Protestant.

Seamus Deane calls this belief of Yeats's "an idea of the peripheral becoming the central culture."[99] A class that is by definition different, excluded from the whole, represents itself as that whole. Once again, Yeats turns the tables, making difference the very basis of identity. The Ascendancy can represent all of Ireland precisely because of its exclusion. Yeats transforms what should be the central weakness of his class into a strength. If Ireland is characterized by its solitude, then the most solitary are logically the purest Irish.

Yeats took Edmund Burke as his guide through this forest of contradictions. There is a good deal of historical irony in this, because Burke
denounced in the Anglo-Irish of his time exactly the pretensions Yeats
was to advance in his own. In 1792, Burke denounced "the resolution of
one set of people in Ireland to consider themselves as the sole citizens in
the commonwealth. . . . "[100] Nonetheless, Yeats was to find in Burke
the best expression of what Swift called "the universal bent and current
of a people" (EX, p. 292). This idea is nothing more than a reworking of
the nationalism of Yeats's youth. He even called the "universal bent and
current" by the name "national spirit" (EX, p. 357). The national spirit is
distinct from any momentary majority in a body of representatives, but,
because it must be represented in action in some manner, Yeats vests it in
a particular class: "The will of the State, whether it build a cage for a dead
bird or remain in the bird itself, must always, whether interpreted by
Burke or Marx, find expression through some governing class or company identified with that 'bent and current', with those 'elemental
forms', whether by interest or training. The men of Swift's day would
have added that class or company must be placed by wealth above fear
and toil . . . " (EX, pp. 357–358).
     A nation, in Burke's words "is a choice not of one day, or one set of
people, not a tumultuary and giddy choice; it is a deliberate election of
the ages and of generations; it is a constitution made by what is ten
thousand times better than choice, it is made by the peculiar circumstances, occasions, tempers, dispositions, and moral, civil, and social
habitudes of the people, which disclose themselves only in a long space of
time."[101] This essentially social and historical definition of a nation bases
all value on continuity, on agreement arrived at over a long period. As
such, it loses its force in times of revolutionary change and dispute. Thus
Yeats was in the position of believing that the "universal bent and current" of the people had been abandoned by the people themselves, so that
it could only be reasserted by an insurgent minority. But Yeats also faced
another situation unanticipated in Burke's formula. Another group also
thought itself the representative of the "universal bent and current" of the
people, only it felt that the people in question were Catholic, not Protestant, Irish by language and descent and not English. How can a single
state combine two organic nations, each with its own bent and current?
     Thus the real irony of Yeats's last years is that he faced, in Fianna Fail
and Eamon de Valera, a nemesis with a value system almost exactly the
same as his own. As at the very beginning of his political career, Yeats
became most vituperative when he found in others aspects of himself.
Nothing makes this more clear than Yeats's late propaganda on behalf of
the family. Cullingford traces Yeats's political use of the family to Burke,
who made it one of his metaphors of the organic state, "a permanent
body composed of transitory parts."[102] As Yeats said in plans drawn up

for the Blueshirts, "An organization to be lasting & powerful must resemble a group of families or else a single family."[103] *On the Boiler* is Yeats's weird manifesto on behalf of this metaphor, a work in which he aims to "restore the responsibilities of the family" (OTB, p. 29). The concept on which Yeats bases his propaganda in this pamphlet is "innate intelligence or mother-wit" (OTB, p. 17). One of the painful ironies of this work is that, despite its denunciation of mathematics in voting and representation, it can blithely assure its readers that mother-wit "can be measured, in children especially, with great accuracy" (OTB, pp. 17, 26). Another, even more painful, is that the disciple of Swift can allow himself to say that, because progress will "enable everybody without effort to procure all necessities of life and so remove the last check upon the multiplication of the uneducatable masses, it will become the duty of the educated classes to seize and control one or more of those necessities" (OTB, p. 19). Obviously, "A Modest Proposal" was not one of Yeats's favorite works by Swift.

Late in life, then, Yeats comes to see the health of the family as synonymous with the health of the state, and in this pamphlet he carries the analogy far enough to demand selective breeding so as to keep the state strong. It is not necessary to connect these ideas to those of the Nazis to feel their terror. *On the Boiler* shows what happens when Burke's idea of the state as family is transported into a world divided by competing families. It is almost impossible to keep in mind while reading *On the Boiler* that less than ten years earlier, Yeats had defended his class in the course of a speech opposing the outlawing of divorce. So far has he come from that brief liberal fling that he is capable of empowering the state to restrict not just the legal form of marriage but its biological form as well.

Most important of all, however, is the fact that *On the Boiler* was outrageous to the new Irish state only in its particular allegiances and not in its principles. At exactly the same time that Yeats was publishing his pamphlet, de Valera was promulgating a new constitution, which read in part: "The State recognizes the Family as the natural primary and fundamental unit group of society, and as a moral institution possessing inalienable and imprescriptable rights, antecedent and superior to all positive law."[104] On this principle, which vested rights not in the individual but in the family, the new state outlawed divorce and, in a move that might have distressed the Yeats who worried about the overbreeding of the masses, birth control. In other words, the political principles for which Yeats was fighting in *On the Boiler* were in fact those of the state he opposed. The difference, of course, is that between competing definitions of the "bent and current" of the people, different notions of who is of the family. Though Yeats denounced de Valera as a mathematics professor who had given Ireland over to government by the numbers, the head of

Fianna Fail was in fact the expression in triumphant government of the organic nationalism Yeats believed in from beginning to end. That this party used nationalism systematically to exclude the very group Yeats named as the people itself was not just a defeat for Yeats but his own failure as well, the failure of nationalism to include difference within identity.

The late poems, elegiac and bitter, are Yeats's final attempt, one full of the consciousness of failure, to reconcile these opposites. One of the most successful elegies is "The Municipal Gallery Revisited." In its stroll through the picture gallery, the poem sums up the Irish history of Yeats's era:

> Around me the images of thirty years:
> An ambush; pilgrims at the water-side;
> Casement upon trial, half hidden by the bars,
> Guarded; Griffith staring in hysterical pride;
> Kevin O'Higgins' countenance that wears
> A gentle questioning look that cannot hide
> A soul incapable of remorse or rest;
> A revolutionary soldier kneeling to be blessed . . .
>   (VP, p. 601, ll. 1–8)

The list is in a way an indictment of Irish history for having provided its children with nothing but conflict. Ambush, trials for treason, assassination, revolution, and, perhaps in the image of Griffith's hysteria, the *Playboy* riots, all emphasize the violence and misery of modern Irish history. The rough parataxis of the stanza appropriately conveys the same sense, avoiding coordination as if these events could not be composed into some sensible narrative. Instead they reenact over and over, in the same terms, a history of death and defeat.

Yet somehow in the course of the poem Yeats transforms this history into that of friendship. The remarkable trick on which this poem is based is its transition from a history of civil war and revolution to a history of friendship:

> come to this hallowed place
> Where my friends' portraits hang and look thereon;
> Ireland's history in their lineaments trace;
> Think where man's glory most begins and ends,
> And say my glory was I had such friends.

The images of the first stanza are long forgotten in this celebration, almost as if Yeats is consciously replacing them with a more congenial vision. The nature of the verse changes as well, falling into the richly coordinated syntax Yeats mastered so completely. Though it retains in the clauses linked by semi-colons something of the parataxis of the first stanza, this conclusion embeds each clause in an involved syntax of address in which agreement is virtually extorted by the form.

The change from first stanza to last is accomplished in part by an aestheticization of politics. Looking at the pictures of the first stanza, Yeats exclaims,

> "This is not," I say,
> "The dead Ireland of my youth, but an Ireland
> The poets have imagined, terrible and gay."
>   (ll. 10–12)

Poetry has the ability to make the dead live and also to make the terrible, that which causes death, gay. It resolves abstract opposites, terror and gaiety, and also practical ones such as the opposition between Griffith and O'Higgins. All parties can be included in the poet's Ireland, where Arthur Griffith, leader of the mob that attacked Synge, can wear the aristocrat's virtue, "pride." Already, then, in the second stanza, Yeats dissolves the conflicts that seem synonymous with Irish history to make a history in which the specific contents of conflict take second place to the splendor of commitment.

Yet the aesthetic history thus produced turns out to be exclusive after all. As the poem progresses, it concentrates on Yeats's triumvirate of friends: Synge, Lady Gregory, and Yeats himself. The three are unified in their belief that literature comes "from contact with the soil" (L, 43). Thus Synge, who had no real home for much of his life, can be called "that rooted man" (l. 48), whereas Lady Gregory's house is the home of "Deep-rooted things" (l. 37). All good literature, "all that we said or sang" (l. 42) draws its strength, Yeats believes, from such contact with the soil. What the three touch in the soil is the "universal bent and current" of the Irish people, the nationalistic ethos that is in fact what serves to unify all the disparate parties presented at the beginning of the poem. Yeats is able to lump together men with quite different, even mutually exclusive, political programs because he sees Irish history in terms of truths embodied in the soil.

Such an ethos should be inclusive of a whole people, but Yeats limits it in class terms, "Dream of the noble and the beggar-man" (l. 47), and even more strictly to certain individuals: "We three alone in modern times had brought / Everything down to that sole test again . . . " (ll. 45–46). Ireland, it turns out, is the private preserve of three people, who give it a history of harmony by their friendship for one another. Yeats composes the chaos of actual Irish history by reducing it to a tiny group, which can represent alone the authentic Irishry. Once again, then, unity – "*All* that we did, *all* that we said or sang" – comes out of antithesis: "We three alone." Yet it is hard to believe that the tiny unity of the three friends actually includes in some way the violence of the first stanza. Instead of trying, through all failure and self-contradiction, to include the violent and conflictual within a unity, Yeats here creates a harmony simply by ignoring its opposite. The poem achieves its beautiful calm by this exclusion, and few would wish it different. It is pleasant as well to hear Yeats ask for judgment on the score of friendship and not on the score of his many antipathies, particularly vicious at the time he wrote this poem. But calm and pleasure are certainly bought at some cost.

A very different tone dominates "The Statues." The whole poem requires more commentary than it repays, but the last stanza can serve here to represent the bitter side of Yeats's late politics. When Pearse summons Cuchulain to his side in the Dublin Post Office in 1916 he summons a personification of Irish nationalism, a mystical identification with a mythical past. Yeats calls on the same spirit when he grandly speaks as "We Irish" (VP, p. 611, l. 28). The phrase assumes that one voice can speak for the Irish. Borrowed from Berkeley, it indicates an unspoken agreement, a familial discipline: "We Irish do not hold with this" (UP, 2:458). It forces a unity the poem almost immediately dissolves. For the Irish, it seems, are different from "this filthy modern tide" (l. 29). But the Irish are, of course, a modern people with a modern state. Yeats does not ignore this, but instead forcibly redefines the true Irish as anti-modern. Thus in one stanza, Yeats calls upon his people in a grandly inclusive term, "We Irish," and also defines them by antithesis, ruling out of the Irish race all those not opposed to the filthy modern tide. The Irish are not the citizens of a state, but a "sect." The family, in other words, unifies when seen from the inside, but ruthlessly divides when seen from outside. The true Irish "climb to our proper dark" (l. 31), as if darkness and seclusion were the real home of the race and not the soil after all.

"The Statues" seems a particularly unhappy example of the curse of Irish politics, because it claims to represent at one and the same time a "sect" and all the Irish. To define one's class, or religion, or linguistic group simultaneously against some opposition and as the true Ireland is to continue the logical partition now represented by Northern Ireland. For Yeats, "The Statues" marks a somewhat hysterical attempt to close the gap between sect and nation, part and whole, while simultaneously insisting on forcing it farther open. It seems appropriate that the poem is also one of Yeats's most fully anti-modern works, one that takes "modern" easily and naturally as a term of opprobrium. For modernism in politics means the coexistence of different sects within a single state. Unfortunately, Yeats does speak for the Irish in his refusal to accept this state. As at the very beginning, conflicts in his poetry are one reenactment in the seemingly endless reenactment of Irish discord.

The Protestant Ascendancy is as much a logical solution to this discord as an actual class. It resolves the tension between liberal individualism and nationalism by making the nation synonymous with certain isolated individuals, just as it resolves the conflict of one class with the rest of the state by making that class into the state. But a logical solution does not always easily become a practical one. If the Ascendancy were truly the Irish nation, its opinions would guide the new state. But this did not happen because, according to Yeats, democracy had substituted a purely metonymical definition of wholeness for his synecdoche. The answer was for synecdoche to assert its figurative power. If the Ascendancy represented true Irishness and the fledgling democracy some false imposition, then action taken in the name of the Ascendancy served Ireland. Yeats could serve his country by opposing it.

At almost all times in his life, whatever his immediate political allegiances, Yeats thought in terms of a paradoxical figure whereby a part distinguished by its difference from the whole came to represent that whole. Thus the same figure could stand for difference, division, heterogeneity and also for identity, unity, and a tyranny of the same. On the surface this might seem a realization of the Hegelian dream of reconciliation between part and whole, but Yeats's solution, like many versions of the Hegelian scheme, led only to a limited and tyrannical reconciliation. By the logic of Yeats's paradoxical figure, the more his class met with opposition the more truly in the right it was, because it represented by virtue of difference. Thus force and violence finally become their own justification.

The movement offering the most violent reconciliation of part and whole was, of course, fascism. Yeats's brand of exclusive nationalism did, in fact, come close to one side of fascist doctrine. The potential for Irish nationalism to do so is illustrated in a very odd chapter of Odon Por's *Fascism,* published in 1923. Por, whose work had a strong influence on Ezra Pound, divides his sixth chapter between Macchiavelli and AE. The link between Macchiavelli and AE, between authority and cultural nationalism, is Mussolini.[105] Thus Por sees AE's book *The National Being* as a virtual blueprint for Italian Fascism. That Por could have compared statements by Mussolini, dictator of the Italian people, to those of AE, whose work with dairy cooperatives was conducted largely on his bicycle, shows how the extremes of cultural nationalism might meet, how such doctrines might serve an authoritarian right and a vague but well-intentioned left.

This correspondence also explains how the influence could have run in the other direction, from Mussolini to Yeats. As early as 1924, Yeats proclaimed Mussolini's movement as the natural and inevitable counterforce to centuries of "centrifugal" individualism and thus as the successor to the moribund democracies of Europe. He was even thrilled by the mass response to Mussolini, because this mass seemed united by its abhorrence of liberty as defined by the democracies (UP, 2:433–435). Subsequently, he was eager to see connections between the intellectual foundations of Italian Fascism, as he found them in Croce and Gentile, and Swift (EX, p. 354). Italian Fascism seemed at times an actualization of Swift's belief in the "bent and current of a people." It promised a historical method of organizing society, one in tune with the historical, collective character of its inhabitants, instead of the abstract system favored under democracy.

At the same time, however, Yeats was capable of praising Mussolini as the leader of "individualist Italy" (L, p. 693). Like Pound, who may well have influenced Yeats in this direction, he saw in Mussolini a symbol of the revolt against the masses, against human standardization. Yeats told Thomas McGreevy he "believed that Mussolini represented the rise of the individual man as against what he considered the anti-human party machine."[106] Both Mussolini and Gentile gave the impression that they meant to turn the individual loose in a new Italy. "We return to the individual," Mussolini declared. "We oppose everything that oppresses and mortifies the individual."[107] Cullingford treats Yeats's individualism as if it tempered his interest in fascism, but it seems instead that fascism attracted Yeats precisely because it allowed him to indulge both his nationalism and his individualism, because, in fact, it served as the last, most extravagant, reconciliation of a conflict present in his thought from the beginning.

If this is the case, then why was Yeats's association with fascism, in the form of General O'Duffy's Blueshirts, so brief? Though Yeats was enthusiastic about the Blueshirts at one time, this enthusiasm seems not to have lasted beyond a few months in 1933. The most common explanation is that Yeats finally decided that fascism was but another mass movement, one not so different in this respect from communism or even liberal democracy itself. In the full flush of his enthusiasm for the Blueshirts, Yeats declared that his movement would need "militants, marching men."[108] Even in 1934, when his feelings had cooled somewhat, he insisted on the necessity of "force, marching men" (VP, p. 837). But, as Paul Scott Stanfield has shown, Yeats had used the phrase "marching feet" as early as 1902 to signify the actions of an unthinking mass, and he was to use it later to criticize communism. Thus it may be, as Stanfield suggests most cogently, that Yeats ended by seeing in fascism merely another manifestation of the mob.[109] Fascism was insufficiently anti-democratic for Yeats, insufficiently distinct from the other mass movements of the century.

Other testimony from these years suggests a further, more complex, explanation. This is to be found in Yeats's "Genealogical Tree of Revolution," a table reflecting notes he made on politics during 1933.[110] According to the table, the path to revolution begins with Nicholas of Cusa, whose antinomies are restated by Kant and then solved, at least putatively, by Hegel. From Hegel's solution come two movements, laid out on the tree in parallel, contrasting categories. On the left, both politically and spatially, dialectical materialism interprets Hegel's dialectic as the "conflict of classes," a historical struggle within which each class negates its predecessor, thus justifying hatred of the past and finally tyranny in the guise of the proletariat. On the right, Yeats placed what he called "Italian Philosophy," by which he meant Hegel as interpreted by Croce and Gentile. In this philosophy the dialectic is rejected because conflict is not explained in terms of immanent contradiction but rather as the clash of distinct, separate entities, what Yeats calls here "positives." The final aim of dialectical materialism is, of course, communism, and that of "Italian Philosophy" is fascism.

Even in the bare form that now survives, the table shows that Yeats traced the political conflicts of his century to the Kantian antinomies and to Hegel's attempt to resolve them. Conflict between subject and object, part and whole, freedom and history, right and duty, underlay other, more programmatic, conflicts between parties and persuasions. Moreover, the chart shows that Yeats understood that left and right are linked by their common attempt to resolve in practice antinomies that Hegel had solved in theory, a solution he saw the modern state enacting in actuality.[111] Though the table implies that left and right are to be considered equal, the right-hand side is clearly favored insofar as its philosophy leads to the condemnation of hatred, to a historical process in which each class bequeaths its "gifts" to the whole, to the honoring of a past that communism considers "criminal." Though there are certain inconsistencies in the presentation of the "Italian Philosophy," it seems to come much closer to Yeats's own beliefs, especially in seeing "individual, class, nation a process of the whole" and not "lost in the whole" as under communism. In other words, fascism resolves the antinomies left in modern politics by dissolving the liberal opposition of individual and community, but not by dissolving it completely into a mere undifferentiated whole, as Yeats felt communism did. Instead, individual and community are related as expressions of one another, just as classes rise, one by one, and then return to enrich the whole.

The "Italian Philosophy" is not, however, the last entry in Yeats's table. Below and presumably beyond both it and communism, beyond the parallel opposition of left and right, is another category: "A Race Philosophy." The first supposition of this philosophy is that "the antinomies cannot be solved." Here Yeats turns Vico on his head by asserting that both family and individual are forces of nature and therefore unknowable, "not transparent to reason." Thus the antinomies represented here by the single clash of family and individual cannot be resolved because their relationship cannot be theorized. The most that government can do is to palliate the conflict by mildly restraining each side. Despite the hints in the table that fascism attracts Yeats because of its greater respect for both sides of the social and political dichotomies, he finally rejects or supersedes fascism because of a conviction that these cannot be equally served. There is no reconciliation. Yeats finally abandons fascism because his fanaticism about his mutually contradictory values is so great that no concrete reconciliation could satisfy it.

In this sense, the table marks the end of Yeats's development in politics. The table is, on one hand, an admission of bafflement and defeat, because there is finally nothing for politics to do in the future it foresees. Because all attempts to resolve conflict have failed, it seems that all must continue to fail. But Yeats does not seem particularly downcast by this failure. Instead, he sanctifies it, as Eliot was to do after him. The clash of individual and family is, according to comments appended to the table, bred into the race as an eternal condition. Thus Yeats sees clearly the results of the modern project, as they have been seen since Hegel, but he interprets these results as an unchangeable, almost biological situation. For all his fanaticism, then, the real danger of Yeats's politics is that they will merely confirm the status quo. Though the table professes to provide the genealogy of revolution, though it ends by enshrining conflict as its one constant, by that very sanctification it solidifies the liberal system Yeats hated more than anything.

Yeats plots out on this table a diagram of his own life in politics. Beginning with a desire to overcome the antitheses left by liberalism, it ramified in many directions as he aged: from the socialism he briefly embraced under Morris' influence to the cultural nationalism of the Irish Literary Revival and then to militant aristocratic conservatism and finally fascism. In a way, Yeats was driven on from one program or solution to another by the failure of each to resolve the contradictions of liberalism. Each solution simply restated at a higher level the fundamental oppositions that both tormented Yeats and gave his life its vitality. For a moment in *The Tower* he seemed to sense that it was these very contradictions that he shared most crucially with his fellow Irishmen and that might, therefore, serve as the reconciliation they seemed to preclude. But he finally chose to refer the whole problem to another, higher level, where human problems become features of eternity and seem sacred because they resist solution.

2

T.S. Eliot: Conservatism

In *After Strange Gods,* that notorious battle-cry against the unorthodox, Eliot names as "the struggle of our time" the effort "to re-establish a vital connexion between the individual and the race; the struggle, in a word, against Liberalism."[1] In this way, Eliot announces clearly what had been implicit in his work for a long time. The distress he reveals over the liberal divorce of individual and race had been working in him since his student days, and the reconciliation of these two estranged entities was the first philosophical problem he confronted. For Eliot, as for Yeats, the desire to solve this problem sprung at least in part from his own anomalous position. He was an urban expatriate who prescribed for others a settled life on the soil, a cosmopolitan, famed for garbling together half the languages of humankind, who preached the virtues of a rooted tradition, and a painfully private religionist who saw religion as a cohesive social force. Eliot's genius was to insist that these apparent contradictions are in fact identities, that community can only come about through detachment, tradition only through the individual talent, ethics only through specific historical facts. His most complex works in criticism and in poetry attempt to make good these claims and thus to find a new basis for his own life as an individual, a member of the educated elite, and a poet.

Eliot's early teachers all made quite clear the fact that the gap between the individual and the world was an immediate political problem as well as a philosophical puzzle. This is especially true of Irving Babbitt, who called the reconciliation of these two estranged entities "the ultimate problem of thought,"[2] but it is also true of F.H. Bradley, as Eliot reveals in his 1927 review of *Ethical Studies.* In this review, Eliot singles out "the social basis of Bradley's distinction" as the most crucial and valuable part of his accomplishment. That "social basis" is Bradley's attack in *Ethical*

74

Studies on "the whole Utilitarian mind," on what Eliot calls "that great temple in Philistia" (SE, p. 362). When Eliot made his own raids on the temple he followed the battle-plan laid out in *Ethical Studies* and, beyond it, in a whole series of attempts to overcome the divisions of liberalism.

Bradley's *Ethical Studies* is, as Richard Wollheim says, "the most Hegelian of all his writings."[3] In this work, Bradley seems to follow very closely the pattern of Hegel's essay *Natural Law,* which, according to H.B. Acton, "impressed him greatly."[4] Hegel objected to attempts to abstract human beings by removing all that "belonging to particular manners, to history, to civilization, and even to the state" to leave "man in the image of the bare state of nature."[5] *Natural Law* therefore takes issue with Enlightenment attempts to ground ethical conduct and political right in abstract conditions created a priori.[6] In *Ethical Studies,* Bradley dismisses pleasure as a source of ethics, demolishing Utilitarianism as Hegel demolishes earlier "empirical" theories of morality. Then, following Hegel very explicitly, Bradley turns on Kant and the idea of "Duty for Duty's Sake," or what Hegel calls "formal" ethics.[7] In neither hedonism nor abstract principles is the source of right conduct to be found.[8]

Against these, Bradley opposes as a source "My Station and its Duties." This slogan stands over Bradley's attempt to ground ethics in a specific social context, which would mediate between empirical fact and disembodied value. For Bradley, in this chapter, "an individual man is what he is because of and by virtue of community. . . ."[9] Thus Bradley sets himself against the Utilitarian idea of the self as "an atom, a unit which repels other units . . . that . . . can stand to others, with their pleasures and pains, only in an external relation." Instead, a man "is what he is because he is a born and educated social being, and a member of an individual social organism."[10] Though Bradley goes on to show that there are important ways in which human beings are more than social, the "social basis" of his work still consists, as R.G. Collingwood puts it, in "the doctrine that reality consists neither of isolated particulars nor of abstract universals but of individual facts whose being is historical."[11]

Ethical Studies is Bradley's attempt to reconnect what modern society sees as opposites, to resolve what Lukács calls the antinomies of bourgeois thought: particular and universal, individual and community, fact and value. The goal of such a philosophy is not simply to impose order on the disparate particulars of modern life, but to derive order from them, not to marshal facts under abstract values, but to find value in historical fact. Politically, Bradley recoils with equal horror from the anarchy of mere expedient morality and from abstract definitions of morality that would impose a specious uniformity on humankind. The difficulty, of course, for Bradley as for Lukács, is to find those "individual facts whose being is historical," that holy grail that is neither isolated particular nor abstract universal.

This difficulty exercised Eliot in his dissertation on Bradley, in which he drenched both subject and object in an acid bath of skepticism, and also in his early poetry, especially in "The Love Song of J. Alfred Prufrock." The psychological tortures of this poem come from the painful suspension of its protagonist between fragmentation and generalization, two opposite but equally inescapable falsifications of human experience. In a recent essay on the politics of modernism, Bruce Robbins complains that "The Love Song of J. Alfred Prufrock" "has yet to be read, after the modernist fashion, against the grain. So read, the poem can be seen to contain, alongside 'that fragmentation which is characteristic of human experience generally' (J. Hillis Miller), what might be called fragments of totality. . . ."[12] To truly read the poem "against the grain," however, would be to realize that alongside its celebrated fragmentation the poem contains, not bits and pieces of totality, but a deep horror of it. Prufrock recoils equally from fragment and whole. His defeat comes from his inability to find a mediation between them.

The general fragmentation of "The Love Song of J. Alfred Prufrock" is obvious and notorious. The poem seems a perfect example of what Terry Eagleton calls the modern "transition from metaphor to metonymy: unable any longer to totalize his experience in some heroic figure, the bourgeois is forced to let it trickle away into objects related to him by sheer contiguity."[13] Everything in "Prufrock" trickles away into parts related to one another only by contiguity. Spatial progress in the poem is diffident or deferred, a "scuttling" accomplished by a pair of claws disembodied so violently they remain "ragged."[14] In the famous opening, "the evening is spread out against the sky / Like a patient etherised upon a table," and the simile makes an equation between being spread out and being etherised that continues elsewhere in the poem when the evening, now a bad patient, "malingers, / Stretched on the floor, here beside you and me." There it "sleeps so peacefully! / Smoothed by long fingers. . . ." This suspension is a rhetorical as well as a spatial and emotional condition. The "streets that follow like a tedious argument / Of insidious intent" lead not to a conclusion but to a question, a question too "overwhelming" even to ask. Phrases like the "muttering retreats / Of restless nights" combine physical blockage, emotional unrest, and rhetorical maundering in an equation that seems to make the human being a combination not of angel and beast but of road-map and Roberts' Rules of Order.

In certain lines, metaphor dissolves into metonymy before the reader's eyes. "The yellow fog that rubs its back upon the window-panes" appears clearly to every reader as a cat, but the cat itself is absent, represented explicitly only in parts – back, muzzle, tongue – and by its actions – licking, slipping, leaping, curling. The metaphor has in a sense been hollowed out to be replaced by a series of metonyms, and thus it stands as a rhetorical introduction to what follows. The people in the poem also appear as disembodied parts or ghostly actions. They are "the faces that you meet," the "hands / That lift and drop a question on your plate," the "Arms that are braceleted and white and bare," the "eyes that fix you in a formulated phrase." Prufrock himself fears such a reduction, to use Kenneth Burke's term for the effect of metonymy.[15] The dread questions "How his hair is growing thin!" and "But how his arms and legs are thin" reduce Prufrock to certain body parts, the thinness of which stands in for the diminution caused by the rhetorical figures. What Prufrock fears has already been accomplished by his own rhetoric.

In this poem the horror of sex seems to come in part from its power to metonymize. Like Augustine, Eliot sees sex as the tyranny of one part of the body over the whole.[16] Though Eliot is far too circumspect to name this part, he figures its power in his poetry by the rebelliousness of mere members: hands, arms, eyes. Sexual desire pulls the body apart, so that to give in to it is to suffer permanent dismemberment. This may account for the odd combination in Eliot's work of sexual ennui and libidinous violence. The tyranny of one part scatters all the others, reducing the whole to impotence. In this way, the violence of sex robs the individual of the integrity necessary to action.

An oddly similar relationship of part to whole governs Prufrock's conception of time. In a burst of confidence he asserts, "In a minute there is time / For decisions and revisions which a minute will reverse." Yet he seems to quail before the very amplitude of possibility contained in time, so that all these decisions and revisions are foreclosed before they can be made. Thus Prufrock's prospective confidence in the fullness of time becomes a retrospective conviction that "I have known them all already, known them all: – / Have known the evenings, mornings, afternoons. . . ." To know "all" already is to be paralyzed, disabled, because "all" is not full of possibility but paradoxically empty, constituted as it is by pure repetition, part on part on part. In a figure that exactly parallels the bodily metonymies, time becomes a collection of individual parts, just as the poem's human denizens had been little more than parts: "And I have known the eyes already, known them all"; "And I have known the arms already known them all." The instantaneous movement from part to whole, from eyes, arms, evenings, mornings, to "all," expresses the emptiness between, the gap between dispersed parts and an oppressive whole made of purely serial repetition. The very reduction of human beings to parts of themselves and of time to episodes makes it impossible to conceive of any whole different from this empty, repetitious "all." As Burke says, metonymy substitutes quantity for quality,[17] so that instead of living life Prufrock feels "I have measured out my life with coffee spoons."

Eliot's oppressive repetition of the word *all* expresses not some plenitude but this emptiness. Richard Ellmann has remarked how Yeats's repetitions of *all* in "In Memory of Major Robert Gregory" "help lend an aura of universal genius to a young man who may have been only a universal dabbler."[18] *All* is in some sense the key word of Yeats's poem, carrying with it the insistence on completeness that is Yeats's theme. The word is so useful because it can easily expand the singular to the level of the general. As William Empson remarks in his essay "All in Paradise Lost," "the word presumes economy of means; it raises the thing in hand absolutely without needing to list all the others." On the other hand, the expansiveness of *all* also contains the opposite possibility of contraction. Empson says Milton uses the word so much because he "is an absolutist, an all-or-none man."[19] Eliot's absolutism is, if possible, even more absolute than Milton's; for him, it is not all or none, but all and none. Since Prufrock's *all* is a mere sum, an aggregate, it actually signifies the very opposite of what it seems to say. Whenever it seems to name all it in fact reduces all to nothing. All becomes one of Eliot's chief rhymes, yet pairing it with "fall" and "sprawl" as he does highlights the paradoxical emptiness of the word, all the emptier for its many repetitions.

There finally comes a moment in the poem that is, as it were, "after all," after "the cups, the marmalade, the tea," after the metonymical clutter, when Prufrock might have declared, "I am Lazarus, come from the dead, / Come back to tell you all, I shall tell you all" to one who might have replied, "That is not what I meant at all. / That is not it, at all." Eliot's "after all" seems very literal in this passage, for the moment he is hoping to achieve comes *after* all the others, after the negative *all,* the series of identical encounters represented here by a string of metonyms. The paragraph suggests that all is not all after all, that there may be one who breaks out of the metonymic series into uniqueness: "After the sunsets and the dooryards and the sprinkled streets, / After the novels, after the teacups, after the skirts that trail along the floor – ." After metonymy comes wholeness, "all" rhymed with the "ball" of the entire universe, but this all is in the hands of one unique individual, the Lazarus who has gone beyond all time by dying and who now comes "back to tell you all." The uniqueness of Lazarus's act, the way it breaks the chain of time, makes a truly expansive "all" possible again. Only through the particular, the truly different, is the whole apprehensible.

This "all" seems to collapse in incomprehension, however, when confronted, albeit conjecturally, with the "one" who says "That is not it, at

all." And yet Eliot's syntax is so obscure here as to allow another possibility, that he actually welcomes, even longs for, just this sort of contradiction. In fact, the odd drift here from the conditional perfect into a kind
of timeless subjunctive – "If one . . . should say" – suggests that the
episode might yet happen. If "one" refuses to become "all," should
refuse the proffered habitual thing, then the metonymic chain is broken
and all is restored. The uniqueness of this act resurrects wholeness, just as
a repetitive sameness had annihilated it.

Prufrock therefore suffers as much from a sense of oppressive totality
as he does from fragmentation. The chain of metonymic substitution that
so horribly contains him constitutes a negative plenitude, an all indistinguishable from nothing.[20] There is nothing in Prufrock's world or his
sensibility to stop the oscillation of part and whole, to break the instantaneous transition from dispersed fragments to uniform totality.
Only difference, a certain "one" not assimilable to the categories of the
others, can save him, but true difference is the one thing that Prufrock
cannot bring himself to believe in.

More than just a figure of speech, metonymy structures "Prufrock" in
the larger sense made famous by Roman Jakobson. For Jakobson, of
course, poetry is more metaphoric than prose, more dependent on equiv-
alences and parallels than the form that must to some extent include
purely contingent details. Poetic structures themselves reinforce this metaphoric bias. Jakobson says, "the phonic equivalence of rhyming words
prompts the question of semantic similarity and contrast."[21] Eliot seems
almost to flaunt his rhymes, which follow no set pattern but dominate
the poem nonetheless. From the snidely perfect "In the room the women
come and go / Talking of Michelangelo," the rhymes, by their phonic
equivalence, emphasize not so much the similarity or contrast between
the rhyme words themselves as a general semantic closure that mirrors
the spatial and temporal closure expressed thematically in the sentence. "I
grow old . . . I grow old . . . / I shall wear the bottoms of my trousers
rolled" enacts temporal repetition and closure both syntactically and in
rhyme. Rhyme, these rhymes seem to say, is a habit and thus the perfect
expression for a life ruthlessly enclosed in habits. As A.D. Moody puts
it, "the couplet insists on the fixed facts."[22] Only the irony with which
Eliot advertises his own subjection to rhyme as a past poetic practice
separates him from his characters, as if the poetry could become new by
trifling with the old.

Yet the search for similarity or contrast that Jakobson says is motivated
by rhyme is continually frustrated as well. The "Michelangelo" couplet
seems formed not so much on contrast as on mere contingency, as if the
subject of conversation might well have been anything. Similarly, decisions to wear one's trousers rolled or to eat a peach betray their own

accidental quality as nonce decisions. Within the closure offered by habit is an equal and opposite subjection to chance. Within the structure of rhyme and also within the syntactical parallels is a wasteland of metonymic details, unconnected to one another or even to their paired rhyme words. Structurally speaking, then, the poem contains a myriad of contingent details within a comically rigid phonic scheme, playing one off against the other as if to physically demonstrate the conflict between fragmentation and empty totality. For this is the result of the poem's play with traditional verse devices, that it expresses structurally a society both ruthlessly totalized and helplessly fragmented. In historical terms, the poetry displays individuals absolutely governed by habit and yet also helplessly wayward. In any real sense, the sort of particular, historical fact that Bradley desires does not exist in "Prufrock," only isolated moments and the negative totality represented by the deadly tolling of the word *all*.

Prufrock's squirmings may seem to have little to do with politics of any kind. Yet the self-contradictory fact that Prufrock's loneliness is matched by his utter integration into a repressively repetitive society does have political implications. Even Prufrock's decadence, the very ennui that makes him seem so distant from anything so rough as politics, can be seen to represent the modern contradiction between freedom and necessity, in which one is free precisely to the extent that one has no power.[23] The larger philosophical and social context of these contradictions appears in the earliest political work Eliot is known to have produced, the Extension lectures of 1916. In these lectures, now represented only by syllabi and outlines, Eliot takes aim at Rousseau, and at the simultaneous "escape from the world of fact, and devotion to brute fact" that he sees as the legacy of Rousseau in politics, religion and literature.[24] Prufrock obviously suffers in the grip of this contradictory escape into subjection, because both he and the poem that contains him escape what Moody calls "the fixed facts" only insofar as they also eagerly submit to them. But the lecture outlines also make visible beyond Prufrock the larger contradiction between idealism and realism, the individual and the world, fact and value, that Eliot followed Bradley in hoping to resolve. Bradley's program to put "individual facts whose being is historical" where modern society puts either "escape from the world of fact, or devotion to brute fact" is meant to mediate between mutually exclusive but equally inescapable falsifications of human experience. Eliot's lectures outline a political, ethical, and literary effort to find this resolution, so obviously and painfully absent from "Prufrock."

It seems quite impossible, given Eliot's class and sensibilities, all too accurately represented even in the form of travesty in "Prufrock," that this program might be a revolutionary one. But Prufrock's tortures are not so different from those suffered in a book Lukács was writing at about the same time, a book whose very title, *The Soul and the Forms,* evokes the oppositions that Prufrock cannot resolve. Though Eliot and Lukács could hardly have been known to one another at this early date, the Extension lectures show Eliot's awareness of the fact that left and right concur in the fight against the contradictions of modern society. Eliot identifies two wings in this fight, two tendencies, "one toward syndicalism, more radical than nineteenth-century socialism, the other toward monarchy. Both currents express revolt against the same state of affairs, and consequently tend to meet." He concludes in a later lecture that "contemporary socialism has much in common with royalism." Thus the writer who was so portentously to identify himself as a "royalist in politics" had much earlier identified royalism with socialism.[25]

Late in his life, Lukács was to take Eliot's poetry as one example of modernist pessimism, a merely passive suffering in the face of injustice and oppression.[26] "Prufrock" seems a perfect instance of such apolitical withdrawal. Yet Lukács's antagonism obscures the fact that the two writers begin with very similar philosophical analyses of modern contradictions, both presided over by Hegel. And though it is certainly true that the two diverged once it came to practical solutions, both gave the aesthetic an important role in resolving the contradictions Hegel had identified.[27] Both men desire from literature at least an attempted synthesis of fragment and whole, but Lukács will find this in the great bourgeois works of the nineteenth century, in which representative individuals inhabit a normative totality, whereas Eliot looked for his version of the classic in the modern condition itself. In fact, the very withdrawal that irked Lukács was to become an indispensable part of Eliot's aesthetic crusade. Eliot will base his literary order on what seems to Lukács spasmodic and idiosyncratic, and in so doing he will attempt to achieve the reconciliation both men pursued.

2. THE CRITIC AND THE CRISIS OF HISTORICISM

On the most immediately practical level, the purpose of Eliot's early criticism was to make a place within an inhospitable literary establishment for the poetry Eliot wanted to write.[28] The reader sees in these essays the young American rudely shouldering his way into a gathering to which he had not been invited. Of course, the young American was so successful that he was soon sending out the invitations himself. This success is hard to account for, especially because Eliot used two quite different, seemingly incompatible, arguments to advance his work and that of his generation. On one hand, he argued that it deserved a hearing because it was new and different. In "*Ulysses,* Order, and Myth," for example, Eliot praises Joyce and Lewis, and by implication the important poem he had just published himself, for sensing the changed conditions of a new age. On the other hand, he claimed that the new literature wasn't new at all. Thus Lewis and Joyce could be enlisted in the ranks of the "classicism" that Eliot had been advertising since at least 1916.

The power of the early essays comes from their almost casual transformation of this apparent logical weakness into a polemical strength. There is no conflict between the classic and the modern if even the classic is time-bound, available only in particular forms at particular times, as a goal that successful literature achieves "according to the possibilities of its place and time" (UOM, p. 482). Insisting that the apparent contrast between the classic and the modern is in fact an identity allows Eliot to close two other troublesome gaps, that between particular and universal and that between fact and value. For if the particular virtues of the present no longer exist in contradistinction to timeless values, but rather as an instance of them, then adherence to the new and different is not just a temporal necessity, a respect for facts, but an ethical imperative as well. One might advocate the modern simply because it *is* new, the accurate reflection of changed times, but also because all literature *should be* new, in order to remain classical.

To resolve these dichotomies in this way is to dissolve the apparent contrast in the title of Eliot's most famous essay, "Tradition and the Individual Talent." It is, in other words, to provide the reconciliation so painfully absent from "Prufrock" by showing that individual and community, particular and universal, fact and value, freedom and history, are not at odds but in magnificent collusion. Not incidentally, such a resolution might explain why the seemingly extrinsic, in the person of this lonely young American, should come to dominate the intrinsic, so that he should come in time to symbolize British letters. Eliot said later in his life that an American can more easily become a true European than any native-born European.[29] He had already shown how an expatriate American can easily take English tradition as a cudgel against contemporary English letters.

From the very beginning, Eliot's criticism was dominated by Bradley's adoption in "The Presuppositions of Critical History" of Hegel's famous dictum that human beings can no more elude their historical context than one could "jump over Rhodes."[30] But Eliot adopts this idea not just as a necessity but also as an imperative, a value to be counterposed to abstract principles and mere empiricism. In this sense, then, Eliot enlists himself and his criticism in Bradley's program to put "individual facts whose being is historical" where modern society has put either mere facts or an escape from facts.

In a manuscript prepared as a doctoral student at Harvard, Eliot quotes with approval Durkheim's assertion that each society "constitutes a new individuality, and all these distinct individualities, being heterogeneous, can not fuse into one continuous series, nor, above all, into a single series."[31] For this reason, Eliot's work on interpretation in Josiah Royce's seminar at Harvard emphasized the incommensurability of different interpretations.[32] The most famous of his early essays, seemingly devoted to defining "tradition," as if there were only one, begins by insisting that "Every nation, every race, has not only its own creative, but its own critical turn of mind . . ." (SE, p. 3). Eliot could even reconcile himself, for a moment at least, to the Russian revolution, on the grounds that "there are and have been various cultures, and that the difference between our culture and an alien culture is different from the difference between culture and anarchy."[33]

For Eliot, then, all human activities are racial, temporal, and cultural particulars. Though he sympathized with and learned from Irving Babbitt's attack on Rousseauism, Eliot criticized Babbitt's humanism as another abstraction, which tore its subjects from "their contexts of race, place, and time" (SE, p. 386). A good deal of Eliot's mature criticism insists that without such contexts things simply disappear. In a *Criterion* commentary published in 1937 he says, "I cannot think of art . . . but as racial and local; and an art which is not representative of a particular people, but 'international', or an art which does not represent a particular civilization, but only an abstract civilization-in-general, may lose its sources of vitality."[34]

Bradley makes the ethical implications of such historical particularity clear when he insists "that the morality of one time is not that of another time, that the men considered good in one age might in another age not be thought good, that what would be right for us here might be mean and base in another country."[35] Like Bradley, Eliot did not flinch from the realization that local, racial, and temporal particularism made atemporal standards and values impossible. According to Jeffrey M. Perl and Andrew P. Tuck, "A reader used to thinking of Eliot as an absolutist Anglo-Catholic may be interested to know that 'relativist' was the only label that Eliot was willing to accept for himself during this formative period."[36] Indeed, in a letter sent to Norbert Wiener in 1915, Eliot gives his assent to a paper Wiener had written on relativism, and confesses the strength of "my relativism," which, he says, had utterly garbled his thesis on Bradley.[37]

Whether or not relativism had garbled the thesis is difficult to say, but it certainly affected Eliot's sense of poetic value. In "Donne in Our Time," Eliot says, "there is not one permanent and impersonal kind of naturalness and one of artificiality . . . what is natural to-day is artificial to-morrow."[38] In *The Use of Poetry and the Use of Criticism,* he mocks Addison for attempting to fix and determine the meanings of words and therefore the standards to be applied to literature. "It is an elementary error," he says, with all the sad wisdom of an age far distant from poor Addison's, "to think that we have discovered as objective laws what we have merely imposed by private legislation." A recurrent theme of this work, which aims in some respect to fix and determine the uses of poetry and criticism, is that one cannot "*explain* poetry by discovering its natural laws" because "poetry can recognize no such laws." There is "no one essence of poetry, for which we can find the formula" and which would allow poets to "be ranked according to their possession of a greater or lesser quantity of this essence." "Every effort to formulate the common element is limited by the limitations of particular men in particular times and at particular places" (UPUC, pp. 60, 139, 98, 142).

For a rather large group of critics and scholars, such particulars are harmonized in Eliot's writing by inclusion within a "system."[39] Such analyses depend on an interpretation of Bradley that undervalues his "unsystematic and skeptical tendencies"[40] and then argues from Bradley's example to Eliot. James Longenbach admits that "it would be wrong to think of Eliot as a 'systematic' critic,"[41] but this is not simply because Eliot's essays come as responses to particular occasions or because he was ruled by a kind of English diffidence that put a rhetorical brake on systematic pronouncements. Eliot explicitly opposed himself to the making of systems. Metaphysical systems, he observed at the end of his dissertation, "are condemned to go up like a rocket and come down like a stick."[42] Longenbach is able to cite Eliot's disapproval of impressionistic critics like Arthur Symons, but, as the discussion of Addison has already shown, he was equally harsh with critics who worked according to a system. In arguing that Eliot actively avoided systematic theorizing, Victor P.H. Li cites a passage from the 1919 essay on Ben Jonson, in which Eliot criticizes Jonson for codifying "as a formula and a programme of reform, what he chose to do himself." Eliot also criticizes attempts to understand Jonson's work that do not see that what is important in it is that which "escapes the formulae" (SE, p. 136).[43] Here Eliot clearly values what escapes or exceeds the system, and he mocks, as he did in the case of Addison, attempts to make personal impulse and taste into anything more consistent.[44]

Eliot even more rigorously opposes the idea that there might be one system large and comprehensive enough to include all cultures and so to permit rational comparisons between them. His belief in the value of cultural specificity leads Eliot naturally to cultural relativism.[45] As a literary critic, Eliot puts a good deal of emphasis on *taste,* on the unconscious complex of habits, beliefs, and prejudices that gives a specific character to each time and place. To attempt to transcend the limits of taste is, in his eyes, mere folly. There is, he says in "Donne in Our Time," an objective order of merit by which poets might be ranked on some Judgment Day, but "at any particular time, and we exist only in particular moments of time, good taste consists, not in attaining to the vision of Judgement Day. . . ."[46] Two years later, in *The Use of Poetry and the Use of Criticism,* Eliot maintains that "'Pure' artistic appreciation is to my thinking only an ideal, when not merely a figment, and must be so long as the appreciation of art is an affair of limited and transient human beings existing in space and time" (UPUC, p. 109). The accomplishment of perfect taste, by which each poet might be appreciated in objective relationship to every other poet, is not just impossible, but wrong: "We may even say that to have better 'taste' in poetry than belongs to one's state of development, is not to 'taste' anything at all" (UPUC, p. 36). Taste, Eliot says, "cannot be isolated from one's other interests and passions . . . and must be limited as one's self is limited" (UPUC, p. 36). Both a necessity and an imperative, cultural specificity limits the appreciation of poetry emotionally, almost viscerally.

Faced with the fact of cultural diversity, Eliot advances an uncompromising cultural relativism of the sort that is synonymous with historicism. Patrick Gardiner, among many others, traces contemporary cultural relativism to Herder's reaction "against the assumptions of the European Enlightenment" that human nature and/or reason exist unchanging through all the ages and across all borders.[47] Carl Wellman suggests that cultural relativism can lead to two quite different conclusions about ethical or moral values, that all are valid or that none are.[48] Cultural relativism presents a grave moral danger to historicists because it could lead to such a disbelief in value or morality itself, even in the limited morality of a particular culture.

Philosophers sometimes hold that relativism of any kind refutes itself, because it would have to relativize even itself and therefore undermine its own authority.[49] Whether this is true or not, cultural relativists certainly suffer from self-inflicted wounds whenever they try to affirm the norms of any given society. Having undermined the idea of normative values, relativists have little authority on which to call in the affirmation of any particular set of values. One way around this problem is to recast relativism itself as an absolute. Bernard Williams calls this position "vulgar relativism," and charges that it depends on two mutually contradictory principles, that "right" is relative to a given society "and that (therefore) it is wrong for people in one society to condemn, interfere with, etc., the values of another society." Williams describes the central error of this position as the attempt "to conjure out of the fact that societies have differing attitudes and values an *a priori* nonrelative principle to determine the attitude of one society to another."[50]

If advocating such incompatible propositions makes one a "vulgar relativist," then most historicists would merit the term. Historicists relativize everything except cultural specificity, which remains as the only absolute value. As Eliot himself puts it, "The *absolute* value is that each area should have its characteristic culture" (NDC, p. 53).[51] Societies are ranked, then, according to their degree of cultural specificity and self-containment, the extent to which all cultural practices, values, and beliefs come out of the conditions of that society alone. If the only wrong is to violate the specificity of particular cultures, then those cultures will be best that have maintained themselves behind the most impermeable barriers.

Large-scale moral discriminations between whole societies can therefore be made according to this one metaethical value, that each culture should have its own distinct character. In accordance with this value, ancient Greece becomes the paradigm of paradigms, the culture most perfectly self-contained, specifically adjusted to its own soil, climate, and historical background. A perfect German or English society might not resemble ancient Greece in any particular, but would rival Greece in being purely English or German. Because no one set of values will necessarily conduce to cultural unity more than another set, societies can differ quite drastically while still approaching perfection. The surest way of destroying such perfection, however, is to impose from outside some abstract, atemporal set of beliefs on the specific conditions of the society.

As Williams suggests, however, this solution puts its proponent in the contradictory position of making the same values both relative and absolute. Historicism can stop cultural relativism short of complete skepticism only by making the former an absolute moral value. Looked at from without, a society's values are purely relative, but looked at from within they are absolute, the more absolute the more relative they are to the specific conditions of that society. Although historicism may encourage diversity on one level, it reprehends it on another. As Williams says, relativism of this sort has definite "conservative implications."[52] But this conservatism is of a peculiar brand because it counsels continuity and uniformity without reference to any particular value or ideal. A society's values are confirmed simply because they are a society's values, arbitrary though they may be. Therefore, what seems from one point of view as dangerously close to moral anarchy can easily become a kind of pure authoritarianism, pure because it does not and cannot appeal to any justification outside itself.[53]

In other words, the very mechanisms that historicism proposes to resolve the liberal dichotomies recreate these dichotomies. Instead of synthesizing particular and general, fact and value, historicism reproduces the opposition between them. The political implications of this failure are obvious, for historicism can mock its own promise in two different ways, either paralyzing action by relativizing all value or empowering a tyranny by making particular values absolute. The implications for literary politics, for the adjudication of literary value and the arrangement of literary history, are just as acute. These implications emerge in the very essays that seem Eliot's most triumphant negotiations between the particular values of modernity and the absolute value of tradition.

In "The Metaphysical Poets," Eliot picks his way delicately through these contradictions. This brief book review is a clever historical manifesto for modern poetry of the kind Eliot himself was writing, and its defense of the modern rests on a historicist belief. "It is not a permanent necessity," Eliot says, "that poets should be interested in philosophy, or in any other subject" (SE, p. 248). Poetry varies, and should vary, this statement implies, with the age. Therefore, it is perfectly appropriate "that poets in our civilization, as it exists at present, must be *difficult*. Our civilization comprehends great variety and complexity, and this variety and complexity, playing upon a refined sensibility, must produce various and complex results" (SE, p. 248). Eliot's emphasis on the complexity and variety of the age should not mask his dependence on a theory of social congruence: Poetry and the age necessarily match.

The whole essay, of course, depends on such a sociological view of poetry. Tennyson and Browning differ from Donne and Lord Herbert of Cherbury, Eliot tells us, because of something that happened to "the mind of Europe" (SE, p. 247). In the seventeenth century the famous "dissociation of sensibility set in," a very curious description that makes dissociation sound more like petrifaction. In 1947, Eliot added that the dissociation "had something to do with the Civil War . . . that it is a consequence of the same causes which brought about the Civil War; that we must seek the causes in Europe, not in England alone; and for what these causes were, we may dig and dig until we get to a depth at which words and concepts fail us."[54] The digging must be so deep because cultures are wholes, because no one cause can ever be isolated out of the complex, because analysis destroys the very subject it seeks to understand. On this purely descriptive level the essay relies on historicist assumptions: Each age differs, held together as a unity by virtually invisible ties of commonality. It might certainly be argued that implicit within the essay lies a perfectly sound defense of Tennyson and Browning, even of Milton and Dryden. If modern poets must be difficult, then Tennyson and Browning had to be discursive. They can hardly be blamed for something that happened to the age as a whole, and, in fact, normative judgments of this kind are inappropriate when different ages are so incommensurable.

Eliot's essay is not, however, primarily descriptive but polemical. Frank Kermode argues that Eliot seeks in history a period with qualities like those he wanted in his poetry; the discovery of such a period obviously gives historical weight to contemporary techniques that seem departures.[55] However, this justification of the modern clashes with the other justification Eliot gives, that modern poetry must be as modern as the age. In order to align the contemporary with some authorizing historical exemplar, Eliot makes the historical into the normative: What Donne and Lord Herbert did because they couldn't help it becomes an imperative task that poets *should* perform. In fact, the historical difference between Donne and Tennyson becomes in one of the most well-known passages an ahistorical difference between the "ordinary man's experience" and that of "the poet" (SE, p. 247). Presumably, there were "ordinary" men in Donne's England so that the "mind of Europe" could not then have been so perfectly unified as Eliot asserts. What is expressed at one point as a divide between two historical periods is made here into a permanent distinction of value between the ordinary and the artistic.[56] In short, Eliot asserts both that all ages are congruent, unified for good or ill through all their manifestations, and that cultural unity is a hard-won achievement of a few golden ages. The historicist principle of cultural specificity and unity has become an ahistorical, normative value.

Literary modernism also has two very different roles, as an involuntary response to the conditions of modern Europe and as the almost providential cure for several centuries of moral dissolution. The poets who follow Dryden, Eliot says, "do not feel their thought as immediately as the odour of a rose" (SE, p. 247). Here Eliot's dissociation of sensibility declares itself as a modern version of the split in human nature deplored as early as Schiller's *Aesthetic Letters*. For Eliot, as for Schiller, modernization exacts a fearful price as material progress develops certain faculties and turns them against certain others. Unfortunately, Eliot's polemic merely advertises the division in his own sensibility; his very ability to see and note his own creative responses betrays a division. But the implicit program of the essay suggests that modern art has already begun to heal the split caused by modernization. Baudelaire, Eliot suggests, more closely approximates Donne than Tennyson. This means that somehow modernization negates itself, that the very conditions of variety and complexity that threaten poetry will also defuse their own threat.

Eliot's ability to accomplish this trick depends on his having made dissociation and unity both specific cultural and historical facts and atemporal standards. The "dissociation of sensibility" seems to stand like a great divide between the metaphysicals and the moderns. However, Eliot defends the metaphysicals from Johnson's censure by asserting that "after the dissociation, they put the material together again in a new unity" (SE, p. 245). The virtues of the metaphysicals turn out to depend as much on dissociation as on unity, for these poets do not simply bask in cultural and psychological homogeneity but instead wrench together disparate facts.

Modern poetry will be able to do this again, it seems, *because of* the historical dissociation and not in spite of it. Modern poets, living in a situation of great "variety and complexity" must "dislocate" language to achieve their meaning (SE, p. 248). In so doing, "we get something that looks very much like the conceit . . . a method curiously similar to that of the 'metaphysical poets'" (SE, pp. 248–249). The results of the dissociation of sensibility turn out to look a lot like what preceded the dissociation. In other words, all good poetry, modern or not, will perform the task that Eliot implies elsewhere in the essay is the peculiar task of the moderns. Dissociation, like unity, is both historical and ahistorical or normative at the same time.

"Tradition and the Individual Talent" depends even more completely on such transformations. In "Tradition and the Individual Talent," in the balance between the two terms of the title, Eliot again illustrates the historicist dilemma, caught between the particular and the general, the relative and the absolute. His elegant solution depends on his ability to show that tradition *is* the individual talent, that by being individual the modernist becomes, willy-nilly, traditional. As he says himself, "the most individual parts" of a poet's work "may be those in which the dead poets, his ancestors, assert their immortality most vigorously" (SE, p. 4). The elegance of this solution begins to fray and even tear a bit when the concept of the individual is stretched beyond reasonable limits. When the individual must function both as a specific particular, locked in history, and as an ahistorical normative standard, Eliot exposes despite himself the difficulties of making a value system out of historicism.

In his essay, Eliot speaks of an "ideal order" of literary "monuments" (SE, p. 5), which sounds like a free-standing library of objective facts. The "simultaneous order" of European literature becomes an order, however, as a "sense," a "feeling," "a sense of the timeless as well as the temporal and of the timeless and the temporal together" (SE, p. 4). When Eliot says of the great dead writers that "they are that which we know" (SE, p. 6), he aims a witticism at the present, but he also makes clear that the past is that which is known by the present. The essay therefore moves quite naturally from the definition of tradition as a self-unifying whole to the metaphor of the mind as such, as a receptacle that stores up particulars "until all the particles which can unite to form a new compound are present together" (SE, p. 8). As he says in "The Metaphysical Poets," such minds "are always forming new wholes" (SE, p. 247) like the constantly re-forming whole of tradition.

Thus Chris Baldick calls Eliot's model of tradition a "subjective correlative," an individual unity that figures as prototype for a larger, seemingly impersonal unity.[57] That the individual mind is Eliot's model for tradition is signified by his use throughout his career of expressions like "the mind of England" (SE, p. 332), "the whole mind of society" (SE, p. 354), "the mind of a whole people" (UPUC, p. 22). Use of terms like "maturity," applied in "What Is a Classic?" equally to individuals and to periods and literatures, extends the analogy (OPP, p. 55).

The real continuity behind history, Eliot thus suggests, is that of the individual mind. Though its contents change, and must change, the mind remains as a principle of wholeness. He says the mind of Europe is "a mind which changes" (SE, p. 6), but he does not want to accept the logical conclusion, that ahistorical standards are therefore inappropriate to a constantly changing mind. What remains in Eliot's analysis as an unchanging, normative standard is the wholeness of the mind, its ability to fuse new material with the old. By this standard, Eliot enables himself to reject Tennyson and Browning on the grounds of intellectual and emotional disunity while praising Donne and Marvell. But "Tradition and the Individual Talent" presents the mind as *always* forming new wholes. Wholeness is both an ideal, reached only at the peaks of history, and a neutral function, always accomplished.[58] Moreover, as an ideal it is without content, being purely relational. Though Eliot rejects the idea of an unchanging human nature, he surreptitiously depends on his own definition of ideal human nature in making literary discriminations.

These contradictions are concretely expressed in "Tradition and the Individual Talent" and elsewhere in Eliot's inconsistency about the degree to which tradition can be conscious. He says in "The Function of Criticism" that there is "an unconscious community" between the true artists of any time, but that this community could also be brought about consciously (SE, p. 13). In "What Is a Classic?" he calls maturity "an ordered though unconscious progress of a language," but then says that maturity of mind needs "consciousness of history" (OPP, p. 56). In "Religion and Literature," he demands a literature that would be "*un*consciously, rather than deliberately and defiantly, Christian," but then complains against censorship that "acts only from custom and habit, not from decided theological and moral principles."[59]

"Tradition and the Individual Talent" itself contains the most important such inconsistency. There, Eliot says flatly, "Tradition . . . cannot be inherited, and if you want it you must obtain it by great labour" (SE, p. 4). In fact, the only difference between the present and the past is "that the conscious present is an awareness of the past. . ." (SE, p. 6). The famous platinum analogy, in which the mind of the poet resembles the catalyst in a chemical reaction, seems to contradict this assertion, however, because the mind remains "inert, neutral, and unchanged" through the course of its chemical experiences (SE, p. 7). Actually, the more apt analogy for the mind of the poet is the chamber in which the gases are mixed, "a receptacle for seizing and storing up numberless feelings, phrases, images, which remain there until all the particles which can unite to form a new compound are present together" (SE, p. 8). Here the mind is seen as a neutral container, the receiver and not the creator of ideas and emotions. As Murray Krieger puts it, "the poet can give us nothing that was not in our world before his entrance upon it."[60]

The motive force behind the chemical combinations seems to inhere in the chemicals and not in the poet's mind. If these experiences and emotions reform themselves within an inert container, leaving the catalyst unchanged, then the process must be an unconscious one. And, in fact, Eliot quarrels with Wordsworth at the end of his essay, arguing that the recollection of experiences by the poet "does not happen consciously or of deliberation" (SE, p. 10). And yet, "there is a great deal, in the writing of poetry, which must be conscious and deliberate." Here Eliot apparently means that the bad poet is apt to spend too much time worrying over his ideas and emotions and not enough time on his craft, which he tends to take for granted. But the assurance that "the bad poet is usually unconscious when he ought to be conscious, and conscious when he ought to be unconscious" seems nothing more than a desperate sleight-of-hand, especially because it is not followed by any specifications about the seemingly imperative boundaries between the conscious and unconscious tasks.

Something fundamental in Eliot's argument makes this conflict inevitable. On one hand, the tradition he offers in his essay must be a conscious one. Eliot could hardly identify a completely unconscious tradition for us. Even if the ties he speaks of are primarily unconscious, they must be capable of being brought to consciousness or the essay itself would be an impossibility. Beyond this, the simple fact that Eliot advocates conformity to tradition as a program means that the tradition must be consciously elaborated. Otherwise, Eliot's polemic could not evoke an effective response. Eliot phrases his polemic in terms of greater consciousness and awareness: "The poet must be very conscious of the main current; . . . He must be quite aware . . .; He must be aware . . ." (SE, pp. 5–6). Eliot calls his professional readers to awareness: "The poet who is aware of this will be aware of great difficulties and responsibilities" (SE, p. 5). If conformity to the past is largely an unconscious bequest, then no poet need be aware of or troubled by difficulties.[61] In fact, Eliot feels it necessary to defend himself against the idea that he requires excessive erudition of his poet; he allows that such work must not encroach on the poet's "necessary laziness" (SE, p. 6).

Why then does Eliot choose such a passive metaphor for the poet and quibble with Wordsworth about whether recollection can be deliberate? J. Hillis Miller suggests that "Eliot's praise of unconsciousness seems to be partly a fear of the annihilating effects of a relativistic historical sense. To be aware of the history of one's own culture is admirable, but to see it from the outside as a culture among others is to be so detached from it as to be unable to participate in it."[62] Eliot does not fear relativism, however, but insists on it. His conception of unconscious tradition corresponds to the general standards of historicism, which limit individuals to a specific time and place. To purposely rise above that time and place is to achieve the impossible. But in order to mount a polemic in favor of an unconscious tradition, one must have become conscious of it and therefore have accomplished the impossible. The contradiction in the essay between conscious and unconscious definitions of tradition is the expression of Eliot's difficulty in transforming historicism into a polemical value system.

A.D. Moody explains Eliot's essay by saying that "the poet's mind, as the conscious present, must transcend that more important mind to which he submits."[63] This is to say that the poet, or, more appropriately, the poetic critic, must contain and be contained by tradition, must be alternately part and whole. To do so he must be both conscious and unconscious, individual and general, relative and absolute, modern and timeless. The fruits of modernity, the very byproducts of the collapse of tradition into fragments, must be used to make tradition whole again. This, then, is the program of "Tradition and the Individual Talent" as it is of "The Metaphysical Poets," to use modernity to reverse itself, to go through the divisions left by the lapse of tradition to achieve a new wholeness.

The project founders, however, on Eliot's unwillingness to compromise his relativism, an unwillingness that leads to a project for change and discrimination that is yet denied any standards by which to work. In his essay, Eliot takes a resolutely relativist stand: "Art never improves" (SE, p. 6). This statement seems to put all value judgments, all qualitative discriminations, out of court. But Eliot also has a way of distinguishing "the main current, which does not at all flow invariably through the most distinguished reputations" (SE, pp. 5–6). How to distinguish the "main current" from its eddies and backwaters? The very metaphor of the "current" contains the answer, requiring as it does continuity of flow. That which does not reach the farther stages clearly does not belong to the main current. This solution still leaves, however, the seemingly paradoxical statement that the "most distinguished reputations" might not swell the main current. These, it becomes clear, must be reputations of the "immediate generation before us," "simple currents," which are "soon lost in the sand" (SE, p. 6). How this description can be squared with the previous statement that tradition abandons nothing is one of the major puzzles of Eliot's essay.

Equally puzzling is the role of the modern critic in this process. His role is both to bring the past to consciousness and to serve the "main current" by pointing out the weakness of the simple side currents, noting where they split off and lose force. If art "never improves," then what possible standards has the modern critic for distinguishing side currents from the main one? It seems that the activity of the modern critic is purely self-justifying, for to refuse allegiance to these slightly older currents is to stop them dead, as it were, in the water. Without any specific atemporal standards, the word of the present is law; its simple antipathy constricts and forms the current of tradition. Eliot certainly assumes that each age will be a finer judge than the last of conformity to the past and that historical changes of taste will thus accumulate into a coherent tradition. Why the present should be any keener at this discrimination than the immediate past, from which, after all, the present must distinguish itself in order to exist, is a question unanswered in the essay. Eliot implies that the modern, in the very act of declaring its independence from the immediate past, willy-nilly serves the demands of tradition. In other words, by being new, it constitutes tradition.

Eliot apparently does not want to accept the implications of the idea that "art never improves," the possibility of mere variation without historical direction or accumulation. On the other hand, he refuses to formulate an abstract, atemporal system of standards or even to suggest, except in unguarded moments, that such standards exist. The present, therefore, appears as both relative and absolute, specific in its distinction from the immediate past and general in its enjoyment of traditional amplitude, conscious of its own difference and yet unconsciously congruent with the whole of the past. As both part and whole, the modern confirms tradition simply and purely by being modern. John Crowe Ransom observes dryly that in Eliot's system "even the apparent innovations of poets were really fulfillments of history; which would be a comforting if not very realistic belief."[64]

Eliot's early essays were so seductive in part perhaps because they pandered to such unrealistic beliefs in his audience. To be up-to-date and yet thoroughly classical, individual and yet part of tradition, free of repressive standards and yet armed with a good, strong standard of one's own – these are all tempting prospects. At bottom, Eliot assured his readers that the apparent contradictions of modernity were not contradictions at all, that modern conditions had brought into being a modern art whose role was to dissolve the very conditions of its emergence. The modern poet, simply as a modern and as a poet, would resolve the contradictions that both Eliot and Bradley had tried to resolve in philosophy.

The early essays seem to announce the arrival of the sort of poetry predicted in the Extension lectures, a poetry that would mediate between realism and solipsistic idealism, whose classical form would balance out the excesses Eliot associated with Romanticism. From the beginning, Eliot was able to shape the reception of his own work so that it was read as if it had in fact accomplished these reconciliations, as if it had success-fully completed the traditional task of the aesthetic. As modernism ceased to be a promised future and became a settled present, it became easier to ignore the fact that this apparent reconciliation depended on a relativism so deeply held it constantly imperiled all standards of value. It also became possible to ignore the fact that much of the aesthetic impact of Eliot's poetry came from the almost spectacular way in which it failed to play the role assigned to it in the criticism.

3. THE WASTE LAND

Essays like "Tradition and the Individual Talent" and "The Metaphysical Poets" promise so much that they impose insupportable burdens on the poetry to follow. To announce an aesthetic modernism that will resolve the contradictions of political and social modernism is one thing; to actually provide it, quite another. In order to succeed, Eliot would have to do much more than simply find a form for the fragmented materials of the present, a task *The Waste Land* is traditionally held to have accom-plished. Instead, he would have to find a form that could be distinguished from the false, repressive unity that is the counterpart of modern frag-mentation. Few modern poems succeed as well as *The Waste Land* at depicting this necessary connection between the isolated worker and the anonymous crowd, which is the larger social version of the necessary relationship between fragment and "all" in "Prufrock." But having painted such a vivid picture of this social contradiction seems to make it all the more difficult to resolve aesthetically. Though a number of con-temporary critics feel that Eliot has succeeded in doing just this, it might be more accurate to say that *The Waste Land* vividly illustrates the dif-ference between the necessary connection of opposites like worker and crowd, fragment and form, and a reconciliation of them.

According to Ronald Bush, Eliot began serious work on *The Waste Land* by taking up a fragment he had written several years before:

> London, the swarming life you kill and breed,
> Huddled between the concrete and the sky;
> Responsive to the momentary need,
> Vibrates unconscious to its formal destiny. . .[65]

Though this passage was eventually dropped from "The Fire Sermon" at Pound's suggestion, it serves as a remarkably compact introduction to the entire poem.[66] In this quatrain, London appears as an early version of the force that swarms and breeds at the beginning of the final text. But the city inspires such horror because it breeds *and* kills, and in this it resembles a force that appears prominently in "Gerontion," a poem that was at one time to have introduced *The Waste Land*. In "Gerontion," history "gives when our attention is distracted / And what she gives, gives with such supple confusions / That the giving famishes the craving." In both instances, there is a kind of blighting generosity, a sterile and sterilizing generation. The early quatrain brings out the political vision implicit in "Gerontion," because it is a specifically modern, specifically urban life that is paradoxically fertile and deadly. And "Gerontion" emphasizes the historical vision behind the quatrain, the paradoxical combination it portrays of subjection to "momentary need" and to "formal destiny."[67]

Together, the two passages reveal the spatio-temporal nightmare behind *The Waste Land*. The picture of the London crowd huddled between concrete and sky is a physical realization of a modern plight: Human beings are held in utter subjection to the immediate, their noses in the very concrete, as it were, *and* to vast impersonal forces they cannot perceive. The passage portrays a kind of post-Kantian hell where humanity is fastened by iron links to empirical facts and is also shadowed by immaterial forms. The urban crowd is itself a physical embodiment of this condition, because it piles individuals up into "swarms," vast forms without perceptible character, beyond the ken of the individual, but also prunes humanity back, so that each individual is a barely surviving remnant of the whole.

Accurately portraying this paradoxical condition is the poetic problem of *The Waste Land*, as Eliot conceives it in this early version. This early passage introduces all the major formal problems Eliot was to encounter in composing his poem, problems that have survived as critical controversies. How does the poet portray immediate, contemporary reality and also the "formal destiny" behind it? How does he relate the present moment to the totality of history? What is the relationship between the perceiving consciousness, both the poet and the character fitfully visible within the poem, and the crowd?

Because Eliot began with a collection of loosely related poetic fragments, what he later called "a sprawling, chaotic poem," that all too accurately reflected the social chaos of its subject, the problem facing him was to find the "formal destiny" that animated and unified his collection of scraps.[68] But the real difficulty was to find a form that would not reproduce on an aesthetic level the formal terrorism that had beaten the crowd into a featureless mass. Bush observes that Eliot could hardly abandon the quest for order entirely, because he was "a proponent of Irving Babbitt, T.E. Hulme, Charles Maurras, Georges Sorel, and Julien Benda."[69] But it should be remembered that although Babbitt did teach Eliot the necessity of order, of generalization, Eliot was to criticize Babbitt precisely for over-generalizing, for flattening out the particulars of place and time. The influence of the other members of the list was equally ambiguous. Eliot had long since displayed the ambidextrous nature of Sorel's politics, which he claimed in the Extension lectures might lead to the violence of the general strike or to the order of royalism, and he was to call Hulme both revolutionary and reactionary. Though the Extension lectures use Maurras as an example of centralization, Eliot was later to use him as an example of the very opposite.[70] In short, Bush's list shows something much more complex than a mere desire for order. It shows as well the political background of a desire for a particular kind of order that would remain distinct from the homogenization such thinkers associated with liberal democracy, an order that could be derived from fragmented particulars without violating their specificity.

The same passage suggests a possible solution to this problem in the form of an observer whose vision reconciles what the crowd cannot. The crowd is only conscious of itself and truly living "in the awareness of the observing eye," but such observers can see only because they are even more painfully peculiar than the crowd itself:

> Some minds, aberrant from the normal equipoise
> (London, your people is bound upon the wheel!)
> Record the motions of these pavement toys
> And trace the cryptograms that may be curled
> Within these faint perceptions of the noise
> Of the movement, and the lights![71]

In the unrevised version of this passage preserved with the *Waste Land* manuscript, the "cryptogram" is instead the "painful, ideal meaning" of the pavement toys. Thus Eliot claims for himself the ability to find the ideal in the purely physical motions of the crowd, to perceive the connection they themselves cannot see, and thus to reconcile the contradiction that makes urban life so hellish. This can be done because the poet, the observer, stands both inside and outside London, not "bound upon the wheel" as is the rest of its population. Eliot does not claim greater powers for the poet, only a more extreme aberration that will throw him far enough out on the orbit of urban life that the center might at last become visible. In other words, he situates the poetic observer precisely where his literary criticism would have him, both in and out, a part of the whole only because he is so thoroughly individual. The passage also suggests that to solve these problems would be to dispel the social and historical anxiety with which the whole poetic project began. An aesthetic resolution of part and whole would represent the social reconciliation of individual and crowd, momentary need and formal destiny, fact and ideal meaning.

It is clear that at one point Eliot hoped that the figure of Tiresias might solve his aesthetic difficulties. In the drafts of *The Waste Land,* Tiresias appears just after the passage on London's "swarming life." In fact, he seems to have filled the role assigned in that passage to "the observing eye," the aberrant mind that will record the motions of "these pavement toys." This is perhaps the genesis of Eliot's claim in the notes that "What Tiresias *sees,* in fact, is the substance of the poem." Even at the very earliest stage, however, potential problems with this solution begin to appear. At one point in the draft, Tiresias announces that having "perceived the scene" he knows "the manner of these crawling bugs." Pound thought this "too easy" and removed it,[72] but it revealed a dangerous possibility that remains in the final text, that Tiresias will unify the London crowd only by diminishing its individual members. Of course, to do so would be to recapitulate and reinforce the horror that afflicts the crowd, not to alleviate it.

Tiresias is still often considered to be what Eliot calls him in the notes, "the most important personage in the poem, uniting all the rest." Grover Smith takes this nomination so seriously he has Tiresias chatting with the Countess Marie at the very outset of the poem.[73] But how is this unification accomplished? Is Tiresias an image of reconciliation, as many readings have suggested, or is he merely representative of the necessary but still contradictory connection of individual and community, particular and universal, under modern conditions? Is it possible that as a critic, in the notes to the poem, Eliot suggests the former, whereas he demonstrates as a poet the latter, and that in this contradiction might be seen the gap between Eliot's aesthetic program and the reality of his own poetic work?

In any case, to understand the relationship of particular to general in *The Waste Land* we must, as Levenson says, confront "what comes to the same thing, the problem of Tiresias."[74] After Pound's work, what remained of the crucial London episode that introduces Tiresias was the dramatic scene that begins

> At the violet hour, when the eyes and back
> Turn upward from the desk, when the human engine waits
> Like a taxi throbbing waiting. . . .

(ll. 215–217)

The physical metonyms constitute a mild, rather conventional, critique of the division of labor. Because the worker is tied to the desk, he or she becomes part of a machine, a "human engine." At the same time, the definite articles suggest that this is just one set of human components from among an infinite number of sets. The human subject is both fragmented and generalized at the same time. The feeling given is one of infinite, simultaneous repetitions of a single gesture in which isolated body parts detach themselves from the work that has both held and dispersed them. Here the figure of metonymy is used polemically to depict a metonymized society in which individuals are both dismembered and standardized.[75]

The typist who appears next in the passage is a worker named metonymically for the machine she tends, so merged with it, in fact, that she is called a "typist" even at home. In *The Education,* Henry Adams proclaims his astonishment at the denizens of the new American cities: "new types, – or type-writers, – telephone and telegraph-girls, shop-clerks, factory hands, running into millions on millions. . . ."[76] Eliot's point here seems very close to Adams's. Eliot's woman is also a "type," identified with her type-writer so thoroughly she becomes it. She *is* a machine, acting as she does with "automatic hand." The typist is horrifying both because she is reduced by the conditions of labor to a mere part and because she is infinitely multiple. In fact, her very status as a "type" is dependent on a prior reduction from whole to part. She can become one member of Adams's faceless crowd only by being first reduced to a "hand."

The typist is the very type of metonymy, of the social system that accumulates its members by mere aggregation. Yet this "type" is linked syntactically to Tiresias as well. In fact, the sentence surrenders its nominal subject, Tiresias, in favor of her. The evening hour "strives / Homeward, and brings the sailor home from sea, / The typist home at teatime, clears her breakfast, lights / Her stove, and lays out food in tins" (ll. 221–223). The typist shifts in mid-line from object to subject, from passive to active. Does the evening hour clear her breakfast, or should the reader search even farther back for an appropriate subject, to Tiresias himself? Though this would hardly clarify the syntax, Tiresias could function logically as both subject and object, seen and seer, because, as the notes tell us, he *is* the typist: "All the women are one woman, and the two sexes meet in Tiresias." The confused syntax represents this process of identification, erasing ordinary boundaries between active and passive, subject and object.

On what basis can the typist merge with all other men and women to become part of Tiresias? In other words, what is the figurative relationship between the whole he represents and the part acted by the typist? The process of figurative identification seems similar to that in "Prufrock," where women are also represented as mere "arms" and where all women are also one woman. As in "Prufrock," the expansion to "all" depends on a prior reduction of individual human beings to standardized parts. Just as Prufrock has "known them all already, known them all," Tiresias has "foresuffered all." His gift of prophecy, however, depends on the supposition that human behavior is repetitive, that "all" is in fact the mere repetition of a single act into infinity, enacted "on this same divan or bed." What, therefore, is the real difference between the industrial system, in which "all the women are one woman" and the identification represented by Tiresias? In which case is the typist less of a type?

The poem itself suggests that there may be no difference because Tiresias and the "human engine" are one and the same:

> When the human engine waits
> Like a taxi throbbing waiting,
> I Tiresias, though blind, throbbing between two lives . . .
> (ll. 216–218)

By means of this intricate chiasmus, Eliot links the human engine that waits to Tiresias who throbs through the middle term of the taxi, which both waits and throbs. In so doing, Eliot suggests a link between the reduced conditions of the modern worker and the mythical hermaphrodite who includes all experience. The passage contains within itself a representation of this link in Tiresias's throbbing "between two lives." Tiresias appears here almost as a metaphor for metaphor, throbbing between two lives as the common term that joins them. But the activity of joining, the throbbing that seems to evoke human longing, is in fact the noise of the taxi engine, the drumming of its pistons a travesty of human sexual activity. In this way, the passage mocks its own insertion of Tiresias between two lives by positioning the taxi as the true medium between individual and race, present and eternity. Even stylistically, the passage undermines its own assertion of metaphorical identification by merely juxtaposing the two elements that both terms share: There is no "between" between throbbing and waiting, no comma or other punctuation, and yet this is where the all important connection between Tiresias and the modern worker is accomplished. Read in this way, the passage suggests that the process by which Tiresias represents all men and women is no different from the process by which the modern industrial machine conglomerates them into one mass, that what looks like metaphorical representation is but the additive accumulation typical of industrialism.

The typist, that is to say, is just as much a type within the "inclusive human consciousness" represented by Tiresias as she is within the routines of her office. The same thing is true of the typist's lover. Tiresias is able to understand the young man carbuncular, "one of the low," because he has "walked among the lowest of the dead." He is able to understand human beings, in other words, only insofar as they are types. The uniformity of modern industrialized life is therefore but one instance of the uniformity of all human life. Adorno makes this point when he says of Kafka, "The absence of choice and of memory which characterizes the life of white collar workers in the huge cities of the twentieth century becomes, as later in Eliot's 'Waste Land', the image of an archaic past."

That archaic past is not the one the Victorians fondly identified with Athens but one in which human beings are "driven together like animals."[77] Adorno may well be thinking of Tiresias, in whom a sterile conglomeration of male and female represents an ancient situation still repeated in the modern city, inside, in the loveless sex of the typist and her young man, and outside, in the inorganic relationships of the crowd.

Tiresias was certainly at one point to have served the very function Eliot assigned to modern literature in his early essays. As an observing eye that is both of the crowd and outside it, he is to reconcile individual and community, part and whole, freedom and necessity. The directions Eliot included in his notes to the poem suggest that Eliot hoped even after the poem was written that Tiresias could fill this role. But the Tiresias he has actually portrayed in the poem itself is instead the incarnation of the failure of reconciliation, a mere juxtaposition of part and whole that dramatizes the gulf between them. As a dramatic figure, Tiresias demonstrates two equal but opposite fears that both gripped Eliot, a fear of fragmentation and loneliness and a fear of featureless uniformity. In the modern world, it seems, freedom cannot be had without fragmentation and loneliness, and community cannot be had without coercion and conformity.

Such an interpretation of Tiresias's role in *The Waste Land* calls into question a common idea about the poem first suggested by Eliot himself. In *"Ulysses,* Order, and Myth," Eliot describes the famous "mythical method" by which the disorder of contemporary reality is to be gathered up into a coherent aesthetic form. Thus *The Waste Land* is often read as backing its apparent disorder with some image of an ultimate historical order. As Hugh Kenner puts it: "Eras and cultures resemble one another, and from their resemblances we collect a normative sense of what it can mean to live in a civilization."[78] In other words, tradition, like Tiresias in the conventional interpretation of him, is a normative whole made up out of the resemblances between particular historical times. In this way, criticism provides the resolution Eliot so devoutly wished for when he began his poem, a resolution in which the particular and the general would shake off their modern, contradictory relationship and assume a new one of organic reciprocity. But this norm, this fruitful interpenetration of temporal particularity and eternity, is precisely what Eliot does not provide.

The opening lines of "The Fire Sermon" might be taken as a representative example. These lines constitute for Stephen Spender a "negative statement which with the imagination one reads as both negative and positive"[79]:

Sweet Thames, run softly, till I end my song.
The river bears no empty bottles, sandwich papers,

Silk handkerchiefs, cardboard boxes, cigarette ends
Or other testimony of summer nights. The nymphs are departed.
                                                    (ll. 172–176)

Eliot's vision superimposes the vividly realized trash of the modern
Thames onto the absence of such trash from Spenser's river. The past, we
understand this passage to say, was full, whole, unbesmirched by the
detritus of the present. Yet such fullness appears in the poem only as an
absence, whereas the emptiness of the present seems sharp and real. The
present is represented metonymically as parts of parts, each one of which
figures the incompleteness of the modern world. But the purely additive
nature of the metonymic list also makes it impossible to definitively stop
adding to it. The river fills with these absent items and thus serves as a
figure for the negative plenitude, the empty totality, of the modern age.

The river's barrenness, the fact that it does not "bear" the freight of
modern trash, signifies its purity, but also, perversely, its fullness. The
more it does not bear, the more beautiful it seems in contrast. Its refusal
of the present preserves a continuity the modern world destroys. On the
other hand, the plenitude of modern times, its sheer industrial productivity, appears as a paradoxical emptiness. Within such tortured paradoxes
how to distinguish the past's fruitful barrenness from the present's barren
fruitfulness? Tradition appears in the form of the contradictory force
Eliot confronted at the very beginning of his work on *The Waste Land,* a
force that is at once barren and oppressively fruitful, that both breeds and
kills. Tradition, in other words, suffers from the same paradoxes that
fracture present-day London itself.

This figure, in whom positive and negative become one, was once to
have begun *The Waste Land,* and it actually does introduce the final version of the poem in the guise of the Cumaean sibyl. In the story of the
sibyl, who asks for as many years of life as there are grains of sand in a
handful, plenitude turns into a curse, because she forgets to ask for
eternal youth as well. Thus the full hand is empty, the uncountable grains
a figure for an interminable life of sheer extension, fear in "a handful of
dust." The handful of dust is in a sense a metaphor of metonymy, the
isolated hand a figure of the dismemberment caused by time that refuses
to add up, the grains of sand a figure for a life where the multiple is
merely the aggregate, never the organic. All the isolated, metonymized
hands of *The Waste Land,* such as the "automatic hand" with which the
typist plays her gramophone, figure a failure of tradition, of "handing
over," because tradition is now empty, a continuity inseparable from
bland repetition. Instead of Kenner's easy accumulation of the best into a
stable norm, there is something much more like the situation described
by Adorno: "The best, which is forgotten, is remembered and imprisoned in a bottle like the Cumaean sibyll. Except that in the process it

changes into the worst: 'I want to die', and that is denied it. Made eternal, the transient is overtaken by a curse."[80] The particular, that is to say, joins the general only in a negative plenitude, an "all" as empty as that in "Prufrock."

Eliot's essays of this period seem to promise a poetry in which present and past, modernity and tradition, will seamlessly join with one another, resolving modern contradictions by dissolving the modern into tradition and vice versa. But *The Waste Land* actually portrays a relationship in which tradition resembles modernity only in reproducing its contradictions. Tradition itself is just as paradoxically blighting and smothering as the contemporary London that had once begun the poem. There is no whole that can be distinguished from the repressive, false whole of contemporary reality.

If so, then perhaps the only real hope in a poem like *The Waste Land* is to use this very failure as a kind of stand-in for reconciliation. Perhaps *The Waste Land* and "*Ulysses,* Order, and Myth," the essay so often used to interpret the poem, should be re-read. Though it is true that Eliot announces the "mythical method" as a means of ordering and controlling the chaos of modern life, it is also true that the works he praises for introducing the method are not themselves particularly orderly. Eliot praises Joyce and Lewis not for reconstituting the novel but rather for dismantling it, for composing works "more formless than those of a dozen clever writers" (UOM, p. 483). The "mythical method" thus appears as a way of arriving at new forms by accelerating the destruction of current forms. It is therefore transitional, as what Eliot calls "a step toward making the modern world possible for art, toward that order and form" so longingly imagined in the essay (UOM, p. 483). As a transition, it is actually destructive, more formless than what it replaces. The "order" of "*Ulysses,* Order, and Myth" does not appear *in* the text of *Ulysses* but is instead promised by its very lack of order. In short, Eliot may not expect modern writers to resolve in aesthetic terms the contradictions of modern life but rather to imply by aesthetic disorder a resolution that cannot be achieved under present conditions.

Read in this way, "*Ulysses,* Order, and Myth" very closely resembles Lukács's *Theory of the Novel,* another work that announces the death of the novel and the distant promise of a "renewed epic" to replace it.[81] For both writers, the novel is the form of an age of formlessness, or, as Eliot puts it, "the expression of an age which had not sufficiently lost all form to feel the need of something stricter." But both Eliot and Lukács deny that a new form can be achieved by returning to the past. Eliot remarks quite snidely that a writer can seem to be classical by rejecting modern materials and "selecting only mummified stuff from a museum" (UOM,

p. 482), but this is clearly not his way. Though Lukács begins *Theory of the Novel* with a rapturous hymn to Greek completeness and rounded-ness, he opposes "any resurrection of the Greek world."[82] Instead, both writers derive a new stricter form from the novel's formlessness. Lukács insists that "the very disintegration and inadequacy of the world is the precondition for the existence of art and its becoming conscious," and that new forms must somehow "carry the fragmentary nature of the world's structure into the world of forms" (TN, pp. 38–39).

The relationship between this dismantled novelistic form and the myth suggested by it is therefore an ironic one, because it is the very disintegra-tion into ultimate formlessness of the novel that signifies the unified form of the renewed epic. The final step in Lukács's theory of the novel is therefore a theory of irony. For Lukács, wholeness is present by negative implication in the chaos of the novel. There is, he says, a "unified world in the mutual relativity of elements essentially alien to one another" (TN, p. 75).[83] Lukács calls irony "a negative mysticism to be found in times without a god" (TN, p. 90).[84] Because the wholeness of the lost world cannot be revived directly, it can only be glimpsed in inverted terms in the very disintegration that makes it impossible. Irony acquires, accord-ing to Paul de Man, "the positive power of an absence."[85]

Eliot suggests something like this in his dissertation, where he says that it is the relative that impels us toward the Absolute.[86] Thus there may be a different sort of relation of particular and general in *The Waste Land,* one in which the general is pulled from the very intractability of the particu-lar, community from a common loneliness. The relationship between particular and general would not be a positive one but rather a negative one, because the particular can never transcend itself without falsification, and yet that very negativity would function as an inverted form of com-monality. Though Eliot pledged himself to true reconciliation, a "nega-tive mysticism" of this kind is the only sort of consolation that he allows into the text of *The Waste Land*.

Whatever promise might be contained in "What the Thunder Said" is inextricably involved with the most extreme negativity it depicts. The last section of *The Waste Land* begins by considering the crucifixion as a finality, not as a prelude to resurrection: "He who was living is now dead." Yet, after a long exilic passage through many lines of dry rock without water, the reader emerges onto the road to Emmaus, where the risen Christ is truly, though ambiguously, present: "Who is the third who walks always beside you?" (l. 360). Eliot suggests by his use of this particular part of the resurrection story that Christ is present in our very doubts and confusions about him; he is the third who insists on being counted even though it throws off the total. The fact that experience does not add up, these lines suggest, is our best evidence of the hand of God, not the symmetry and order of the cosmos but its excess over human forms of order.[87]

The figure of the risen Christ is, moreover, "hooded" and sexually ambiguous. The hood recurs a few lines later in a passage that seems to recoil from the waves of communist revolution then washing over Europe, a passage in which "maternal lamentation" merges with "hooded hordes" swarming over the dry earth (ll. 368–369). If the "maternal lamentation" is that of the Virgin Mary, in her well-known pose over the body of Christ, and if the hood is the same that so recently hid the risen Christ, are the "hordes" somehow to be associated with the resurrection? Is Eliot somehow drawing from his most gruesome representation of social disorder a promise of spiritual rebirth? The rest of this section is littered with "empty cisterns and exhausted wells" (l. 385), dried-up sources of water that are clearly parallel to the "empty chapel" bereft of its god. But just these exhausted sources give rise to "voices singing out," to lightning and finally to rain. In other words, *The Waste Land* does not include any hints of salvation until the very bottom has been reached, and then it seems to suggest that salvation comes only out of the very exhaustion of the negative. It seems as though Eliot can logically conceive of only one absolute, the negative, but that the very existence of an absolute in any form suggests the possibility of something beyond mere chaos.

There is some reason to believe that Eliot had something like this in mind at the end of *The Waste Land*. The long drought is ended by "a damp gust / Bringing rain" (ll. 394–395), and yet two lines later the leaves still "Waited for rain." There is a voice from heaven, yet at the end of its statement, the human protagonist still sits on the shore waiting for answers. The last section builds to an obvious climax that it refuses to accept. Indeed, it reopens matters with a last verse paragraph of startling disorder. It may be, however, that such disorder contains an answer of greater validity than those given by the voice of thunder. The final word, "Shantih," is, by definition, beyond understanding, ineffable. Its meaning seems to exist, in fact, only in contradistinction to the wild cacophony of languages and styles preceding it. J.M. Bernstein says, paraphrasing Walter Benjamin, "The plurality of languages signifies an original unity of language,"[88] and such a relationship seems to exist here, where the unity of the single word from the root language of the West exists only in opposition to the plurality of languages around it. It is as if Eliot could only approach peace through conflict, as if he could only grasp linguistic unity as an implication of linguistic disorder, and, finally, as if he could imagine social solidarity only by extension of social chaos. Disorder thus becomes not a fault to be overcome, but a necessary moment in the process of arriving at order.[89]

As Adorno puts it, in a statement that owes an obvious debt to the early Lukács: "The whole, as a positive entity, cannot be antithetically extracted from an estranged and splintered reality by means of the will and power of the individual; if it is not to degenerate into deception and ideology, it must assume the form of negation."[90] The original ambition of *The Waste Land,* to reconcile the contradictions of London life by assuming a position outside it, is therefore doomed to failure. The individual cannot, by any expenditure of might and main, think his way out of the society that contains him. Only irony can suggest what cannot really be achieved. The relationship of part to whole in *The Waste Land* is therefore not metaphorical but ironic, because the reconciliation of part and whole, like that of individual and community or concrete fact and "formal destiny," is only an impossibility implied by the mutual exclusiveness of the two terms of the relationship.

The most obvious objection to this solution is that it merely justifies a complete abdication. Bernstein says that Lukács's theory of irony "appears to lack the power to turn the negating power of irony into something positive."[91] Eliot's poem has been attacked for years for similar reasons, for a failing the left once called "defeatism."[92] The obscurity of the poem has also seemed to some a retreat into an elite enclave. But the original readers of the poem reacted somewhat differently. A.L. Morton and other young communists like Edgell Rickword were thrilled by the "strange and unexpected transitions of the poem, even by its obscurity; it was in this sense 'a liberating experience.'" For such readers, Eliot was "a standard around which certain forces of revolt gathered."[93] Morton's opinion is not particularly idiosyncratic. Q.D. Leavis implied in "The Discipline of Letters" that "the resistance to Eliot's poetry came from the same quarter as the attempts to break the General Strike."[94] In *Contemporary Techniques of Poetry,* Robert Graves places Eliot's work with that of left-wing writers committed to revolution.[95]

Stylistic disorientation did, in such readings, figure political freedom. But readers like John Cornford, who joined the Communist Party after reading *The Waste Land,* were not responding to a theory of individual freedom. The thrill felt by Cornford, Morton, and Rickword must have come in part from the dialectical process Adorno describes in defending modernist literature from Lukács: "loneliness will turn into its opposite: the solitary consciousness potentially destroys and transcends itself by revealing itself in works of art as the hidden truth common to all men."[96] Morton and Rickword recognize in the isolated lives of the typist and the young man a common fate and thus make solidarity out of fragmentation. In the same way, stylistic discontinuity can become a "standard" around which people might "gather," a disunity that paradoxically brings about unity. This quite different totality exists by implication in contradistinction to the repetitive, constrictive totality explicitly present in the poem. Such, at any rate, was the resolution wrung from the poem by some of its early readers, who were as desperate for a resolution of particular and general as Eliot himself.

The very negativity of modern contradictions now serves as a unifying factor, the very absence of reconciliation filling the role Eliot once assigned to the aesthetic. Does the resemblance of this solution to Lukács's negative theology mean that Eliot might also have taken the next step with Lukács into the Communist Party? Morton and readers like him were shocked and disappointed when Eliot announced his conversion to the Anglican church just when they were expecting him to embrace Marxism. Such an expectation seems unimaginable now, when Eliot's conservatism looms over his poetry, obscuring the promise Morton and others found in it. Yet the ability of the poetry to suggest a politics so wildly at odds with what eventually emerged is more illuminating than it might seem.

4. ELIOT'S CONSERVATISM

At about the time that Morton was hoping Eliot might announce his conversion to Marxism, he delivered instead his famous triply reactionary credo, calling himself a "classicist in literature, royalist in politics, and anglo-catholic in religion."[97] A statement so overtly definitive, so pugnaciously comprehensive, so proudly conservative, seems to settle the matter beyond any possible confusion, disabusing any who, like Morton, may have jumped to the wrong conclusions about Eliot's work. In actual fact, however, the three terms are not at all as bluntly self-evident as they appear. In "*Ulysses,* Order, and Myth" it might be recalled, Eliot made classicism itself historically relative, achieved "according to the possibilities of its place and time" (UOM, p. 482). In the Extension lectures of 1916, Eliot had repeatedly compared royalism to socialism, so that a declaration in favor of royalism might not have utterly excluded the end Morton devoutly wished for. And Anglo-Catholicism should be distinguished from Roman Catholicism as Eliot did in "Thoughts After Lambeth," by its greater inconsistency and lack of system: "The admission of inconsistencies, sometimes ridiculed as indifference to logic and coherence, of which the English mind is often accused, may be largely the admission of inconsistencies inherent in life itself, and of the impossibility of overcoming them by the imposition of a uniformity greater than life will bear" (SE, p. 322). At all three points, then, the famous credo is subject to qualification, most especially of the kind suggested by the last quotation, which admits into every system the inevitable exceptions.

Would it be possible to see in this very tolerance of the exceptional and inconsistent a political belief more comprehensive than classicism, royalism and Anglo-Catholicism? F.H. Bradley, to take one example, also opposed abstract political principles on principle. As Peter Nicholson says, Bradley attacked Utilitarianism for setting up a systematic political or moral code that "mistakenly treats moral judgments as reflective instead of intuitive."[98] Political wisdom, according to this philosophy, cannot be taught or learned but must be imbibed. Roger Scruton, who cites Bradley's *Ethical Studies,* puts the same idea in this way: "What rules there are can be interpreted only in terms of a background of custom, habit, convention and a certain 'style' which shows how things are done."[99] Politics, therefore, is the art of the particular. There can be no universal rules for regulating human intercourse.

The same "philosophy" is advocated by three of the figures to whom Eliot explicitly pledged his political allegiance in 1926: Hulme, Babbitt, and Maurras.[100] Despite his hatred of humanism, his appeal to suprahuman standards in conduct and in art, and his passion for order, Hulme did not believe that it is possible to formulate a systematic philosophy that would govern all questions in every context. As Richard Shusterman points out, Hulme divided philosophy from practical life, which he felt was governed by various *Weltanschauungen,* attitudes or interpretive styles. Evading these so as to assume an attitude of pure philosophic neutrality is, according to Hulme, not only impossible but wrong. Shusterman therefore ascribes to Hulme an "unsystematic, historicist, hermeneutic philosophy" that influences Eliot not toward atemporal standards of order but "towards an increasingly historicist and hermeneutical outlook."[101]

Babbitt's political position seems most clearly reflected in *Democracy and Leadership,* first given as lectures between 1920 and 1923. This was the book Eliot cited in 1926 when he listed those works that defined his notion of "classicism." In this book, Babbitt sets himself against "naturalism," by which he means appeal to nature as a source of authority. He includes the concept of "natural rights" on "the list of abstract and metaphysical conceptions that have dominated so much modern political thinking."[102] Against such abstract principles, Babbitt ranges himself along with Burke, who derives ethical standards from "the accumulated experience of the past that has become embodied in the habits and usages that the superficial rationalist would dismiss as prejudice."[103] In fact, Babbitt makes Burke sound very much like Eliot as someone who "saw how much of the wisdom of life consists in an imaginative assumption of the experience of the past in such fashion as to bring it to bear as a living force upon the present."[104] The trick of politics, according to Babbitt's analysis, is to animate prejudice, not to overcome it but to keep it in a living relationship to the facts of the present so that it will never settle into mere principle.

Maurras, as William Chace puts it, "waged a lifelong struggle against the enemies of France and culture as he saw them: individualism, *les droits de l'homme,* parliaments, religious liberty, democracy, and internationalism."[105] The Rights of Man were at the heart of the struggle with the Dreyfusards from which Maurras and the Action Française emerged as a powerful force. While the idea of abstract, inalienable rights appeared to the Dreyfusards as a check against arbitrary authority, Maurras felt that "the atomized society in which individuals appeared as free and separate entities before the law actually wrenched the individual away from such natural societies as his family, his trade, and his region, only to incorporate him into a much vaster and less natural one."[106] Such individuals "had been 'liberated' only to become an item in the books of a vast, distant bureaucracy, indifferent to his real being and needs." Like Babbitt, Maurras blamed not just political revolutionaries but "capitalism and its plutocrats" for this situation, because industrial capitalism tore its human raw material from a traditional context and set it "free" in the great vacuum of the modern city.[107]

Together these examples constitute a conservative dogma that is historicist in that it opposes historically particular societies and their usages to abstract political principles such as those of liberalism. Karl Mannheim sees historicism as essentially "of *conservative* origin. It arose everywhere as a political argument against the revolutionary breach with the past."[108] Mannheim distinguishes two different sources of political authority, nature and history, and aligns these with "a disjunction between liberal and conservative thinking."[109] Robert Nisbet draws the same connection between the authority of history and conservatism as distinct from modern revolutionary movements drawing their authority from nature.[110] The appeal of the latter to natural law, to inherent rights due to the individual, draws from its opponents a response that relies on traditional rights bound to a particular historical context. Pietro Rossi therefore speaks of "the parallel polemic" of historicism and conservatism "against natural law and the Enlightenment."[111] A good example of such a polemic is Michael Oakeshott's *Rationalism in Politics,* in which an anti-traditional and ahistorical rationalism is blamed for nearly everything wrong with the modern world.[112]

The common theme in these various examples is the conservative opposition to liberalism on the grounds that it tries to impose ahistorical, abstract, and rigid political principles on communities that can in fact be governed successfully only by something far more intuitive. Eliot himself developed a similar philosophy, though it is not enunciated in any one place. In fact, the very elusiveness of Eliot's political thought, the marked tendency in it to resist definition and consistency, is one characteristic that puts it solidly within conservative doctrine, which could hardly be systematically argued without falling into self-contradiction.[113]

Eliot opposed the founding liberal belief that "Private morals are not only private, but wholly negative" because it resulted in a situation in which "there is no community . . . and therefore only imperfect individuals."[114] Instead he saw the relationship between private and public as a positive one, so much so that he advances the seemingly paradoxical view that "it is when society is really united that eccentricity is possible."[115] Where the liberal opposition of individual to community produces both uniformity and individual isolation, traditionally united societies, those governed by the sort of unspoken agreements described by Bradley and Babbitt, had room for true exceptions precisely because they were not governed by specifically enunciated formal standards.

The view taken here of traditional societies is every bit as rosy as that in Yeats's fantasies, but Eliot was also aware of the inherent dangers of his position. The essence of that position is the belief that communities cannot be unified if the true interests of the individual are opposed by definition to those of other individuals. Regulative mechanisms and abstract rules of procedure cannot substitute for a common body of belief: "After all, the purpose of government is, or ought to be, the happiness of the governed *in a good life*." Theoretically, a community governed under a definition of the good life, a community, that is, whose politics pre-dated the liberal separation of moral and ethical questions from political ones, would be both unified and free. But, as Eliot says, "it is as immoral to *compel* a man to lead the good life – which of course being compulsory would not be really good – as to allow him to ruin himself."[116] What Eliot recognizes here is the inherent danger posed by the substitution of positive freedom for modern negative freedom. As Isaiah Berlin argues, this substitution can, in the modern world, easily lead to coercion of individuals in the name of their better selves.[117] And, as Yeats discovered, agitating on behalf of common beliefs in a divided society deepens and solidifies its divisions. On the other hand, how is society to prevent individuals from "ruining" themselves, especially individuals who "go bad" simply because they do not share the prevalent definition of the good life?

Thus it is practice, which seems at times the very core of the conservative value system, that exposes the contradictions of contemporary conservatism. Bradley refuses to allow any abstraction of ethical or political principles from practice, from that which is ethical because it is "done." But in the modern world, where what is "done" is open to dispute, this refusal amounts to an abdication, because it removes the conservative from the open debate by which these matters are at least provisionally settled. On the other hand, a conservative who explicitly argues his position refutes himself by demonstrating the absence of the unspoken agreements he advocates. Oakeshott admits, "only in a society already deeply infected with Rationalism will the conversion of the traditional resources of resistance to the tyranny of Rationalism into a self-conscious ideology be considered a strengthening of those resources."[118] As Scruton laments, "the conservative who has risen above the fragments of his inheritance and reflected on the desolation that has been wrought in it, cannot return to an innocence which his own thinking has destroyed."[119] When even the conservative position has been rationalized on the liberal model, the triumph of liberalism is complete.

This dilemma governs Eliot's involvement in practical politics and in part explains his seemingly perverse attitude toward it. He frequently lamented the damage done to Maurras's ideas by their practical application, and he tended to avoid practical involvement himself.[120] His commentaries in the *Criterion* seem at times to suggest that all political movements, no matter how different in theory, converge in practice and become indistinguishable in the mass marketplace.[121] Behind this skepticism lies the conservative belief that ethics cannot be "put into practice" because any truly ethical system will simply exist in and as the historical birthright of a people. By the same token, a truly ethical system can be neither established nor advanced by argument. Thus Eliot's lofty disinclination to convince: "I am not arguing or reasoning, or engaging in controversy with those whose views are radically opposed to such as mine. In our time, controversy seems to me, on really fundamental matters, to be futile" (ASG, p. 11). Why, then, did Eliot write so much on social and political issues? Why did he pour himself out in regular polemics in the *Criterion,* in the controversies of the Anglican Church, and as spokesman for a united Europe? Surely Eliot realized that the unconscious system of ethics he truly desired had not existed in the industrialized West for some time. His polemical writing is, therefore, on one level always a self-reflexive meditation on this problem: What can be done by the conscious effort of a militant conservative intellectual to revive what was once second nature? And, of course, behind this theoretical question lurked the practicalities of Eliot's own historically, politically, and geographically anomalous position as an urbanized expatriate preaching settled habits, traditional pieties, and the healthy influence of the land.

In short, Eliot's position as a displaced person precisely reflected the theoretical dilemma of conservatism, for all contemporary conservatives are displaced in the sense that they live in exile from the historical community they celebrate. Moreover, conscious political activity simply exacerbates this alienation, because such activity demonstrates the demise of historical agreement and the pervasiveness of theoretical argument. Eliot frequently reflected on this dilemma in his political writings. As he said in *After Strange Gods,* "At the moment when one writes, one is what one is, and the damage of a lifetime, and of having been born into an unsettled society, cannot be repaired at the moment of composition" (ASG, p. 27). The American intellectual, he admitted at about the same time, "must be an expatriate."[122] By the end of the Second World War, however, Eliot had managed to convince himself that this very weakness was in fact the intellectual's greatest strength.

In "The Man of Letters and the Future of Europe," published in 1945, Eliot poses the hero of his title against the social problems that had become his major preoccupation. Chief among these is the centralization, the loss of local and regional character, caused by industrialism. The paradoxical results of industrialism and the political machinery that serves it are alienation, as men are uprooted "from their ancestral habitat," and uniformity, as they are mingled in "one large metropolis."[123] The dilemma facing opponents of this system is to combat both ills at once, to conceive of a kind of unity that would not reproduce the "bad" unity of industrial capitalism and political totalitarianism. In the essay, Eliot specifically takes up questions much on his mind at the time: the balance of region and nation, of nations within Europe, of elite and community. The "man of letters" he argues is peculiarly well suited to offer solutions to each of these problems. Because "he should be able to take the longer view than either the politician or the local patriot," the man of letters should be able to balance out the claims of region and nation. The man of letters should also know that "neither in a complete and universal uniformity, nor in an isolated self-sufficiency, can culture flourish; that a local and a general culture are so far from being in conflict, that they are truly necessary to each other."

Why is the man of letters so peculiarly suited to the achievement of these difficult resolutions? The answer seems to be that the very alienation Eliot once complained of now serves to negate itself. The man of letters can take the "longer view" because he is both in and out of society, of the region and the nation, of the nation and of Europe. Thus Eliot was to say, some years later, that the truly European poet "is at the same time no less, but in a way rather more positively a man of his particular race, country and local culture. . ." (OPP, p. 217). This formula could also be read in reverse, as Eliot had insisted as far back as 1918: "It is the final perfection, the consummation of an American to become, not an Englishman, but a European – something which no born European, nor person of any European nationality, can become."[124] What is this but an utter reversal of Eliot's lament that the American intellectual must be an expatriate, or, rather, not a reversal but a Hegelian transformation whereby the very isolation of the American intellectual becomes a predisposition to a greater catholicity than any rooted European can manage?

In this sense, the man of letters stands as Eliot's triumphant solution to the central theoretical problem in his politics, the achievement of a system "capable of disciplining the individual and at the same time increasing his possibilities of development as an independent member of society."[125] For the man of letters these two imperatives, discipline and individual self-fulfillment, are not in conflict but rather in necessary collusion. Not only does this resolution soothe Eliot's own personal anxiety as an uprooted intellectual, but it also dispels the all-too-popular notion that letters are irrelevant to society. Eliot can see this very irrelevance as the primary strength of letters, empowered by its very distance from practical considerations. Thus Eliot proves an even more subtle Hegelian than Bradley, for he makes the very isolation and separation of the conservative into his centrality, as he makes the independence of letters the basis of its social utility.

Notes towards the Definition of Culture is a massive test of Eliot's belief that the man of letters can use this position to suggest solutions to a baffled populace. In writing *Notes,* Eliot becomes a kind of Tiresias, both in and out of society, able to use his position to resolve what society cannot. Eliot also uses *Notes* to argue explicitly that society should be directed by a class that occupies a similar position. The difficulties Eliot experiences in describing such a class, a class that would understand and direct the general interest simply by consulting its own special interests, shows how weak the man of letters finally is against the contradictions of his time.

The goal of Eliot's *Notes* is to describe an ideal relationship between particulars and generalities at the level of politics, social relations, and religion. *Notes* is therefore a work that attempts to put back together what liberalism has divided, a task Eliot had been working on since 1916. As Eliot says, one of the recurrent themes of his essay is "that a people should be neither too united nor too divided, if its culture is to flourish" (NDC, p. 49). The argument therefore carefully balances out the relations of the elite to the other classes, of regions to the country as a whole, and of sects within a particular religion.

The balance is, however, off from the beginning, because unity "can perhaps best be approached through a consideration of the useful diversities" (NDC, p. 51). This is more than an organizational gambit. The logical bedrock of the conservative position is its belief in the value of particular cultures. As Eliot puts it: "The *absolute* value is that each area should have its characteristic culture, which should also harmonize with, and enrich, the cultures of neighbouring areas" (NDC, p. 53). Because

Eliot begins with this as his one absolute value, he quite naturally finds "national culture to be the resultant of an indefinite number of local cultures which, when themselves analysed, are composed of still smaller local cultures" (NDC, p. 60). In this system, the general results from the combination of the various local particulars. In fact, the general is nothing more than the particulars in relation: "The parts of Britain must have, in one sense, a common culture, though this common culture is only actual in diverse local manifestations. . ." (NDC, p. 62). The general exists only in and as the particular. Eliot is quite unwilling to suppose a level of national culture with any elements that do not belong to one particular local culture. At the highest level, the common culture is not positive but purely relational: "We are therefore pressed to maintain the ideal of a world culture, while admitting that it is something we cannot *imagine*. We can only conceive it as the logical term of relations between cultures" (NDC, p. 62). Actually, even the national culture as Eliot describes it is unimaginable, because it too exists only in and as the relations between particular local cultures.

To suggest that local cultures are held together finally by their relations to one another is to offer a tautology. The unity Eliot describes in his essay is both logically and actually empty. And yet the essay constantly implies a level of unity, an agency beyond class, region and sect, capable of conscious independent action. If not for the possibility of such action, Eliot's essay would have no purpose. He is in fact quite sharp at noticing these discrepancies in others. Taking to task a report of the Oxford Conference on Church, Community and State, he says, "we should keep a sharp eye on this personified 'community' which is the repository of authority" (NDC, p. 98). He asks of another such report, "who is to determine what are the needs of the age?" (NDC, p. 99). And yet he says of the efforts of regions to shape their own religious forms that these "should neither be wholly suppressed nor left wholly unchecked" (NDC, p. 83). Who is to suppress or check if not someone in power who is beyond all regions? In his concern not to suggest the desirability of a "uniform culture," Eliot gives such an attenuated version of the common culture as to deprive it of the agencies he himself sees as necessary to unity.

In Eliot's system, which purposely lacks a general level independent of all the parts, society can only be directed by one of its parts, acting on behalf of all the others. Though Eliot suggests that all the parts of each unity sustain and express that unity, one class, one region, and one sect embody more of the whole than all their fellows. The role of the upper class elite is "to bring about a further development of the culture in organic complexity: culture at a more conscious level, but still the same culture" (NDC, p. 36). Eliot cautions his readers "that we should not consider the upper levels as possessing *more* culture than the lower, but as representing a more conscious culture and a greater specialisation of culture" (NDC, p. 47). However, Eliot elsewhere rules out this greater consciousness of culture. From what standpoint is the "governing class" (NDC, p. 45) to govern if the unity of all particulars is so ineffable as to be unimaginable? Over and over, Eliot says that culture is ideally unconscious, that it "is the one thing that we cannot deliberately aim at" (NDC, p. 17). If so, what are the governing classes to do with their greater consciousness?

Eliot's difficulties here come from the convergence of two great paradoxes facing anti-liberal political programs. Having phrased diversity and cultural particularity in such uncompromising terms, Eliot can only allow a unity that is negative, merely relational. Anything else would have to violate some particular and might well become the uniform culture that he sees as the result of liberalism.[126] This unity must, of course, be unconscious because, as Eliot says at length in his dispute with Mannheim over the nature of elites, planning of any kind soon becomes the social engineering inseparable from liberalism. Eliot's other problem is that his own work testifies to the fact that the society he wants is already gone. He speaks in favor of maintenance, but to advocate the unconscious is merely to advertise its absence. *Notes towards the Definition of Culture* is a rearguard action nipping at the heels of a triumphant liberal society. The conservatism it advocates does not really conserve, but attempts to retrieve the lost. This, of course, is a conscious process, carried on in constant battle with opposing forces. The often noticed inconsistency about whether culture is conscious or unconscious comes from this deeper political problem.[127]

Eliot's solution in *Notes towards the Definition of Culture* resembles, although in a weirdly inverted way, a solution Marx bequeathed to Lukács. In *The Use of Poetry and the Use of Criticism,* Eliot speaks of the present as a time "when power is in the hands of a class so democratised that whilst still a class it represents itself to be the whole nation" (UPUC, p. 22). His criticism of the middle class exactly parallels that of Marx: "For each new class which puts itself in the place of one ruling before it, is compelled, merely in order to carry through its aim, to represent its interest as the common interest of all the members of society. . . ." But for Marx, a revolutionary class really does become the universal class because its revolution represents aims that have not "yet been able to develop as the particular interest of a particular class."[128] Each succeeding revolution represents wider and wider interests until the proletariat finally makes a revolution that benefits all classes, liberating even the bourgeoisie from the rule of capital. Lukács adopts and elaborates this analysis in *History and Class Consciousness,* where he develops his well-known concept of the proletariat as subject and object of historical change. The concept is so seductive because it links particular and general, praxis and theory, deriving political principles from the concrete material experience of a particular class. Eliot unwittingly repeats the Marxist critique of the bourgeoisie as a false universal class, and then counterposes a kind of mirror image to Marxism by placing not the proletariat but the upper class as the universal class. Though the differences are obviously huge, Eliot speaking for the deposed class and the past, Lukács for the oppressed class and the future, the two positions share certain difficulties.

Seyla Benhabib criticizes Marx for first making all interests into class interests and then assuming "that there is a real subject of history to whom we ascribe 'universal' interests." As a normative conception, the universal human interest can only be defined "theoretically and *a priori*"[129] and not as the result of the life history of any specific class. In both cases, that of Eliot and that of Marx, the theoretical gap between normative definitions of human interest and the specific interests of real classes is filled by letting the specific interests of one class stand in for the absent, unformulated generality. But this is to lift the specific class out of history, out of all that has made it specific, and to set it over against the other classes in a privileged position. Benhabib observes that in Hegel the universal is not willed by the people but "is *administered* for them by a 'universal class,'" that of the civil service.[130] This role of administration is given to the party in Marxism–Leninism and to the upper class elite by Eliot, which in each case act for a class that is not a class but somehow the whole. What was relative to the specific life history of particular people in a particular class position becomes absolute, the only absolute, in fact, in two systems that disclaim absolutes.

Eliot describes exactly this situation in *Notes towards the Definition of Culture* and perhaps even more clearly in *The Idea of a Christian Society*. There Eliot conceives of a future society that would be comprised of a Christian State, a Christian Community, and a Community of Christians. The state would not be ecclesiastical, but would simply accept Christianity as the "frame" of all political action. The "frame," however, would be maintained by the Community of Christians. Eliot calls this group "the Church within the Church," and says it is to be composed of "the consciously and thoughtfully practising Christians, especially those of intellectual and spiritual superiority."[131] Eliot believes that few human beings are equal to the rigors of Christian belief, and that those few who are should share ultimate political power to be exercised through moral suasion. Eliot says of the Community of Christians that it is made up of "the more conscious, more spiritually and intellectually developed" of the clergy and the laity. By common beliefs and aspirations they will "influence and be influenced by each other, and collectively . . . form the conscious mind and the conscience of the nation."[132] Eliot's ruling elite resembles Hegel's universal class as a kind of disinterested civil service and Marx's universal class as well, because membership is to some degree connected with birth and education.

As their names imply, the Christian Community and the Community of Christians are in one sense identical. No fundamental property separates them, nothing that one possesses to the exclusion of the other. The Community of Christians is nothing more than the Christian Community intensified, raised to a higher power. The Community of Christians is formed by the common culture it shares with the larger Community. It is a universal class acting out the aspirations of the whole, and as such it then turns and forms the larger culture as well. It directs that which has given it form. The situation is clearly circular. Eliot admits, perhaps even desires, as much, but he does not admit to other difficulties. It would seem that the whole system must be based on the norms of the Christian religion. Very little, however, is said about Christian belief or dogma in this book, which is perhaps understandable considering its focus on Christian *society*. As Shusterman says, "Eliot did not invoke God to secure the possibility of permanently stable and absolutely objective knowledge of matters of this world."[133] On the other hand, Eliot's analysis implicitly relies on standards of judgment that are not enunciated anywhere. What is meant by "more conscious, more spiritually and intellectually developed?" Is being conscious something that human beings enjoy in gradation? Is spiritual development to be understood as measurable? Is it the same as intellectual and conscious development or is it a moral quality? Here Eliot evades the fact that his elite is to be chosen by norms that are not specifically Christian and that in fact sometimes seem heretical in that they suppose some people to be incapable of receiving salvation.

Eliot also evades the fact that his Community of Christians would have to be chosen. He speaks of it in the accents of passive classification: it "would contain"; it "would include." How would it be constituted? In *Notes,* Eliot says that "some qualitative differences between individuals must still be recognized, and . . . the superior individuals must be formed into suitable groups, endowed with appropriate powers, and perhaps with varied emoluments and honours" (NDC, p. 34). Here it can be seen how Eliot slips back and forth between quantitative and qualitative differences and also how much work the passive voice does for him. For in both *Idea* and *Notes* he leaves unspecified who is to recognize differences between individuals and who is to form them into suitable groups. The only answer is to suppose another Community, perhaps the Community of the Community of Christians, which would direct this division. Then, of course, yet another group would have to choose that one and so on ad infinitum. Eliot's attempt to constitute a universal class founders on his inability to specify either the norms or the agencies by which that class would be constituted and directed. His analysis relies on a ghostly group without any real norms that directs the whole from behind the stage. The analysis also implicitly sets this group outside history, outside social processes, as an administrative body not subject to its or any other administration. In this sense, Eliot's social system becomes authoritarian. No more than Lukács is he able to escape the authoritarian implications of investing all the claims of humanity in a "universal" class.

Eliot's social criticism is an attempt, like that of Lukács, to resolve the "antinomies of bourgeois thought," to rejoin the severed antitheses of particular and general and to make their relationship concrete and historical instead of abstract. That he is finally unable to accomplish these syntheses signifies the difficulties facing anti-liberal critiques of the left and the right, which seem destined to fall into relativism or into reliance on covert value systems and mystified authorities. Eliot is himself aware of his difficulties. One of the purposes of *Notes* is to "maintain two contradictory propositions: that religion and culture are aspects of one unity, and that they are two different and contrasted things" (NDC, pp. 68–69). What he says here of culture and religion might be said of all the antitheses he tries to link in Hegelian identities of identity and difference. But, Eliot admits, "The way of looking at culture and religion which I have been trying to adumbrate is so difficult that I am not sure I grasp it myself except in flashes . . ." (NDC, p. 29). What finally resolves the difficulty is not a philosophical or poetic solution but a religious mystery, the Incarnation. Eliot suggests that culture is essentially "the incarnation (so to speak) of the religion of a people" (NDC, p. 27). Repeating the term elsewhere he says, "I cannot think of any other which would convey so well the intention to avoid *relation* on the one hand and *identification* on the other" (NDC, p. 32). The concept of incarnation keeps religion and culture suspended between identity and diversity. The one and the many are not reconciled or identified; the religious metaphor simply sanctifies their logical opposition.

The political analyses culminating in *Notes towards the Definition of Culture* and *The Idea of a Christian Society* end in failure, with mystification on one hand and authoritarianism on the other. Could these two tendencies have coalesced and made Eliot a fascist? Unlike Yeats, Eliot had plenty of time to make himself clear, to align himself, as Pound did, with fascism in its quintessence. Yet Eliot's response remained decidedly lukewarm. There was apparently a flicker of interest in Oswald Mosley, the indigenous British fascist, but this did not last long.[134] A number of comments toward the end of the twenties indicated that Eliot preferred fascism "in practice" to communism in practice, though he disdained both as systems of ideas.[135] Finally, there is the oft-quoted statement that "Most of the concepts which might have attracted me in fascism I seem already to have found, in a more digestible form, in the work of Charles Maurras."[136] A good deal seems to hang on Eliot's digestion and why it found Maurras more palatable than fascism.

Eliot edges away from fascism in two rather different directions. On one hand, he complains that it offers nothing as convenient as kingship to incarnate the character of the people. Yet, on the other hand, he complains that "the aim of fascism seems to be centralization. The theory of the *Action Française* carries decentralization to its farthest possible point. . . ."[137] But it should be clear from all that has been said here about Eliot's political beliefs that this apparent contradiction is for him no contradiction at all. The appeal of Maurras and the *Action Française* is its apparent ability to combine kingship and decentralization, to argue at once that the nation needs a single human being as its representative cultural personality and that it should be allowed to lapse into a collection of local communities. Just how far this process might go is suggested by Eliot's own hopes for a future in which America "falls apart into its natural components, divisions which would not be simply those of the old North and South and still less those of the forty-eight states."[138] These divisions would probably be quite small, so that people will "have local attachments to their small domains and small communities, and remain, generation after generation, in the same place."[139]

Eliot was, on one hand, insufficiently nationalistic to be a fascist, and insufficiently interested in the kind of national economic organization proposed by French and Italian fascists.[140] In this sense, conservatism biases Eliot against fascism as cultural nationalism biased Yeats in favor of it. Another index of the difference between conservatism and fascism is the divide that opened between French neo-fascists and the *Action Française,* which was considered insufficiently revolutionary. The most biting comment against Maurras could also have been used against Eliot: "A monarchist is never a true fascist. . . . A monarchist is never a modern."[141] Fascism was *more* modern than Eliot was willing to be in his social and political opinions, and it was, for all its authoritarianism, a mass movement, one whose modes of organization were unlikely to appeal to someone who longed for local control.

It seems at times that Eliot disdains fascism simply because too many people believe in it. He frequently lumps it together with communism as simply another of the byproducts of the degradation of capitalism. In a way, kingship seems a perfect goal for Eliot insofar as it can never be adulterated by practical application. But it also expresses his desire for a greater centralization than fascism, as a mass movement, could promise.

Eliot believed that political and cultural life could be regenerated only by a strict asceticism that "should not only be practiced by the few, but imposed upon the many. . . ." Although he was aware of the dangers of forcing human beings to live according to their higher interests, he also felt that a new system would have to be imposed upon "the many; imposed in the name of something in which they must be made to believe."[142] If the king were not naturally the incarnation of the people, in other words, he would become so by force and indoctrination.

In this rather perverse way, Eliot outflanks fascism by demanding greater decentralization and local autonomy and also by demanding greater spiritual authority, to be centralized in a king. Fascism, that is to say, failed to reconcile the two imperatives that animated Eliot's political thought. He simply insisted too dogmatically on both centralization and decentralization, particular and general, for any political system with any real chance of actual application to satisfy him. In fact, it was Britain's war against fascism that seemed to offer Eliot his final opportunity to reconcile these opposites.

5. "LITTLE GIDDING"

The Waste Land began with a sense of entrapment between "momentary need" and "formal destiny"; *Four Quartets* begins with a claim that resolves this painful contradiction. If the past is not lost but remains implicit in the present, if the present implies a future toward which everything tends, then the rude accidents of practical life and the distant machinations of destiny are not in conflict at all. Destiny, a term Lyndall Gordon says is prominent in Eliot's essays of this period, includes accident as a necessary moment of its own unity.[143] The accidents of the past, accidents like Eliot's marriage to Vivienne Haigh-Wood that seem to expose the individual's subjection to brutal contingency, are revealed as necessary episodes in the master plan.

In "Burnt Norton" as originally published at the end of Eliot's *Collected Poems* of 1936, this claim had a very different effect than it has now, at the beginning of *Four Quartets*. What was a retrospective claim based on a completed body of evidence became, once Eliot decided to replace it at the beginning of a sequence to be written and published in installments, a prospective claim to be tested against a growing body of evidence. What looks settled and even smug was therefore part of a tremendous gamble, a test of the power of poetry to reconcile the immediate and the eternal. The formal coherence of *Four Quartets* would, if achieved, stand for the interdependence of chance and necessity, of contingencies like the Second World War and the teleological pattern of all history. Eliot had such difficulty composing "Little Gidding" because the stakes were so high: as the final installment it had to complete the aesthetic pattern while also inserting the war, still very much in progress, into English history. As Terry Eagleton puts it, "The tensions between concrete and abstract meanings in *Four Quartets,* between a focussed moment and its sustaining context, has an evident relation to a problem at the core of the poem: the relation between an existential present and the sense of a totalised historical pattern."[144]

In this sense, *Four Quartets* was Eliot's ultimate test of the power of the aesthetic to resolve not just the conflicts of his own life but also the contradictions of his place and time. Eliot suggests as much in the famous passage at the end of "Little Gidding":

> The end is where we start from. And every phrase
> And sentence that is right (where every word is at home
> Taking its place to support the others,
> The word neither diffident nor ostentatious,
> An easy commerce of the old and the new,
> The common word exact without vulgarity,
> The formal word precise but not pedantic,
> The complete consort dancing together)
> Every phrase and every sentence is an end and a beginning.
> (LG, V)

A sentence that is right reconciles old and new, common and peculiar, individual and consort.

This passage seems to pose as a triumphant conclusion, as if it were the kind of writing it describes. Most critics take the same position toward *Four Quartets* as a whole. M.H. Abrams, to take an influential example, sees the sequence as a successful quest for "a reconciliation of the divided and warring contraries that constitute the world of motion and time."[145] Yet it seems odd that Eliot's own statement of this principle should appear in the poem as an interruption, a parenthesis so long it forces the sentence containing it to begin again. If good writing is that in which every word is "at home, / Taking its place to support the others," what kind of writing is *this,* which clearly lacks a proper place in the sentence that includes it? This inconsistency suggests the survival of contradiction even in the passage that announces its resolution. It might also suggest, however dimly, an admission of failure, because the opposites survive no matter how carefully Eliot balances them out.

Such an admission would not be inappropriate to "Little Gidding," a poem that cost Eliot tremendous effort, one that was to round off and complete the sequence but that threatened instead to expose how oddly splayed it was between topical reference and formal design. Like Eliot's other works, *Four Quartets* coagulated gradually. Eliot had not planned to add to "Burnt Norton" until the war intervened. "In 1939 if there hadn't been a war I would probably have tried to write another play. . . ." But a sequence of poems, each one divided into segments, could be composed in the fits and starts determined by the war: "I could write them in sections and I didn't have to have quite the same continuity; it didn't matter if a day or two elapsed when I did not write, as they frequently did, while I did war jobs."[146]

The development of *Four Quartets* was therefore tied to the rhythms of wartime routine, but each section was also tied to its specific moment in the course of the war. Angus Calder shows how deeply embedded each quartet is in its own particular moment. "East Coker" has to do with the Phony War and the Army in training, "Dry Salvages" with the exploits of the British Navy, "Little Gidding," obviously, with the Blitz.[147] The powerful effect the quartets had on publication came from this topical reference.

Poems formed out of historical contingency and to a great extent written about it cannot easily shed their peculiar contexts to become a simple unity. Perhaps they were never meant to. Bush suggests that "the last three of the *Four Quartets* were never intended to enlarge upon a private vision of grace." Instead, Bush sees "East Coker" as almost savagely contradicting "Burnt Norton" as fatuous and inadequate.[148] William Spanos maintains that *Four Quartets* looks quite different read "temporally rather than spatially."[149] But Eliot did indeed attempt to impose "spatial," metaphorical patterns on his temporal material: four places, four seasons, four elements. Yet these are hardly the sorts of patterns to accomplish the reconciliation promised in "Burnt Norton." Gordon says of the four elements, "This is a late, and I think, superficial organizing idea."[150] Like the Grail legend in *The Waste Land,* these redundant quadrilaterals were superimposed on a poem already almost complete. Though Eliot claimed he had used these "only for convenience sake," they actually caused him a good deal of difficulty, especially toward the end, when his choices were most restricted. This difficulty is significant because it shows how hard it was for Eliot to reconcile the momentary realities of the war and the formal patterns he chose to impose on them. In short, *Four Quartets* is no more a solution than *The Waste Land.* Its very engagement in history, in the practical life of England under the Blitz, made reconciliation impossible.

The social contradictions most oppressive to Eliot appear in the topical section of each quartet, the third. Together, these sections seem an expansion and revision of the "Unreal City" episode in "Burial of the Dead." Once again a crowd stumbles forward to its work through a purgatorial city. In each case, the section focuses on transportation, usually on the London Tube. As in *The Waste Land,* the subjection of man to machine produces a uniform collectivity in which each member is merely a part of a crowd of parts, of "time-ridden faces . . . empty of meaning. . ." (BN,

III). Through a familiar metonymy, these people become mere faces, parts of themselves. The figural reduction makes them so light they blow aside like trash: "Men and bits of paper, whirled by the cold wind." Eliot's syntax marches these workers around a ring of repetition at the same time that it dismembers them with paradoxes: "Distracted from distraction by distraction."

The most horrible thing about such a life is that it works with a deadly determinism – "the world moves / In appetency, on its metalled ways" – and with absolute randomness, "whirled by the cold wind." To commute by train is to give up all direction and self-control to the schedule while simultaneously being abandoned to your own devices. Thus Eliot represents the effect of modern industrialized civilization, which fragments and fuses at once. The fusion, of course, is merely a mechanical one, the empty "all" repeated in the third section of "East Coker": "They all go into the dark . . . And we all go with them."

The vision of "Little Gidding" was, among other things, to solve these contradictions. The preliminary prose sketch Eliot jotted down for the poem includes this passage:

> They vanish, the individuals, and
> our feeling for them sinks into the
> flame which refines. They emerge
> in another pattern & recreated & reconciled
> redeemed, having their meaning to-
> gether not apart, in a union
> which is of beams from the central
> fire. And the others with them
> contemporaneous.[151]

Having vanished into the redeeming and reconciling fire, individuals have their meaning together, no longer as social atoms but as members of a spiritual community, a union held by a radiant center. This community exists in time as well, joining the living and the dead, making them all contemporaries. As Eliot expanded this sketch, which became the basis for Part III of the final text, he added an important element: detachment. A brief note, "Detachment / & attachment / only a hair's width apart," becomes in the final text these lines:

> There are three conditions which often look alike
> Yet differ completely, flourish in the same hedgerow:
> Attachment to self and to things and to persons, detachment
> From self and from things and from persons; and, growing between
>   them, indifference
> Which resembles the others as death resembles life,
> Being between two lives . . .

Gordon and Moody both cite as a gloss to these lines another preparatory note: "Alone – the ice cap / Separated from the surfaces of human beings

/ To be reunited in the communion." Gordon adds an idea from the first draft of "East Coker": "one must be 'separated' for 'a further union, a deeper communion.' "[152]

It seems from these lines and the glosses from Eliot's notes that the third section of "Little Gidding" is to be an explicit answer to the third section of the first three of the quartets. Those sections tended to focus on the modern crowd, especially on its paradoxical combination of loneliness and conformity, waywardness and automatism. The third section of "Little Gidding" argues that detachment and attachment, independence and unity, indifference and commitment, are unified in a dialectical relationship of similarity and dissimilarity at once. The logic may seem rather finely drawn, but in poetic terms Eliot is simply making an argument he has made before in the person of Tiresias. The passage even quotes the appropriate phrase from *The Waste Land:* "between two lives." Tiresias throbs "between two lives" and between life and death and thus he can observe and unify all since he is both in and out, part and whole. In his essays, Eliot had put the individual critic in the same position, the position assigned to "the man of letters" in his social writings. Here, Eliot makes his most complex claim for the "detachment" of the individual man of letters, which is also a claim for the detachment of the individual per se. Communion, he suggests, only comes about through detachment. The contradiction dividing the modern crowd now becomes a fruitful dialectical relationship.

History itself had, in a sense, forced this solution on Eliot. As Gordon reports, the original plan of "Little Gidding" had put all the emphasis on detachment alone: "There is nothing, initially, about communal feeling: that came later."[153] But this desire for "emotional withdrawal" was thwarted by the war, which forced on Eliot a certain practical engagement and also presented him with a powerful example of fellow-feeling: "It was under these unique conditions that Eliot was making an effort, through *Little Gidding,* to feel his way into that sense of community."[154] Eliot's background, as well as his temperament, made this difficult. Even at this late date, Eliot felt himself to be a "metic," a resident foreigner.[155] But he also had at hand an old argument, which he now dusted off and applied to Kipling and, by implication, to himself. Kipling's "universal foreignness" gave him, Eliot argued, "the freshness of vision of the stranger" (OPP, pp. 242, 247).[156] Foreignness, like detachment, breeds a deeper communion, a more fundamental attachment than those taken for granted by those born English. Thus Eliot could be more truly English than the English precisely because he had not been born in England. The approach to community is made through difference, on which Eliot still insists.

The reader can almost see this change take place as Part III advances, modulating from the singular first person pronoun into the collective and from the repeated clause "If I think" to the syntactically anomalous question "Why should we celebrate." What begins as private meditation becomes a public interrogation, almost as if the community has forced second thoughts on the poet. In content, the passage describes a similar vacillation:

> If I think, again, of this place,
> And of people, not wholly commendable,
> Of no immediate kin or kindness,
> But some of peculiar genius,
> All touched by a common genius,
> United in the strife which divided them. . .

The poetry seesaws in its characterization of the people, who are not kin but are linked, though this link is "peculiar" and touches only some, though, on the other hand, "all" have a "common genius." The logic of this tenuous balancing act between the peculiar and the common only becomes clear at the end of the sentence, where Eliot claims that the people are united precisely by what divides them. This generalizes the argument for detachment, inserting peculiarity, difference, and strife into community as its necessary basis.

Perhaps bearing his own situation in mind, Eliot juggles different ideas about history in the same passage: "History may be servitude, / History may be freedom." What the section says about personal memory, that its chief use is "liberation, . . . expanding of love beyond desire" is also applied to collective memory. History is not continuity but rather progressive recreation of the past; only in this sense is a future possible. Tradition therefore depends on renewal, on the conflict that seems at times to wipe out the past. The defeated are therefore just as much a part of history as the victorious: "Whatever we inherit from the fortunate / We have taken from the defeated. . . ." In this way, history wraps opposing parties, different periods, antithetical movements into "a single party" that depends for its continuity on the strife within it.

Yet it is at this point that Part III begins to seem *too* powerful a resolution. Does it suffice to take the warring opposites of modern life and simply declare them to be dialectically necessary to one another? Read more broadly, Part III appears as a fulcrum, a point of balance, between Part II and Part IV, a compromise that may well falsify both. It is hard to read back from the conclusion of Part III to the magnificent vision of Part II, which represents the testimony of one "between two lives," one from the defeated side in history who comes forth to declare what Eliot himself might inherit from that defeat. The compound ghost, "the spirit unappeased and peregrine / Between two worlds become much like each other," is W.B. Yeats, but also Tiresias, and, as the section makes clear, Eliot himself. The ghost is a wanderer between life and death, but also between countries, between England and Ireland or England and the United States. Eliot's argument in Section III is that this suspended position is a strength, and he claimed this strength specifically for Yeats in the lecture he wrote while working on "Little Gidding." There he awarded to Yeats the impersonality "of the poet who, out of intense and personal experience, is able to express a general truth; retaining all the particularity of his experience, to make of it a general symbol" (OPP, p. 299).[157] Thus impersonality comes to depend on personality, generality on particularity, in a dialectical process most peculiarly possible for those who, like Eliot and Yeats, live between worlds.

Yet the "general" truth the ghost has to deliver in the poem is bitterly contradictory of this bland confidence. The wandering ghost remembers eternally his own "impotence of rage" at the folly of humankind and, perhaps even more lacerating, the shame of being celebrated by a crowd of fools. There is no useful or exalting relationship between the solitary spirit and its fellows: hurt or false approval are the mutually exclusive yet horribly linked possibilities. Instead of mediating "between two lives" as the detached consciousness is supposed to in Part III, the ghost wanders "From wrong to wrong. . . ." The only resolution is offered by escape into "that refining fire." This fire is certainly Dante's purgatorial blaze, but the religious meaning of Dante's fire is shadowed by the literary use to which Eliot puts it. Yeats refines himself "in measure," in poetry, and the horror of personal failure is compensated for by this sense of aesthetic success, just as the isolation of the poet in his own time is balanced out by the community of poetry so masterfully evoked by this section's web of literary echoes. The ghost enters a blaze composed of the words of all his predecessors, a blaze that refines because it is the work of poetry to "purify the dialect of the tribe." But the irony is that the section has already mocked *this* sort of purification: "Your lifetime's effort," the ghost tells Eliot, issues in nought. In order to come to a satisfactory conclusion, the section circles back to a compensation that it has already debunked.

It is difficult for any solution to stand up to the bitterness poured out by the ghost. On the other hand, Part IV seems to propose a solution so grand and so total as to obliterate all bitterness. The phraseology of entrapment – "From wrong to wrong" – is transformed in Part IV:

> The only hope, or else despair
> Lies in the choice of pyre or pyre –
> To be redeemed from fire by fire.

One might almost see the double necessity of fire in this passage as a metapoetic confession, for it was the fourth of the four elements and thus a necessary component of Eliot's scheme for "Little Gidding." Eliot's suffering as craftsman under the ineluctable nature of his own devices appears here, perhaps, as the suffering of the sinner under that which will both entrap and enable him. Necessity itself is transfigured as possibility.

Yet there are fissures even in this relentlessly closed resolution. The phrase "or else despair" rests in a powerfully ambiguous syntactical position. It would seem, on first reading, to suggest that despair is the alternative to hope, the fate of those who refuse the choice of pyre or pyre. But the phrase could also mean that despair is the equivalent of hope, a paradoxical synonym for it, which would make just as much sense when the choice is simply that between pyres. Wouldn't Eliot's dialectic decree a combined reading, in which despair becomes the precondition of hope as defeat is the precondition of victory or detachment the precondition of community? Yet despair and hope truly are antithetical if anything can be, because to despair would be to lose all possibility of the salvation offered in this section by love. Despair is, in fact, what Eliot is trying to defeat, what the ghost of Part II so chillingly left him in legacy, what he most needs to counter in the reading audience of his poem, pummeled by the Blitz. But despair cannot be worked into his solution: Its syntactical ambiguity reveals the anomalous position it holds in the whole argument.

The very toughness of this section, the brutal way it wraps love up in destructive fire preventing any easy choice between the good and the bad in life, may defeat it. The resolving paradoxes seem inhumanly cold next to the reality of fire, and the alarming conflation of German bombers and pentecostal dove at the beginning of the section seems too boldly cruel. The baroque drama of this allegory reveals in its imagistic violence the pressures the poem is now struggling unsuccessfully to balance out. Eliot gambles everything on a stylistic stunt, on the hope that by calling death and salvation by the same name he can surprise his readers into sensing their paradoxical union. But the very extremity of the rhetoric here shows how far Eliot has still to go, how much the whole gamble of *Four Quartets* remains up in the air.

In the end, the poem climbs down from this height. Section V returns to "East Coker" by quoting from it, and to Section III of "Little Gidding" itself:

> We die with the dying:
> See, they depart, and we go with them.
> We are born with the dead:
> See, they return, and bring us with them.

This marks a return to compromise, to the balance of Section III between the bitter rejection of practical life in Section II and the utter obliteration of bitterness by an even more determined hope in Section IV. It also marks, as Christopher Ricks has noted, a return to the early work of Ezra Pound, to "The Return," a favorite of both Yeats and Eliot.[158] Pound might well have been present even in Section II, for the purgatorial fire of Dante's Canto 26 was one of the passages he and Eliot cherished together. "Little Gidding" is therefore intriguingly suspended between Yeats and Pound, and the negative example of the latter might have been even more striking to Eliot than that of the former. In 1942, Pound had taken the role of the "peregrine" to its furthest possible extreme. On Rome Radio he was in fact making Eliot's argument that the isolated, detached observer had a better perspective than the native citizen. For Pound, the logical end of the argument of detachment was to make treason synonymous with patriotism. Is Eliot's invocation of his old friend meant to make a similar argument, to reintegrate even this rebellious remnant of the avant-garde into the European community? If the dead and defeated return and in so doing give birth to us, could even Pound's actions be worked back into the fabric of English history? Has Eliot already accomplished this by weaving Pound's words into the fabric of his poem?

Eliot's enlistment of both Yeats and Pound in his final poetic attempt to reconcile these opposites shows how much the three poets share, for all their differences. In each case, the isolation of the individual, the tensions of class division, and the apparent separation of poetry from the world of practical politics, are all salved by a political aesthetic in which the part becomes the whole, representing it precisely because of its difference. *Four Quartets* is perhaps the most elaborate poetic exposition of that aesthetic and one of the most successful. But the end to which such beliefs took Ezra Pound was so extreme that the mere allusion to him unsettles the quartets' massively achieved conclusion. Eliot claims that "the fire and the rose are one," and he is bold enough to suggest that the German bombers and the pentecostal dove are one. Would he have said as much even a few years later, when "fire" would inevitably have evoked the extermination camps? Can this atrocity be worked back into the divine scheme, and is there room in Europe's "single party" even for Ezra Pound, even for the very least of those who made the camps possible? These are questions barely suggested here, but ones that strike to the heart of this work and the work of Eliot's old friend.

3

Ezra Pound: Fascism

At about the time that Eliot was delivering his Extension lectures and Yeats was first making contact with the hidden dictators of *A Vision,* Ezra Pound was writing a series of articles entitled "Provincialism the Enemy."[1] The three projects seem uncannily synchronized, as if Yeats's occult interlocuters were in fact in general contact with the intelligentsia of Europe. Eliot's concern was the contradictory status of modern man, suspended between a real subjection to facts and an idealistic escape from them. In their own way, the spirits were saying the same thing to Yeats, who noted down their prediction of an imminent break when the conflict of primary and antithetical reaches its natural extreme. For Pound, this extreme already existed in the intellectual method he called *Kultur,* which subjects its students to a rain of atomized facts *and* to overwhelming abstract generalizations. Such a synchronization might seem even more occult if extended to include Lukács, who described, a year or two later, the peculiar relationship of total abstraction and isolated facts characteristic of capitalism.[2]

At the very least, these parallels suggest a common European dissatisfaction, a sense of loneliness and dislocation matched by an equally intense feeling of oppression and conformity. Lukács's answer was dialectics, a method that would produce a concrete totality linking empirical fact and ideal, concrete particular and generalization, individual and community. In less overtly dogmatic ways, the three poets attempted something similar, though dialectic sometimes looked a lot like mere contradiction. Eliot praised the Action Française in 1916 for favoring centralization; thirty years later he still admired this group, but this time because it stood for decentralization. The contradiction simply exposes the two moments of a system Eliot clearly hoped would both unify and set free. Yeats's occult advisers helped him formulate a critique of "abstract systematization," but this critique itself was always called "the

System."[3] Yeats never shrunk from contradiction, but he would at least have wanted his unsystematic system to fruitfully join spontaneity and consistency, instead of merely suffering their opposition.

Pound's essays, published in the *New Age* in 1917, give particularly clear examples of the contradictions caused by these mixed motives. As such, they can introduce this idiosyncratic body of thought, systematically unsystematic, pithy, particular, and gaseously abstract at once, by showing how common were its conflicts. In "Provincialism the Enemy," Pound's real enemy is the philosophical and political system that splays the European individual of 1917 between incompatible but equally inescapable alternatives. Like Yeats and Eliot, to whom he was particularly close in these years, Pound produced an alternative that succeeds only in reinstating the contradictions it was supposed to resolve.[4]

At the outset, Pound defines provincialism as "(a) An ignorance of the manners, customs and nature of people living outside one's own village, parish or nation. (b) A desire to coerce others into uniformity" (SP, p. 189). On the surface, these two clauses seem in conflict, one emphasizing the dangers of excessive particularity, insularity and localism, the other concerned with excessive uniformity. Provincialism is Pound's name for a near-sighted intolerance he associates particularly with the outskirts, which insist in their ignorance that they are in fact the center, but also for the smug intolerance of the center, which denies the outskirts their individual character.

Provincialism sins against the most basic dogma of historicism, the right of all places and periods to their own standards. When Pound enlists himself against "provincialism of time" (SP, p. 198), the essays reveal themselves as part of his defense of modernism against the short-sighted demand that all periods abide by the same rules.[5] Thus the emphasis seems to fall most heavily on the second part of his definition of provincialism, and his essays seem to defend difference against the claims of uniformity. In these essays and in his career as a whole, however, Pound drifts into just the opposite position. From his defiance of tyranny *over* the part, Pound gradually slides into defying a tyranny *of* the part, into the very uniformity he had originally attacked. As he admits in "Pastiche. The Regional," "the man of good-will may find himself first on one side and then on the other of any given dilemma, first for concentration, then for freedom or for decentralisation. . . ."[6]

In these essays, Pound sets himself against a particular intellectual method, against *Kultur,* which is his shorthand for "orthodoxy, obedience, Deutschland über Alles, infallibility, mouse-trap" (SP, p. 190). *Kultur* stands for the systematic regimentation of particulars under general laws, regularities which readily become sanctions. But *Kultur* also stands for the tyranny of uncoordinated details, for an education bent on "hammering the student into a piece of mechanism for the accretion of details" (SP, p. 195), for the myopic investigation of "some minute particular problem *unconnected* with life, *unconnected* with main principles" (SP, p. 191). More and more as the essays progress, Pound works himself into a lather against "the mind switched off all general considerations, all considerations of the values of life, and switched on to some minute, unvital detail" (SP, p. 192). His outrage against coercive uniformity somehow becomes the exact opposite, a disgust with the uncoordinated and disparate.

In the same essays, Pound also plays out this intellectual conflict in political terms. He begins by setting himself solidly against "the hundred subtle forms of personal oppressions and coercions" and in favor of "personal liberty" and "national differences" (SP, p. 189). He applauds the resistance of England and France to "the yelp of 'nationality'" and "the yelp of 'race'," base appeals they have withstood by admitting that they are made of many different races, which admission also ensures "real respect for personality, for the outline of the individual" (SP, p. 190). Such countries "are civilisation because they, more than other nations, do recognise such diversity" (SP, p. 199). The essays plead for better communications between two capitals, London and Paris, and even for the long-planned tunnel to connect them. Pound claims that closer congress would "tend not to making the two cities alike, but to accentuate their difference. Nothing is more valuable than just this amicable accentuation of difference, and of complementary values" (SP, p. 202).

The idea that communication accentuates and preserves differences by enlightening the provincial is one of the noblest Pound ever expressed. A scholar forced to endure the unremitting bigotry of the radio speeches may bless such lines as these, but the relief is short-lived. For Pound begins to express the ideal of communication in such an uncompromising way as to erase the very differences it was to preserve. If, as Pound says, only "reactionaries desire an isolation" (SP, p. 201), then defense of the local and particular is reactionary. Pound therefore contradicts both Yeats and Eliot by rejoicing that "the United States were not subdivided" (SP, p. 201) and by opposing Irish sectionalism with its reliance on the idea of "local rights" (SP, p. 202). Against regionalism, he counterposes the capital, the metropolis, from which all good things flow (SP, p. 200). In fact, by the end of his series, Pound seems to suggest that there should be only one metropolis, a "lumping of Paris and London into one" (SP, p. 203), and a similar lumping, apparently, of all Europe into one. "Anything which stands in the way of this combination is a reaction and evil" (SP, p. 203). Two years later in "Pastiche. The Regional," the implications of this axiom become clear: "There are (axiom I) two great pulls against civilisation (i.e. any great coherence of concentration), namely, the jealousy of the poor and the jealousy of the province. For *poor* and *province* read also slave and barbarian."[7]

Pound is quite capable, therefore, of identifying civilization with difference and with uniformity almost simultaneously. He is clearly grappling with a system that violates its human members by reducing them and by conglomerating them together. Pound associates *Kultur* with political systems organized for "the condemnable 'good of the state'" (LE, p. 432). *Kultur,* he says, "is all one with the idea that the man is the slave of the State, the 'unit,' the piece of the machine" (SP, p. 192). Under these systems individual human beings become mere units, "'component parts', each capable of an assignable 'function'" (SP, p. 196). Over and over in these essays, Pound denounces the reduction of the individual to the unit, to the status of a "gelded ant" (SP, p. 191), a mere "spindle" (SP, p. 196).[8] As Lukács says, "the personality can do no more than look on helplessly while its own existence is reduced to an isolated particle and fed into an alien system."[9] In other words, the philosophical system that Pound calls *Kultur* is but the intellectual expression of the system that organized workers into production lines in which they play the role of mechanical components.

Thus the struggle against provincialism is, Pound says, "a struggle for the rights of personality" (SP, p. 195), for the right to be "a more complete man" (SP, p. 191). Though he uses the language of individual rights, Pound in fact means something quite different from the sort of thing routinely granted by most democracies: "The contest for 'rights', democracy, etc., in the West, has been little concerned with personality" (SP, p. 194). By "personality," Pound does not mean an individuality protected from the claims of the community, but rather a resolution of individuality and community. He can therefore praise in Confucius what may seem to some readers incompatible ideas: "The thought is for the community. Confucius' constant emphasis is on the value of personality, on the outlines of personality, on the man's rights to preserve the outlines of his personality, and of his duty not to interfere with the personalities of others" (SP, p. 193). Here Pound gropes for a reunion of the two things sundered by *Kultur,* the particular and the general, the individual and the community. He needs the sort of tool Lukács felt he had found in the Hegelian dialectic "to demolish the 'contingent' relation of the parts to the whole."[10] But without any such solution, the essays can only oscillate between the two terms, which, because of Pound's inability or unwillingness to modulate his pronouncements, become more and more starkly opposed.

The very style of Pound's prose writings is an attempt to resolve this conflict. He rather defensively claims of a particular detail in "Pastiche. The Regional" that "Snippets of this kind build up our concept of wrong, of right, of history."[11] But this is true only if the snippets are of the right kind, of the "luminous" kind. This distinction enables Pound to mount an attack on "detail" in prose built up, as he says himself, out of "snippets." Moreover, he can call for definition (GK, p. 50) while in the same work denouncing "separation" (GK, p. 100). He can demand "dissociation" of similar ideas while also resting all knowledge on "man's total perception of relations" (SP, p. 268).[12] Within the space of two pages in *Guide to Kulchur,* Pound denounces "attention absorbed by the detail . . . to the DETRIMENT of the total reason" (GK, p. 90) and also mocks the "triumph of total meaning over detail" when it results in stock phrases and cliches about Greek art (GK, p. 92). The form of these works, with their dogmatic generalizations in a setting of random detail, simply reflects the two-front war Pound wages against generalization and random detail, but, because Pound cannot articulate the resolution he seeks, it also reflects, against Pound's will, the twin adversaries themselves.[13]

The luminous detail is Pound's preeminent example of a resolution of particular and general, where the "perception of a whole age, of a whole congeries and sequence of causes, went into an assemblage of detail" (GK, p. 136). Thus the luminous detail stands against a good deal more than just its intellectual rival, the multitudinous detail. It also serves as a counterexample to the multitude itself, the atomistic crowd and its political counterpart, the authoritarian state. "Provincialism the Enemy" illustrates again and again the connection in Pound's mind between *Kultur* as intellectual method and the failed political system that was in 1917 spectacularly disintegrating all over Europe. Though the luminous detail had figured in Pound's thinking well before this collapse, it came to occupy such a prominent place there because of its political utility, because it could serve as the aesthetic had ever since the last great collapse in European politics, to reconcile the dispersed elements of modern society. This was Pound's project as poet, scholar, and political agitator.

It is not usually acknowledged that Pound comes before his public first as a scholar. The second poem of *A Lume Spento* (1908) is preceded by a page-long note citing Janus of Basel, the Rev. Father Sinistrari, Yeats's "Celtic Twilight," and two Provencal legends (CEP, p. 8). *The Spirit of Romance* (1910) begins with a preface giving Pound's scholarly qualifications, and "I Gather the Limbs of Osiris" (1911–1912) begins by presuming to describe a "New Method in Scholarship" (SR, pp. 5–7; SP, p. 21). At the beginning, Pound confines his revolt inside the boundaries of scholarly study, attempting to reform it. The chosen enemy is the positivistic side of philology. In the preface to *The Spirit of Romance,* Pound tears off "the rags of morphology, epigraphy, *privatleben* and the kindred delights of the archaeological or 'scholarly' mind" (SR, p. 5). He revolts against his own philological training, against the very knowledge displayed as "original research" in *The Spirit of Romance*. This revolt against philology becomes one of the intellectual motifs of Pound's life, becoming a lifelong diatribe against "Germanic" methods of scholarship. An early unpublished poem called "The Logical Conclusion" (CEP, p. 274) sets itself against "the 'Germanic' system of graduate study and insane specialization in the Inanities." The anti-Teutonic bias becomes particularly shrill during the First World War, when, as Chris Baldick has shown, there was a general attempt by Anglo-American scholars to free themselves from the tyranny of German methods. Baldick in fact cites one of Pound's comments, to the effect that the "'university system' of Germany is evil . . . wherever it penetrates" (SP, p. 191), as typical of contemporary scholarly jingoism.[14]

This scholarly quarrel had fearful consequences for Pound, because his opposition to the old method of scholarship led into political commitments undreamed of in 1911. At the beginning, however, Pound's revolt is really a rather narrow shift within a particular tradition. His two principal objections to the "Germanic" system are that it piles up meaningless, isolated facts, and that it conduces to provincialism. In "I Gather the Limbs of Osiris," he calls "the method of multitudinous detail" "the method of yesterday" (SP, p. 21). In "How to Read" (1929), he criticizes this "dead and uncoordinated system" (LE, p. 16). The alternative to multitudinous detail is the "luminous detail" and the cure for provincialism is the "historic sense" of literature. The "method of Luminous Detail" is proposed at the beginning of "I Gather the Limbs of Osiris" as "a method not of common practice, a method not yet clearly or consciously formulated, a method which has been intermittently used by all good scholars since the beginning of time . . . a method most vigorously hostile to the prevailing mode of today" (SP, p. 21). Luminous details are "interpreting" details (SP, p. 22), details whose interpretative value is so clear and obvious that they "are swift and easy of transmission" (SP, p. 23) and can be presented without comment by the scholar who is lucky enough to find them.[15] The distinction, which amounts to a definition, between the luminous detail and "multitudinous detail" should make it clear that the method Pound is proposing is not primarily inductive. It is ranged against the massive induction of "German" scholarship and promises a quick and easy entry into general principles.

Luminous details constitute "intelligence of a period" (SP, p. 22) by touching directly those elusive cultural presumptions that are "in the air" (SP, p. 23). They touch the same cultural level mined by the "donative" writer defined later in the essay, who draws "from the air about him . . . latent forces, or things present but unnoticed, or things perhaps taken for granted but never examined" (SP, p. 25). This tangle of un-acknowledged and perhaps unconscious assumptions is called in "Patria Mia" (1913) "the national chemical, or if the reader be of Victorian sensibility, let us say the 'spirit' or the 'temper' of a nation" (SP, p. 123). Pound varies the metaphor into music, to describe the "American key-note," and finally into painting for "the national colour" (SP, p. 124). The presumption that there is such a thing as a national color, timbre, chem-ical, or temper, that deep within any period or culture there exist unify-ing principles, makes the method of luminous detail possible.

The irony is that Pound has simply moved from one "German" meth-od of scholarship to another. Pound varies his terminology over the years, calling the national chemical the "conscience of a given century" in *ABC of Reading* (1934), and using *Zeitgeist* from time to time before replacing it in *Guide to Kulchur* (1938) with Frobenius's term paideuma.[16] But the overall consistency of his thought is indicated by the reuse of a single example from Jacob Burckhardt. In "I Gather the Limbs," Pound chooses as his first example of a Luminous Detail this passage from *The Civilization of the Renaissance in Italy:* "In this year the Venetians refused to make war upon the Milanese because they held that any war between buyer and seller must prove profitable to neither" (SP, p. 22). Almost thirty years later, in "For a New Paideuma," Pound cites the same anec-dote as an example of the kind of act that, like the paideuma itself, makes history, though the attribution to Burckhardt has dropped away and the roles of the Venetians and the Milanese have been reversed (SP, p. 287).[17]

Pound admired Burckhardt's style, as he says in *Gaudier-Brzeska,*[18] and, despite their very different estimations of Sigismundo Malatesta, Pound and Burckhardt share a common approach to the Renaissance. Burckhardt's descriptions of the way political and artistic power act as equals in the Renaissance, his idea that rulers and artists are alike as self-made men, obviously had a very strong appeal for Pound and dominates essays like "The Renaissance" and "Patria Mia." More important, per-haps, is Burckhardt's basic assumption that the Renaissance can be seen as "a complete and consistent whole."[19] If the whole culture, in this sense, is a work of art, to take Burckhardt's famous term for the state, then it would certainly be possible for later ages to derive their sense of the whole "from fragments."[20] These fragments are the luminous details Pound identifies as the building blocks of his "new" method of scholarship.

In choosing Burckhardt as his example, however, Pound puts himself in yet another "German" tradition of scholarship.[21] Though he prided himself on a realist's approach to history, Burckhardt was, as Gombrich says, dependent on Hegel's "construct of cultural history" to give his concrete investigations their exegetic value. Gombrich points out how Burckhardt takes for granted ideas like the *Zeitgeist*.[22] Thus his "exegetic method" consists of "postulating the unity of all manifestations of a civilization . . . in taking various elements of culture, say Greek architecture and Greek philosophy, and asking how they can be shown to be the expression of the same spirit."[23] Like much of the *Kulturgeschichte* Gombrich discusses, Burckhardt's project attempts to "salvage the Hegelian assumption without accepting Hegelian metaphysics."[24] In Pound's case, the use of certain cultural diagnostics, like the accuracy of writing or the degree of usury, to gauge the health of a culture, comes directly out of this exegetic method, a method that goes back to Winckelmann's attempts to imaginatively reconstruct the whole of ancient Greek civilization from the fragments of antique sculpture. For, as Gombrich says, the assumption of cultural unity is an a priori assumption, the necessary bedrock of all historical investigation of this kind and not the result of research.

As Pound's polemic reveals, cultural unity is a moral or ethical assertion made against the positivism of the nineteenth century. Though Pound often adopted the language of science for his own project, it did in fact rest on belief rather than induction, on interpretation rather than empirical discovery. Pound is able to rely on this belief primarily because it is such an old one. The presumption of cultural unity may, however, in a seemingly paradoxical way, make knowledge and appreciation of the past more difficult. As Joseph N. Riddel puts it, "The very notion of periodicity that characterizes his sense of tradition is a notion of repeated discontinuity and a discontinuous repetition. . . ."[25] If each age must be judged as a unity, and no teleology leads from age to age, then periods can easily seem to present a closed aspect to the present as they do to one another. How can an observer from one cultural unity understand an artifact from another with a completely different spirit? Wouldn't the method of luminous detail lead in the end to a disparate array of cultural facts just as uncoordinated as that produced by the "other" German method of scholarship?

One solution is offered by Wilhelm Dilthey, who claims that in interpretation "the individuality of the exegete and that of the author are not opposed to each other like two incomparable facts. Rather, both have been formed upon the substratum of a general human nature. . . ." In understanding another historical period "the exegete tentatively projects his own sense of life into another historical milieu [and] is able within that perspective, to strengthen and emphasize certain spiritual processes in himself and to minimize others, thus making possible within himself a re-experiencing of an alien form of life."[26] The constant that underlies all

human history and that makes historical understanding possible is human
nature: The exegete touches the past by touching some part of his own
mental experience.

   This sort of imaginative recreation of the past seems to be exactly what
Pound proposes in his early poetry. Knowledge of "many new things"
seems in "The Tree" to be conditioned upon the re-experiencing of
original myths:

> I stood still and was a tree amid the wood
> Knowing the truth of things unseen before,
> Of Daphne and the laurel bow
> And that god-feasting couple olde
> That grew elm-oak amid the wolde.
>   (CEP, p. 35)

Such historical reexperiencing often has a mystical aura in Pound's early
poetry, but within the mysticism is visible the practical outline of his
project as a scholarly poet. In "Prelude: Over the Ognisanti," Pound
figures himself as a dim collector of "shades of songs . . . which shades
of song re-echoed / Within that somewhat barren hall, my heart. . ."
(CEP, p. 59). In "Sandalphon," the "angel of prayer" speaks of his collection of songs sung by the other angels as they die. Gathering these songs
amounts to "Giving to prayer new language / and causing the works to
speak / of the earth-horde's age-lasting longing" (CEP, p. 68). This
figure of the poet as compendium, as echoing and reechoing with songs
of the past, is most specific in "Histrion":

> Thus am I Dante for a space and am
> One Francois Villon, ballad-lord and thief
> Or am such holy ones I may not write . . .
>   (CEP, p. 71).

The poets of the past stand for certain eternal moods that may still be
experienced. The fact that "the souls of all men great / At times pass
through us" argues for the essential stability of human nature, and at the
same time suggests a method whereby the past might be understood.
Dante, Villon, perhaps Christ himself, do not represent experience lost in
the vastness of time, but stand instead as names for different experiences
available in the present. This is the "permanent basis in humanity" that
Pound speaks of in *The Spirit of Romance* (p. 92), a basis in the "psychic
experience" of human beings. The fact that there is "one man who understands Persephone and Demeter, and one who understands the Laurel"
indicates that particular personalities are apt to reexperience particular
myths because such myths are "explications of mood" (SR, p. 92). For all
Pound's mysticism and reverence about the gods, he still defines a god in
"Religio" as "an eternal state of mind" (SR, p. 47). The fact that there are
such states makes historical knowledge, as well as epiphany, possible.

Pound, it seems, knew nothing of Dilthey, but a reference in *Spirit of Romance* may show how his model of historical reexperiencing comes to resemble Dilthey's. In the first chapter, Pound says, "Ovid, before Browning, raises the dead and dissects their mental processes; he walks with the people of myth; Apuleius, in real life, is confused with his fictitious hero" (SR, p. 16). The example of Apuleius comes from Walter Pater, and there is evidence to suggest that Pater has some impact on Pound's notion of historical understanding. In *Marius the Epicurean*, Flavian's reaction to Apuleius is much like Pound's, and seems almost a motto for his early poetry: "Might one recover the earlier manner and sense of [poetic beauty], by a masterful effort to recall all the complexities of the life, moral and intellectual, of an earlier age?"[27] Pater answers Flavian's question elsewhere in a manner that was to be useful to Pound.

Pater attempts to understand a previous historical period by answering these questions: "In whom did the stir, the genius, the sentiment of the period find itself? where was the receptacle of its refinement, its elevation, its taste?" The analysis of this masterwork proceeds by isolating "the virtue by which a picture, a landscape, or a fair personality in life or in a book, produces this special impression of beauty or pleasure. . . ." The asethetic critic succeeds "when he has disengaged that virtue, and noted it, as a chemist notes some natural element. . . ."[28] When this virtue is isolated, then so too will the virtue of the period be, insofar as it is contained in its own stir, genius, and sentiment. Pound borrows Pater's methods and his terms in defining his own new method of scholarship in "I Gather the Limbs of Osiris." Pound speaks of the *"virtu"* of the individual, by which that individual's works bear an unmistakable stamp, the *"virtu* of a given work of art" (SP, p. 28). As Hugh Witemeyer points out, Pound even borrows the chemical metaphor from Pater.[29]

Pater decides that the question of abstract beauty can be set aside in favor of impressionism: the question to be asked is "How is my nature modified by [the word's] presence, and under its influence?"[30] Thus Pound says in "I Gather the Limbs of Osiris" that the artist first comes to a definition of his own *virtu* and then "will be more likely to discern and allow for a peculiar *virtu* in others. The erection of the microcosmos consists in discriminating these other powers and holding them in orderly arrangement about one's own" (SP, p. 29). In fact, all of Pound's literary criticism could be called such a microcosmos, which is nothing more than a focusing of the whole "cosmos of souls" on one point: "The soul of each man is compounded of all the elements of the cosmos of souls. . ." (SP, p. 28). "Histrion" is the poetic manifesto of the microcosmos, which makes historical understanding possible by arranging the whole of human history around the individual personality. Understanding proceeds just as Dilthey suggests when the exegete emphasizes or

diminishes certain responses in himself in order to imaginatively reexperience the past.[31]

The process of imaginative recreation can be observed in a number of
works written before *The Cantos* are properly under way. "Near Perigord," perhaps Pound's most serious attempt at a long poem before
1915, is, as James Longenbach suggests, almost entirely a hermeneutic
exercise.[32] Its ambition is to "have men's hearts up from the dust / And
tell their secrets" (P, p. 151). To effect such a resurrection, the historian
must "read between the lines" of the available evidence. Another poem,
"Provincia Deserta," makes it clear that Pound fills in the gaps between
the lines by his physical recreation of the lives of those involved. By
itself, "Provincia Deserta" seems a lament for the lost days of Provencal
romance, but read in conjunction with "Near Perigord" it can be seen as
the necessary precondition for an interpretative reconstruction of that
life: "I have walked there / thinking of old days" (P, p. 121). Pound says
in 1913, "A man may walk the hill roads and river roads from Limoges
and Charente to Dordogne and Narbonne and learn a little, or more than
a little, of what the country meant to the wandering singers, he may
learn, or think he learns, why so many canzos open with speech of the
weather; or why such a man made war on such and such castles" (LE, p.
95).

Therefore, Part I of "Near Perigord" presents Bertrans and his text as
impenetrable mysteries, but Part II attempts an explanation by putting
the exegete, who is by now the reader, in Bertrans's place. When his
"green cat's-eye lifts toward Montagnac" so does the reader's: "Sunset,
the ribbon-like road lies, in red cross-light / Southward toward Montagnac. . ." (P, p. 154). The reader is given Bertrans's view of the coun-
tryside as evidence that the topography of his possessions is the governing principle behind his seemingly romantic forays. The attempt here is
to "Take the whole man, and ravel out the story" (P, p. 152). "Near
Perigord" ends in uncertainty, as most of Pound's early hermeneutic
exercises do, but the only complete theory offered in the poem is based
on the idea that a very literal physical recreation of a past life may be the
key to understanding it.

One of the reasons "Near Perigord" ends inconclusively is because
there is no one interpreter whose opinion of Bertrans holds authority
over others. There seems to be one Bertrans for every interpreter: Arnaut
Daniel; Richard Coeur de Lion; Dante; Maent; and the poetic voice itself.
Ideally, these various different interpretations should be compatible, because each is one part of the "cosmos of souls." Instead, the various
impressions disintegrate into "a broken bundle of mirrors," a jumble of
inconsistent reflections. The method of imaginative recreation seems to

lead to the sort of chaos Dilthey hoped to avoid, and Pound begins the first version of *The Cantos* by worrying over this failure.

The ur-Cantos take up more completely than any other work the question of hermeneutic method, and they show as well how intimately this question is linked to that of poetic method. Pound begins these poems by confronting Browning because Browning offers a model of poetic form and a method of knowing the past.[33] The first ur-Canto begins in envy of Browning's poetic relationship to Sordello: "You had one whole man? (And I have many fragments, less worth?)" (TC, p. 115). It seems that Browning has a whole man not just because he was clever enough to light upon Sordello first, but because there was something less problematic about his relationship to the past: "You had some basis, had some set belief" (TC, p. 115). Therefore, the poem takes great pains to recapture this past by the means already used in "Near Perigord." "I walk the airy street," Pound says, placing himself at Sirmio to recall Catullus just as he had placed himself in Provence to recall Bertrans de Born (TC, p. 115).

This is, as Bush notices, the peripatetic method of "Provincia Deserta,"[34] but more explicit claims are made for the method of reenactment in this later poem. After a description of some experiences in Venice, Pound exclaims, "So, for what it's worth, I have the background . . ." (TC, p. 117). The "background" is the physical, sensory experience of the world inhabited by the poets of the past. Pound agonizes over the truthfulness of his relationship to these places: "Sweet lie! – Was I there truly? / Did I know Or San Michele?" (TC, p. 120). He does so because the strength and truthfulness of his impressions are the conditions on which he presumes to rescue the past from "the attritions of long time" (TC, p. 120). One question resounds through these poems: "What have I of this life"; "What have we of them"; "What have we now of her?" (TC, pp. 120, 180, 187) To "have" a background is to "have" something of the past, so that the claim of momentary triumph, "we have that world about us," is based as much on the kind of imaginative recreation Pater practiced as it is on mystical experience. The continuity of the natural world, the Como of Catullus or the Provence of Bertrans de Born, and the continuity of human nature seem to guarantee together the retrieval of the past when single sensory experiences out of the cosmos of experience are reenacted by a later poet.

Why, then, does the question of historical knowledge remain as an unsolved problem well into *The Cantos* in their final version? For all the confidence implied by the "So that:" that ends the resurrection scene of Canto 1, the past remains distant in the first few cantos, fitfully experienced through a screen of documents. Pound caps a long history of bringing his poetic heroes into poems as exegetes by finally choosing a real historian, Benedetto Varchi, and placing him at the center of the sequence of Cantos 5–7. In the question of Alessandro de Medici's murder by his cousin Lorenzo, Varchi has the best evidence and the best credentials: "I saw the man, came up with him at Venice, / I, one wanting the facts, / And no mean labour. . ." (5/19).[35] And yet it is Varchi's puzzlement that Pound seizes on, his question "*Se pia? / O empia?*" With this question, Pound adds another to the historian's tasks. The problem is not just to know, because Varchi has ample knowledge of the best kind, but to judge. Looking back from this vantage point, we can see that Pound has always been asking this question: What sort of man was Arnaut Daniel, Bertrans de Born, Sordello? Does Bertrans belong in Dante's hell? Not only does the moral judgment complicate the historian's task, but it obviously strains against the limits of Pound's own historical presumptions. No longer is the past a subject for psychological and aesthetic discrimination, as it was for Pater, but an occasion for moral judgment between good and bad. What is implied is that there is a quasi-theological truth to events that the exegete must find.

Here Pound confronts the implicit relativism of Pater's brand of historicism. Poetic matters are at stake as well as moral ones. As the ur-Cantos show, the question of how to know the past is intimately connected with the poetic question of how to arrange our knowledge in significant form. Pound questions Browning simultaneously on the structure of his poem and on the nature of his relationship to the past. To structure a poem, the poet must know his material *in relation,* otherwise the poem really is no more than the shining catch that Pound proposes to dump out willy-nilly at the beginning of ur-Canto 1. At the very outset, Pound juxtaposes the rag-bag to the diorama of Browning's *Sordello,* a model of purely linear history, and the poem vacillates between a random arrangement of the past and a fitful recreation of it in real time. The question "How shall we start hence, how begin the progress," is both historical and poetic (TC, p. 119). It asks for a method of reaching back to the past, and simultaneously figures that method as a progress or procession, as if the diorama were to be wound backward. How do we reconstruct the past when our evaluation of it, placing greatest emphasis on what most nearly touches us, precisely reverses chronological order? Thus the question of historical evaluation and historical order are intimately connected and both must be decided simultaneously with the question of poetic order, which is what Pound attempts to do in the ur-Cantos.

Pound struggles in these early cantos against the provincialism of the present, which can be overcome only by a method of connecting seemingly disparate facts. But the method of Luminous Detail is biased in just the wrong direction. The idea of individual *virtu* leads directly to the

conclusion that "we have one Catullus, one Villon" (SP, p. 28), and if so
that there is no way of judging Catullus and Villon in the same balance.
In an early attempt to define the method of Luminous Detail, Pound
imagines a naive spectator in a "room containing a picture by Fra An-
gelico, a picture by Rembrandt, one by Velasquez, Memling, Rafael,
Monet, Beardsley, Hokusai, Whistler, and a fine example of the art of
some forgotten Egyptian" (SP, p. 24). The spectator is confused because
"These things obey no common apparent law." Pound's spectator is the
modern spectator of history, confronting a group of masterworks purposely scrambled in terms of time and place. How is he to get his bearings without the sense of teleological development provided by the
chronological series? Pound's answer here is radically relativistic: All
these works produce "power," "none 'better,' none 'worse,' all different"
(SP, p. 25). He concludes unhelpfully, not answering his own questions,
that the rules governing all the paintings are "similar and different with
different" works.

Pound adopts the terms of the problem and those of the attempted
solution from Pater. The idea that masterworks are producers of power,
which Pound dresses up in "I Gather the Limbs of Osiris" with modern-
istic engineering terminology, comes from Pater's preface to *The Renaissance,* already discussed here as a source for Pound's ideas in the essay.[36]
Pater calls the great works of art "powers or forces producing pleasurable
sensations, each of a more or less peculiar or unique kind."[37] Pound takes
on Pater's relativism with his connoisseur's language. To the aesthetic
critic Pater says, "All periods, types, schools of taste, are in themselves
equal." "Beauty," he says, "is relative," and it is the job of the critic to
find it in concrete examples, not abstract definitions.[38] As Hans-Georg
Gadamer puts it, "To think historically now means to acknowledge that
each period has its own right to exist, and its own perfection."[39] Such
historical thinking places itself against a teleology with its goal in the
present, and against what Gadamer calls a reverse teleology, where all
virtue is accorded to the antique past. But how can a universal history
exist if there is no purposeful connection between events, and how can
works of art be judged against one another if art has no transcendent
value? In other words, how could the room of paintings in "I Gather the
Limbs of Osiris" ever be arranged in a sensible order? "The task is to
show how these relative values of the ages have become expanded into
something absolute," to quote Dilthey.[40]

The formulation Dilthey gives the task is precisely correct, because
relativism is not to be abandoned or countered, but is to be lifted to a new
level at which its claims acquire the transcendent value of the absolute.
The solution Pound arrives at resembles the one Eliot discovered.[41] If
ages are seen as separate unities, each unified by a particular ethos, then

the different ages might be mediated and judged by the degree of unity they exhibit, the strength of their cohesive principle. Antiquity here retains its normative force because it is usually the Greeks who are accounted the most perfectly unified civilization, but no specific Greek idea or accomplishment need be copied because the degree of unity between features is what is worthy of emulation. In other words, the methodological principle that allows time to be lumped together in ages and periods in the first place acquires the force of a normative value, after having fragmented history into a series of individual wholes. To return to the terms of the previous chapter, Pound becomes a vulgar relativist, one who makes relativism itself into a transcendent ideal, thus making the same conditions both relative and absolute.

Gadamer describes the same solution to relativism as taking "The specific perfection of Greece" – that is, "its rich variety of great individual forms" – and making it the principle that "constitutes the value and meaning of history." Such an ideal "does not contain any particular content, but is based on the formal idea of the greatest variety."[42] The formal principle of unity is lifted here to the very highest level, in that the whole panoply of historical forms can be seen as an expression of a single force, human potential, and the very incommensurability of historical works can be honored as the expansion and expression of an underlying unity. Gadamer calls this a teleology without a telos, and Jauss says that without a teleology it "yet again promises the aesthete a coherent whole."[43] This is the answer to Dilthey's question how relative values can become absolute: "The mind rediscovers itself at ever higher levels of consciousness . . . in every subject of a community, in every system of culture and, finally, in the totality of mind and universal history. . . ."[44] This totality is finally the context within which historical facts can be compared, its variety the principle that historical value approximates.

Each individual writer or artist may have his own "pure color," but all come together on the palette: "I suppose no two men will agree absolutely respecting 'pure color' or 'good color,' but the modern painter recognizes the importance of the palette" (LE, p. 215). The palette combines all the individual works of individual value, none of which is absolute in isolation. In combination, however, they form a value system. Thus combined, they become "axes of reference," relationships between "*the best of each kind*," without invidious comparison between kinds (LE, p. 35). Because it is both impossible and undesirable for a modern poet to copy Dante or Villon, their value as examples is not inherent in their own work but only in them insofar as they represent the full development of possibilities within the whole cosmos of human creativity. They are signposts allowing the later writer to find his way about that cosmos.

Pound approximates here a very old solution to the problem of historicism and value. Vasari unselfconsciously combines a similar notion of artistic particularity wherein Michelangelo's genius differs from Raphael's with a deeper belief that there is one classic standard of beauty.[45] The conflict between these two different ideas of artistic value does not become clear and painful until the sixteenth century, when Lomazzo attempts to harmonize them through an architectural metaphor. Art in Lomazzo's *Idea* appears as an imaginary building with seven columns, one each for the great artists of the Renaissance. Together, the columns form a harmonious structure because each painter excels at one "part of the painting," Leonardo at portraying light, Mantegna at perspective, etc.[46] The scheme works only because the art of painting is seen as a fixed whole with "parts." For the same reason, Pound's metaphor of the palette works only because world literature can be seen as a fixed array, a spectrum, within which each "color" can find its exact position. Different individuals may differ from one another without danger to the absoluteness of value because they relate to one another as parts of a fixed and absolute whole. Lomazzo's model also solves a particular historical problem. Individuals have a historical character in the model: They are creatures of a particular time. But as practitioners of "art," whose boundaries do not change from age to age, they are part of a timeless schema. The historical distance between Mantegna and Titian disappears in the atemporal structure of the building.

All such solutions, however, depend to some extent on the assumption that human nature has fixed boundaries, that it is not a continuous product of historical human experience but the bedrock of it. Even Dilthey, according to Gadamer, bases his belief in the possibility of historical understanding on "the similarity of human nature through the ages."[47] Because there is what Dilthey calls a "substratum of general human nature,"[48] then the space between past and present is not a gulf at all but a continuity. If "every work of art and every historical deed is intelligible because the people who express themselves through them and those who understand them have something in common" then "History is not something separated from life or divided from the present by distance in time."[49] Gadamer himself says that what seems the abyss of time is in fact "filled with the continuity of custom and tradition. . . ."[50] Even Gadamer sees certain works of art losing their historical contingency within this tradition and becoming part of an order of classics, an order of seeming simultaneity like Lomazzo's building.

Pound's "palette" is really nothing more than this sort of fixed substratum. His famous claim in *The Spirit of Romance* that "All ages are contemporaneous" (p. 6) is founded on a belief in "a sort of permanent basis in humanity" (p. 92). Aside from its utility as a principle in *The Cantos*, this belief in a permanent human nature makes comparison between different works of art possible: "art and humanity, remaining ever the same, gave us basis for comparison" (p. 157). Thus Pound has sanction for the imaginary gallery of "I Gather the Limbs of Osiris." What holds together the seemingly random series of painters named in that essay is human nature itself, which can serve as a common term and an enclosing structure because it is always the same. The luminous detail is finally nothing more than a part of this permanent bedrock, part of what Pound calls "the permanent basis of psychology and metaphysics" (SP, p. 23). These details, given by great artists, are the "permanent property" of the race (LE, p. 47). Therefore, what can be seen on one level as clues to a particular historical condition, the life of an isolated period, can be seen on another level as part of the common property of humankind. The luminous detail evades the provinciality of other modes of historical investigation because its evidence can take a place in an array whose fullness and variety count as permanent values.

Hermeneutic method and theory of history touch here, as that which makes historical understanding possible, the basic consistency of human nature, becomes as well the link between events and finally the transcendent value within which events and works of art lose their limited historical character. But Pound's emphasis on the "permanent" nature of such value is so much stronger than anything in Dilthey as to be qualitatively different.[51] Gadamer's notion of the classic is something of an aberration in a system that otherwise insists on the idea that man is a product of his history, and even Dilthey's much more conservative hermeneutic is a good deal more dynamic than anything proposed by Pound. Pound's insistence on the "eternal moods" (CEP, p. 193), the unchanging states of human experience, is so strong that it hardly seems historical at all. He resolves the historical anxiety of the ur-Cantos by insisting that "we have that world about us" (TC, p. 118), not that it can be recovered but that it remains eternally present. If psychological recreation can work this well, why should *The Cantos* include history at all? Could there be any history if human nature is always essentially the same? The method of luminous detail thus solves the problem of historical relativism by banishing history itself. What began as a celebration of the particular ends in obeisance to an eternal unchangeable system of values. For all his diatribes against *Kultur,* Pound simply recreates its contradictory combination of random facts and abstract generalizations. The "new" method of scholarship, which was in any case not as new as Pound claimed, falls victim to all the contradictions of the old.

2. HISTORY, VALUE, AND THE CANTOS

The anxieties attending the early abandoned cantos show how important it was for Pound that his new long work be "a poem including history."

History assumes such an important role not because Pound is a covert traditionalist who hopes to rival the great poets of the past, but because history is the context within which details and universals come together. The new method of scholarship is a historical method because Pound, like Bradley, hopes to put "individual facts whose being is historical" in the gap between particular and general opened up by conventional scholarship and traditional democratic politics. In fact, however, *The Cantos* include history only in a very peculiar and restricted sense, and they come to contain less and less of it as the concerns of the poet become more vehemently archival. One of the great paradoxes of this great and paradoxical poem is its progressive adoption of a static, undifferentiated conception of history even as it comes to depend more and more on undigested atoms of historical evidence. The gap, that is to say, grows instead of diminishing, yet the contradiction to blame is at work from the very beginning.

Except for a few remaining anecdotes from Provence, the dominating historical period of the early *Cantos* is the Renaissance. Benedetto Varchi, a Renaissance historian, voices the central historical question of these cantos: *pia o empia?* The basic structural opposition, however, is not between good and bad acts in the Renaissance, but between the Renaissance as a whole and the present. These cantos intermix the past and the present as if they had enough in common to validate comparison, and the two phases of history thus come to represent alternatives eternally open to humankind. Pound finally decides on an answer to Varchi's question that is expressed as a contrast between the Renaissance and the present, which is finally a contrast between fullness and emptiness.

Jeffrey Perl suggests that Burckhardt views history not as progressive or developmental but as "a cultural ideal" and "the sustained failures or periodic successes in living up to it." Even the cultural ideal, Perl argues, does not emerge from history itself, but is "crafted as an antidote to the nineteenth century and a program for its renewal."[52] Perl's interpretation seems to square with Burckhardt's method of writing history, which avoids narrative by isolating certain periods and analyzing those periods by aligning all the various strands of culture side-by-side, in seeming simultaneity. The method, especially in *The Civilization of the Renaissance in Italy,* attempts to create an image of the golden age as one of spontaneous and simultaneous development. Behind this scheme is not a theory of time but a very simple system of values. As Hayden White puts it, "The unspoken antithesis of this age of achievement and brilliance is the gray world of the historian himself, European society in the second half of the nineteenth century. . . . The Renaissance was everything that the modern world is *not.*"[53] Though this arrangement depends on a value judgment and not on historical interpretation or analysis, the values themselves are peculiarly hollow. Against the emptiness of the present Burckhardt arrays the fullness of one moment of the past, but the primary thrust of his argument is not that the Renaissance is full of something particularly good. Rather, the emphasis falls on fullness and wholeness per se. The Renaissance brings to light "the full, whole nature of man," "man in his totality." This totality includes the individuality "not only of the tyrant or Condottiere himself, but also of the men whom he protected or used as his tools – the secretary, minister, poet, and companion."[54] It can hardly be argued that man in his totality is totally good, and Burckhardt does not flinch from the implications of his ideas. In fact, Burckhardt is free to be brutally frank about many aspects of the Renaissance because he is only glamorizing the coordination between them. This value is, of course, inseparable from Burckhardt's methodology, which relies on such coordination to build up a historical picture out of seemingly unrelated fragments.[55]

Beginning with the same problem of interpretation, and using similar methods, Pound arrives at a very similar conclusion. Canto 5 is the last of a long series of historical puzzlements beginning with a scholarly query about Arnaut Daniel in *The Spirit of Romance*. Just as Pound wonders what sort of man was Bertrans de Born, here Varchi interrogates himself about Lorenzaccio: "Whether for love of Florence . . . Or for a privy spite?" (5/19) Pound assumes Varchi's puzzlement at the end of the canto ("Both sayings run in the wind"), but the question does not remain unanswered in *The Cantos*. Pound uses a contrast to answer it in Canto 7. There Lorenzaccio is compared to the dried-out men of the present, "Being more live than they, more full of flames and voices" (7/27). Like Lorenzaccio's victim, Alessandro de Medici, who was "Eternal watcher of all things" (7/27), a sufferer from "abuleia" (5/19), these men of the present are mere "husks," their words "shells given out by shells" (5/27). Lorenzaccio may be brutal, but at least he is alive.

Pound's decision in Lorenzaccio's favor is part of a general balancing of past and present in terms of emptiness and fullness. He phrases it in perfectly clear and crude terms earlier in Canto 7: "Beer-bottle on the statue's pediment! / That, Fritz, is the era, to-day against the past" (7/25). This, with perhaps some self-mockery in it, is followed by a more serious reformulation: "Against their action, aromas. Rooms, against chronicles." In these rooms live men characterized by their emptiness: "husks," "shells," "locust-casques," "dry pods" (7/27). Speaking of these empty rooms with empty men the rhetoric empties itself:

> Knocking at empty rooms, seeking for buried beauty;
> And the sun-tanned, gracious and well-formed fingers
> Lift no latch of bent bronze, no Empire handle
> Twists for the knocker's fall; no voice to answer.
>
> (7/25)

This passage is sometimes compared to Eliot's "Portrait of a Lady," and Ronald Bush has linked the whole canto to "Gerontion,"[56] but this particular passage is rhetorically equivalent to the remarkable non-description in "The Fire Sermon": "The river bears no empty bottles, sandwich papers, / Silk handkerchiefs, cardboard boxes, cigarette ends / Or other testimony of summer nights."[57] Eliot's landscape somehow lacks even the ephemera so vividly visualized in the poem. Specificity becomes negative here as a seeming fullness is drained dry by the rhetorical turn. Pound will use the same tactic in the Usura Canto, one that is linked very closely to Canto 7.

The standards by which Lorenzaccio should be judged are therefore not those of good and evil, but those of life and death, emptiness and fullness. Lorenzaccio is not only "more live than they" but "more full of flames and voices" (7/27). These standards derive from Burckhardt's sense of Renaissance man as "all-sided" and "complete" and from his contrasting sense of the present as fragmentary and empty. The same standards operate in the Malatesta Cantos as well. Critical debate about the extent to which Pound approves of Sigismundo Malatesta is misguided by an inappropriate set of standards.[58] Ordinary moral discriminations miss the point for the same reason that Varchi's question about Lorenzaccio must be turned instead of answered. Sigismundo's only real vice is to be *too* full, "a bit too POLUMETIS" (9/36). The reiterative imprecations of Pope Pius's denunciation of Sigismundo confirm his essential fullness instead of demonstrating his moral turpitude:

> Lussioroso, incestuoso, perfide, sozzure ac crapulone,
> assassino, ingordo, avaro, superbo, infidel
> fattore di monete false, sodomitico, uxoricido
> and the whole lump lot.
>
> (10/45)

Pius's purely additive style mimics despite itself the style Pound uses elsewhere to demonstrate Sigismundo's resourcefulness: "and that he rejected the whole symbol of the apostles, and that he said the monks ought not to own property / and that he disbelieved in the temporal power. . ." (10/44). Marjorie Perloff speaks of the way the details of the Malatesta Cantos are "flattened" against a kind of screen, effacing the difference between past and present.[59] The omnipresent "and," used as all-purpose connective, also flattens out the difference between conventional good and bad, preserving the truly essential dimension of Sigismundo's life: its fullness. Even Pius confirms this in the very act of enumerating Sigismundo's supposed sins.

As a personality, Sigismundo takes what little form he has from the historical method Pound derives from Burckhardt. The terms of Pound's praise of Sigismundo in *Guide to Kulchur* confess this debt. When Pound speaks of Sigismundo's "all-roundedness" (p. 159), when he praises Sigis-

mundo as "an entire man" (p. 194), he is clearly speaking in terms that
Burckhardt made current, speaking of "all-sided," "many-sided," and
"complete" men as the creation of the Renaissance.[60] Though Burckhardt takes the terms themselves from Renaissance testimony, his elevation of them to the highest significance has clear relation to the needs of
his historical method. The "complete man," like the complete civilization, can be observed in any randomly chosen detail; it can be described
by a collection of seemingly fragmentary observations defying ordinary
chronology. In the same spirit, Pound describes Sigismundo's life by
means of a fortuitously preserved post-bag, and he even exaggerates the
confusion of the contents by way of demonstrating completeness
through heterogeneity. In Guide to Kulchur, Pound says, "The perception
of a whole age, of a whole congeries and sequence of causes, went into an
assemblage of detail. . ." (p. 136). This is true only of "unified" ages such
as the Renaissance is usually held to be, and it is true as well of men if they
are similarly unified. In 1937, Pound spoke of a "full man" as one "who
approaches the Renaissance totalitarianism" (SP, p. 454).[61] His praise of
such men is inseparable from the historical method first enunciated in "I
Gather the Limbs of Osiris"; the essential virtue of such men is only
another version of the historical principle on which the Luminous Detail
depends.[62]

It stands to reason, then, that the same historical principle might give
form to Pound's chosen incarnation of evil. Certainly the habit of using
usury as an index of culture grows out of the earlier method of Luminous
Detail. Pound claims in 1942 that "an expert, looking at a painting . . . should be able to determine the degree of the tolerance of usury
in the society in which it was painted" (SP, p. 323). This claim is based on
the belief that "the character of the man is revealed in every brush-
stroke," and therefore the character of the age itself comes clear in every
detail. As Pound says in Guide to Kulchur, this belief marks his work as
"totalitarian" – that is, based on a belief that cultures are rooted and
linked in simple basic ways. But Pound's handling of this particular
variety of his historical method is somewhat uncertain. In 1937, he says,
"You can probably date any Western work of art by reference to the
ethical estimate of usury prevalent at the time of that work's composition. . ." (SP, p. 76). We can tell what Pound means here, but on the
surface his statement is logically circular. What Pound apparently means
is that given the history of usury and given a group of art works of
varying quality, the latter could be dated by reference to the former. But
somehow in the telling the essential term, quality, has dropped out. The
historiographical system becomes all cause, no symptom, and confesses
itself as almost purely a priori. Usury itself, it should be remembered,
was at one time merely a symptom to Pound of a whole process of decay.

But, as Fredric Jameson says in his analysis of Wyndham Lewis, such theories of history tend "to become mesmerized by their own organizational framework in such a way that they misread the organizational device by which they were able to narrate historical change for the objective force or cause responsible for the change in question."[63] This sort of change certainly occurs in Pound's handling of writing as historical diagnostic: At one time only an index of good culture, writing gradually becomes a cause with the power to drag down civilizations single-handedly. Much the same thing happens with the idea of usury. Often the kind of symptom that can be read directly in the products of a culture, it soon becomes a cause, gathering more and more power to itself in Pound's mind as his purely a priori method confirms his prejudices over and over again.

The shift of usury into this position of central cause also changes the temporal shape of history as Pound sees it. The idea that there are "degrees" of usury implies that history is gradual in its submission to or freedom from this force. Pound often uses a fairly conventional rise-and-fall terminology that would seem to reflect the same belief. But such gradualism depends on the supposition that usury is but one of a large number of historical forces. As it becomes in Pound's mind virtually the *only* such force, history loses its gradual shape and becomes abrupt. There is no rise and fall but a series of drastic shifts, complete breaks in historical continuity. Pound locates the most important of these breaks around 1500 (SP, p. 274, GK, p. 50). Both his desire to personalize history and the drive toward a greater centralization of historical forces lead Pound to place the blame more and more on Leo X (SP, p. 57). In the "Cavalcanti" essay and in Canto 46, Pound narrows the date of absolute decline to 1527, which he seems to place in the papacy of Leo X, though Leo was some years dead by then. In any case, what is important is the narrowing of the forces of historical change to one year and one man: "Thereafter art thickened. Thereafter design went to hell, / Thereafter barocco, thereafter stonecutting desisted" (46/234). The image is one of immediate, catastrophic and total historical change.

Canto 45, the Usura Canto, represents this change stylistically. Here Pound represents linguistically the stark border between pre- and post-usury life, which is also the border between totality and emptiness. As a negative catalogue, Canto 45 greatly expands the techniques used earlier in Canto 7 to contrast past and present: "With usura hath no man a house of good stone . . . hath no man a painted paradise on his church wall . . . seeth no man Gonzaga his heirs and his concubines / no picture is made to endure or to live with . . ." (45/229). Again Pound depicts the present as a negative plenitude, the fullness and multiplicity of the catalogue of the past drained by negative reiteration to nothingness. The

connection between this canto and Canto 7 is made explicit at the end:
"Corpses are set to banquet / at behest of usura" (45/230). These are
certainly the same corpses that in Canto 7 "Bend to the tawdry table, /
Lift up their spoons to mouths, put forks in cutlets, / And make sound
like the sound of voices" (7/27). The fact that these corpses, more dead
than Lorenzaccio, return in Canto 45 signifies that the essential opposition between fullness and emptiness remains operative at this stage of the
long poem. Usury reverses the Renaissance, rendering its fullness and
completion null and void. In this analysis, usury becomes a purely empty
force, because it seems to be defined solely by the real things it can blast
and destroy. There is, unfortunately, no other way to describe emptiness
or nullity. The dependence of usury on its opposite for description and
definition also shows, moreover, how little gradation there is between the
two antagonistic forces.

On the syntagmatic axis the situation of the Usura Canto is one of pure
opposition.[64] No change takes place, no exchange or influence, only the
static confrontation of two mutually inimical forces. Because these forces
exclude one another by definition, because usury is everything that the
full life of the Renaissance is not, and vice versa, there is no real ground
on which they might confront one another. Thus there is very little
genuine syntax in the Usura Canto: "Not by usura St. Trophime /Not
by usura Saint Hilaire . . ." (45/270). This sort of compression results
from Pound's basic conception of usury as much as it does from stylistic
imperatives. In this sense, the Usura Canto resembles the Malatesta Cantos on a very basic level. Though there is a good deal of violent activity in
the Malatesta Cantos, because the clash here is one of men not definitions, the basic situation is still that of deadlocked opposition:

> With the church against him,
> With the Medici bank for itself,
> With wattle Sforza against him. . .
>   (8/32)

The only consistent factor in all of Sigismundo's multifarious activities is
his opposition to the tide of power. Even the merest orneriness is worth
noting, because it is part of the essential contrast between Sigismundo's
fullness and the vacancy of the coming order, a vacancy seen from the
other side in the Usura Canto.

On the paradigmatic axis, however, the two sets of cantos share the
characteristic of infinite substitution. Both sets depend stylistically on
reiteration, on the repetition in a kind of chant of syntactically identical
elements. The Usura Canto modulates from "With usura," repeated
eight times, through "came not by usura," repeated fully or partially
seven times, to a series of archaicized verbs: "rusteth," "gnaweth," etc.
The modulation, especially that series of changes rung on "came not by

usura," is especially artful, which may account for the popularity of this canto. But this art can hardly hide the fact that there is no particular reason for the Usura Canto to be as long as it is, and nothing to prevent its being twice as long. Each line is fundamentally interchangeable with every other line. Behind this stylistic fact lies the ideological fact that all of usury's foes are interchangeable. Usury is not specific in its evil but vastly general, because it stands against life itself: "Usury slayeth the child in the womb" (45/230).

Barthes calls the series of substitutions possible on the paradigmatic axis "a potential mnemonic series, a 'mnemonic treasure,'" and this seems to offer an explanation for Pound's structures.[65] The possibility of substitution depends on memory, on all the cultural associations behind particular terms: For Pound this mnemonic series *is* culture. It is exactly what is imperiled by usury, and so one term of the relation, usury, remains the same throughout the canto whereas the other term is replaced over and over by similar alternates. The same situation obtains in the Malatesta Cantos where Sigismundo confronts a bewildering array of enemies, all of whom are linked by their venality or mean-spiritedness. As in the Usura Canto, the essential structure is additive, openly so in its dependence on "And" to link successive lines. The "and" signifies more than the simple episodic quality of Sigismundo's life; it exposes as well the essential identity of Sigismundo's foes, their interchangeability.

Behind these stylistic and structural arrangements Pound's basic historiographical theory is visible. Because all the real movement in these cantos takes place along the paradigmatic axis – that is, the battle lines are never changed only some of the fighters – history does not appear in terms of change at all. These cantos, despite the sense of historical crisis on which they depend for drama, have an impoverished sense of history as alteration over time. But they have a correspondingly enriched sense of history as memory or conservation. In both sets of cantos, all events are identical to the one great event – the clash of elemental opposites. This clash has a rich history in that it seems to occur simultaneously from the beginning of civilization to its foreseeable end, but it has no real history at all in the sense of genesis or development. The interchangeability of players means that no single player initiated this war, nor has any player ever fundamentally altered its course. Heroes come into prominence in *The Cantos* by aligning themselves, usually against all foes, with predetermined positions of virtue. Men like John Adams, Brooks Adams, Thomas Jefferson, and Benito Mussolini are heroes not so much by act as by definition.

Pound wrote nineteen cantos of Chinese history in the late 1930s because he discovered in Confucian historiography an ancient and venerable tradition that exactly corresponded to the historiography implicit in his earlier cantos. As Michael André Bernstein says, "Confucian historical writing proceeds along two discrete *paradigmatic* axes, one of effective, the other of evil or incompetent, rulers. . . . The names within each group are meant to be interchangeable, offering a set of possible substitutions for one another rather than any syntagmatic, linear progression."[66] The Mandate of Heaven, the source of political legitimacy in China, is purely an either/or proposition, a matter of definition much like usury. As long as the emperor reigns, he enjoys the Mandate, but his fall shows that the Mandate has passed to another: Weak or irresponsible rulers cease to be rulers by definition as well as in fact. Because the standards mysteriously applied by the Mandate never vary, Confucian history is nothing but an endless illustration of a single definition, a vast expansion of the method of the Usura Canto. In practical terms this leads to the static, repetitive oppositions of Pound's China Cantos, the kind of thing accurately encapsulated by the Emperor Tching: "We are up, Hia is down" (53/265). The same sort of see-saw approach characterizes Confucian history of learning, in Pound's redaction: "halls were re-set to Kung-fu-tseu / yet again, allus droppin' 'em and restorin' 'em" (54/284). There is, in other words, very little that looks like history at all in these cantos, where very little changes except the names.

By its very magnitude in time and space, Chinese history seems to confirm for Pound a sense that all history is a clash between eternal antagonists. In Pound's version, Chinese history seems an endless interchange of the same two forces:

> YAO, CHUN, YU controller of waters
> bridge builders, contrivers of roads
>   gave grain to the people
>   kept down the taxes
> Hochang, eunuchs, taoists and ballets
> night-clubs, gimcracks, debauchery
>   Down, down! Han is down
>   Sung is down
> Hochang, eunuchs, and taozers
> empresses' relatives, came then a founder
> saying nothing superfluous
> cleaned out the taozers and grafters, gave grain
>   opened the mountains
> Came taozers, hochang and debauchery. . .
>   (56/302)

The crudity of the language, the unwillingness of the poet to vary phrases like "gave grain" or the list of synonyms for the taoists by more than an iota must signify a desire to emphasize the identity over time of these political forces. Pound must also be straining to force English to surrender its tenses. He says in his preface to the translations from Confucius: "As to the frequent lack of tense indications, the ideogrammic mind assumes that what has been is and will be."[67] Repetitiveness and a relatively weak use of verbs in the passage quoted combine to make it seem timeless. The language of permanence, present in Pound's work from the beginning, is immeasurably strengthened by his exposure to China. What vitality there is in the China Cantos comes from this sense of permanence, from the belief that history matters because whatever was once true remains true.

All history, therefore, takes on for Pound the aspect of an eternal conflict between diametrically opposed forces. Pound's wartime articles, in Peter Nicholls's summary, "return constantly to one main theme: History can be understood only in terms of a perpetual struggle between the pure, 'European' values of Catholicism, and the rootless, 'anti-statal', monopolistic values which Pound attributes to Hebraism and Protestantism."[68] Though Pound sees Catholicism in Italy as being much the same as Confucianism in China, based on reverence for the grain and the social and economic organization enforced by tillage, the similarity extends beyond mere specifics. The ultimate conflict is between the two qualities Pound associates in the earliest cantos with the break between past and present: fullness and emptiness, wholeness and partiality.[69] As he says in "A Visiting Card": "We find two forces in history: one that divides, shatters, and kills, and one that contemplates the unity of the mystery" (SP, p. 306). Evil is simply whatever is partial, whereas the good is more and more associated in Pound's work with the "totalitarian."

Pound's use of this word in the 1930s and 40s is specifically political.[70] He uses it in connection with Mussolini, who originated the word. But Pound sees political ideas like Mussolini's as deriving their legitimacy from something outside politics. Nicholls says of the China Cantos that "the immenseness of China's land-mass sponsors in the Dynastic Cantos a reverence for the authority and institutions which have guaranteed its apparent political stability. . . in the Chinese Cantos the land is an image of totality, at once the source of productivity and 'authentic' labour, and a basis which sustains the all-pervasive forms of law and custom."[71] Pound turns more and more to the land, in defiance of Social Credit dogma, as the image of a timeless totalitarianism, of which the despotism of Mussolini is merely a modern example. The land is a visible, tangible principle of unity, a guiding social principle fully present in the physical world and guaranteed against change. "Shun and Wan had a thousand years between them and when their wills were compared they were as two halves of a tally stick" (SP, p. 89). This extraordinary consistency in the ideas of virtuous men is guaranteed by the fact that "man, earth: two halves of the tally" (82/526). Consistency over time and social unity within time thus come to be synonymous, because social unity is achieved by reverence toward the principle on which all aspects of society ultimately rest. The truly virtuous society, then, has no history. The China Cantos frustrate because they are a massively chronological demonstration of this fact. The irruption of history into the permanent order is, as Gadamer says of much older historiographies, "the result of error in calculation by human reason."[72] Because error is doomed by its very lack of connection to the greater totality, the system soon rights itself, and history ceases for a time to exist.

What seems to be a struggle between two forces can therefore be resolved into an even more static situation. There is in this system but one force; history is made by its periodic absence. "Totality" can have no external alternative; the only alternatives are in fact only parts that refuse to assume their places. Pound's idea of the permanent order resembles what Jauss calls a "self-activating tradition." As Jauss shows, this sort of self-sufficient and self-generating tradition brings with it a historiographical model with "nothing but the continual alteration [sic] of decline and return to classical models and lasting values."[73] In Canto 7, the Malatesta Cantos, the Usura Canto, and the China Cantos, there are no real opposing forces, but one image of fullness and wholeness imperiled by partiality. This is the most extreme extension of the belief on which the Luminous Detail rests, the last step in Pound's elevation of a methodological principle to the prestige of a moral law. In this analysis, historical alternatives to the right are not simply wrong; they cease to exist. As was the case in the rhetoric of Canto 7 or the Usura Canto, the alternative to wholeness is a negative plenitude, something that can only be described by the reality it momentarily displaces.

Though every human being has by definition a place in this totality, its generative principle lies outside humankind. Otherwise, it could never enjoy the permanence for which Pound worships it. What then is the place of human beings in their own history? Pound's phraseology in "A Visiting Card" is revealing: Against partiality there exists that which "contemplates the unity of the mystery" (SP, p. 306). Man's role in his own history is that of contemplation. In his Italian wartime articles, the anti-intellectualism of this belief clearly emerges: "But faith is weakened by debates, [which are] more or less rabbinical and if not rabbinical at least anti-totalitarian. . . . Faith is totalitarian. The mystery is totalitarian. . . . That fatal inclination to want to understand logically and syllogistically what is incomprehensible is Hebrew and Protestant."[74] Because the real tradition is permanent and self-generating, because history is little more than a record of error, humankind's own investigation into the past is of little intellectual value. Its value comes only from its power to provoke worship. Thus the most compelling image of the human use of history comes in Canto 61:

and they received the volumes of history
with a pee-rade with portable cases like tabernacles
the dynastic history with solemnity.
                                        (61/336)
The proper human stance toward history is that of worship. Here the
history books are carried forth like idols to be worshipped as artifacts.
This may not have been precisely what Pound had in mind when he
announced his new method of scholarship in 1911, but the two events are
linked by their own ineluctable history.

   Pound began his search for a new method of historical scholarship by
complaining against authoritarian Germany. The ironic fulfillment of his
project is signified by the alliance he effects with an even more authoritarian Germany. His complaint that *Kultur* turns the individual into
a powerless ant could be even more justly levied against his own totalitarianism, as revealed in the China Cantos. These ironies expose the fatal
tendency of Pound's methods to recreate the situation they were supposed to resolve. This failure is an ethical one, because Pound manifestly
fails to suggest a viable ethical alternative to the paradoxical unification of
relativism and moralism that he hated in modern Europe. And there is a
parallel poetic failure, because *The Cantos* so obviously become just that
grab-bag of odd facts, ruled over by iron generalizations, that Pound set
out to avoid. Most ominous of all, however, is the political failure loom-
ing in Pound's use of the word "totalitarian," a political failure that will
repeat the same paradoxes in a far more serious context.

3. THE FASCIST BARGAIN

Whatever else they might have been, Pound's political activities were an
attempt to resolve the modern conflict of individual and community,
though such a resolution was made almost impossible by his tendency to
phrase each side in the most extreme and dogmatic terms he could find.
At times, Pound would defend the rights of the individual in terms that
sounded suspiciously like those of classic liberalism. "The truth is the
individual," he said in 1911, not at all aware of the potential contradiction
between the form and the substance of his declaration (SP, p. 33). In 1918,
he praised James as the defender of "human liberty, personal liberty, the
rights of the individual against all sorts of intangible bondage" (LE, p.
296). Pound used the phrase "individual rights" in *ABC of Economics* in
1933 (SP, p. 253) and even as late as the radio speeches he could build a
formidable rant about the rights granted in the American constitution
(EPS, p. 110).[75]

   Pound often phrased his individualism as an elitist defense of the artist
against the uncomprehending mass. "The artist," he said in 1919, "is the
antidote for the multitude" (SP, p. 426).[76] But great art also depended, he

never tired of reminding his readers, on a great culture, a centralized collective force at the peak of its powers.[77] Pound's first discussion of the vortex makes it a confluence of "centuries of race consciousness, of agreement, of association" (SP, p. 34). Without such concentrations art "will be individual, separate, and spasmodic" (LE, p. 221). Thus it is also possible for Pound to use the term individual, without explanation or justification, in a negative sense, to complain, as he did in *Guide to Kulchur*, that "our time has overshadowed the mysteries by an over-emphasis on the individual" (GK, p. 299).[78]

Pound resolves this contradiction in much the same way Eliot and Yeats did, by insisting that the collective is most truly present in certain individuals. "The culture of an age," says one of the chapter titles in *Guide to Kulchur*, "is what you can pick up and/or get in touch with, by talk with the most intelligent men of the period" (p. 217), though certain unspecified qualifications are registered by a terminal question mark. These men, many-minded and various, *are* the civilization of which they seem only a part: "The life of the race is concentrated in a few individuals" (SP, p. 38). They are human luminous details, figures for the whole, even if the whole should reject them. Pound laments in his letters that civilization exists now only "in the isolated individual, who occasionally meet one other with a scrap of it concealed on his person or in his study" (L, p. 181). If the isolated individual *is* the whole from which he seems exiled, then there is no contradiction between the specific and the general, the individual and the collective. The many-minded individual, like the luminous detail, resolves the conflict between detail and abstraction.

There is just one short step to take from first asserting that isolated individuals represent the whole even if they are isolated to asserting that they represent it *because* they are isolated. Pound hardly even hesitates before this step. "Any full man," he says in 1937, "any man who approaches the Renaissance totalitarianism . . . is bound to suffer occultation, to remain three-fourths in shadow" (SP, p. 454). He who represents the whole, Pound says, is condemned to remain partial. Like Yeats, he inadvertently exposes the logical contradictions of elitism, in which the elite bases its claims both on its resemblance to and its difference from the mass. Like Yeats and Eliot, he conceives of the elite as a universal class, a minority that represents best because of its difference from the majority.[79]

Pound resolves *this* contradiction by displacing it into the future. For the artist certainly does not represent today's culture, from which he is so thoroughly estranged, but this very estrangement can be seen as proof that he represents tomorrow's culture. "Serious art is unpopular at its birth. But it ultimately forms the mass culture" (SP, p. 231). Armed with this two-part axiom, Pound can transform the quirkish and idiosyncratic into the general: "The artist, the maker is always too far ahead of any revolution, or reaction, or counter-revolution or counter-reaction for his vote to have any immediate result; and no party programme ever contains enough of his programme to give him the least satisfaction. The party that follows him wins; and the speed with which they set about it, is the measure of their practical capacity and intelligence. Blessed are they who pick the right artists and makers" (SP, p. 215).[80] Thus Pound's common metaphor for the artist is the seed, the genetic synecdoche for an entire future (JM, p. 21).

Yet this solution, attractive as it is, entangles Pound in a process of endless deferral in which a real resolution of the gap between individual and collectivity is always just around the corner. It stands to reason that the artist's ideas do go into action only by becoming the unreasoning dogma of the mob of the next age, so that success and failure are simultaneous and synonymous. These ideas would, of course, have to be challenged in their turn by the artists of the next age, in an endless overturning that could never come to rest. Pound's anxieties on this score emerge in his inconsistent attitude toward what he called the "time lag." In *Guide to Kulchur,* he rails against the "time-lag" that prevents certain works from coming into currency (GK, pp. 147, 214). Somewhat inconsistently, he insists that "the truth of a given idea [is] measured by the degree and celerity wherewith it goes into action" (GK, p. 182). But a greater inconsistency lies in the incompatibility of these ideas with his insistence elsewhere that there is always a time lag, that, in fact, the truth of an artist's ideas can be measured by the resistance they cause in the boorish audience. It is quite clear that Pound seized on obscure American statesmen like Van Buren precisely because they had been ignored. Though he complained against the time lag, he also relied on it as proof that a certain set of ideas were too true to be received in their time. The time lag is therefore the temporal version of the gap between individual and collectivity, and, like that other gap, it is both necessary and reprehensible in Pound's thinking.[81]

Pound placed himself in this gap as the one individual who could recognize the future fast enough to speed its coming. He was pathetically, obtusely proud of the brush-off he had received in the halls of Congress, where, he was told, there was nothing for a man like himself to do. In Pound's mind, the inability of Congress to use him marked his importance. But there is obviously a problem in measuring one's political validity by one's lack of influence. Pound constantly preached that historical change is made by the acts of individuals. A renaissance, he said in 1914, "is a thing made by conscious propaganda" (LE, p. 220).[82] What great individuals make, however, is not their own time, which is likely to oppose them, but the next age. Speaking of Frobenius, Pound denied "that the conscious *individual* can have no effect in shaping the paideuma, or at least the next paideuma" (SP, p. 284). The qualification is of the greatest importance, for the conscious individual works in alliance with the future against the present from which it differs. But how does this future emerge from an age so bitterly opposed to its ruling ideas? How does the committed individual make his renaissance against the opposition of his time?

Pound's answers to these questions range from the hopeful to the evasive.[83] In *ABC of Economics,* he creates a beautiful picture in which "the best men . . . place their ideas and policies before the majority with such clarity and persuasiveness that the majority will accept their guidance, i.e. 'be right' " (SP, p. 247). But if the majority does not accept such guidance, it is left to derive whatever bitter pleasure there is in refusing to be right, because "A new learning imposes itself!" (GK, p. 151) In other words, writers and artists are always right because they align themselves with an ineluctable future. But what does this notion do to Pound's voluntarism? Historical change in Pound's thinking, as in Eliot's, is, it now appears, both conscious and unconscious, willed and fated. His image of the artist is of an isolated individual who by sheer will power ushers in a new age of collective greatness against the opposition of the collectivity of the present. It is the isolated individual who really represents the race, who enacts its destiny. Thus the tone of Pound's radio speeches, which constantly accuse his British and American listeners of acting against their own interests and characters. Pound, it seems in these speeches, is the only true American left, one who gained the right to speak for his country by committing treason against it.

Pound's wartime collaboration with the Axis powers represents the most extreme realization of the political ideas he shared with Yeats and Eliot, as fascism represents the most spectacular example of the contradictions they shared. In a 1934 letter to Odon Por, Pound warned, "Never lose sight of the AIM of Fascism, and its great elasticity."[84] It may seem strange to hear a totalitarian doctrine, famed for its intolerance, praised as elastic, but this was precisely its appeal to European intellectuals, especially in its early days. In contemporary political science, the elasticity of fascism is perceived as a problem imperiling classification and understanding.[85] There still is no real consensus on a definition of fascism or even on the list of regimes to be considered fascist. On the left, fascism is understood as an intensification of capitalist domination.[86] But it was often perceived at the time as anti-capitalistic.[87] And a number of modern scholars argue that fascism based its appeal on a skillful conflation of capitalism and its opposition.[88] There are similar debates about fascism and modernization and about the relationship of fascism and liberalism.[89] This inability to account for fascism is itself explanatory. As George Mosse says, "Most intellectuals' commitment to fascism was based on a very real dilemma: The society which surrounded them after 1918 did not seem to work well or even to work at all. . . ."[90] That there is disagreement about fascism means that there is disagreement as to why modern society still does not work. Fascism is so hard to categorize because it promised to resolve all such disagreements by absorbing them; it pretended to solve social controversies by taking both sides.[91]

Italian Fascism, in particular, presented itself as above partisan politics. As Por put it in 1923, "Fascism has no special theory, does not represent the triumph of any particular political system or doctrine, but rather a reaction against all those systems that have ruined Italian political life."[92] Against all previous systems, Fascism also opposed system as such, offering itself as a concrete, pragmatic alternative to the rule of political theory. Mussolini personified this alternative, a man and his intuitions against the abstractions of theory. Mussolini began his rule by boasting that he would deal with the problems of Italy "without restrictive ideological preconceptions."[93] He ended, pathetically, by instructing his advisers never to disagree with him "because contradiction only raises doubts in my mind and diverts me from what I know to be the right path, whereas my own animal instincts are always right."[94] In this sense, Mussolini represents the squalid culmination of Bradley's highly idealist doctrine that politics is intuitive instead of theoretical, just as Pound's anti-intellectualism represents an impolite version of Eliot's emphasis on unconscious communal bonds.

Pound was Mussolini's perfect acolyte, because he worshipped without qualification or doubt the instinct on which Mussolini based his claim to power. For Pound, Mussolini's genius registered in his face, "in the swiftness of mind, in the speed with which his real emotion is shown in his face, so that only a crooked man cd. misinterpret his meaning and his basic intention" (GK, p. 105).[95] Beyond the mere hero-worship evident here is Pound's own conviction that political theory is both useless and dangerous. In 1928 he claimed that "theoretical perfection in a government impels it ineluctably toward tyranny" (SP, p. 220). Freedom, as Pound saw it, advanced against theory, in the American experience as well as the Italian: "Liberty is not defendable on a static theory" (SP, p. 305).[96] Where Mussolini resembled American revolutionaries like Jefferson and Adams was in his moving forward "without regard to abstract ideas" (JM, p. 64), in fact, it might almost be said, against abstract ideas, because these lead, in Pound's mind, to fixed laws that impede the individual.

Instead of such rigid and arbitrary laws, Fascism promised what Al-

fredo Rocco, Minister of Justice, called "an organic and historic concept."[97] Fascism was to replace rule by unchanging generalizations with
rule according to local, historic realities. It was to be flexible and particular where former systems had been rigid and anachronistic. Pound noted
in the late 1930s that "In Italy there is current the adjective 'anti-storico'
to describe unlikely proposals; ideologies hung in a vacuum or contrary
to the natural order of events as conditioned by race, time and geography" (SP, p. 148). This first virtue of Mussolini's he mentions in his
introduction to *Jefferson and/or Mussolini* is "the continual gentle diatribe
against all that is 'anti-storico,' all that is against historic process" (JM,
p. v).[98] Thus Mussolini's intuitions are not wholly arbitrary, but they
achieve greatness because they are rooted in the race, time, and geography of Italy. This single personality represents in distillation a national
character, whose ruling principles are not intellectual or abstract, not
predictable and certainly not codifiable.

Though Fascism purported to be against all political systems, it should
be clear from the foregoing description that it implicitly opposed one
system above all others: liberalism. Por quotes at length a 1923 attack
Mussolini made against liberalism for claiming "an indisputable, scientific truth, applicable in all circumstances and in every time and place."[99]
Thus the attack on system, theory, and ideology is in fact an attack on
liberalism, the one system to make system itself into an ideology. Pound
joined, in his own confused fashion, in this attack: "Liberalism is a running sore, and its surviving proponents are vile beyond printable descriptions" (GK, p. 254). As Robert Casillo says, Pound tended to associate
liberalism with mercantilism and usury.[100] This association reproduces,
at a very elementary level, the common Marxist association of laissez-
faire economics and democratic liberalism, both of which are seen as
impersonal, ahistorical, abstract systems reducing humankind to mere
constituent parts.

In this opposition to liberalism, Fascism betrays traces of its origins on
the left. Por links Fascism and communism, though he realizes some of
his readers will be scandalized by the linkage, because of their common
opposition to liberalism: "Events in Russia and in Italy demonstrate the
possibility of governing altogether outside the ideology of Liberalism
and in a manner entirely opposed to it. Communism and Fascism have
nothing to do with Liberalism."[101] Por repeats a point made by Mussolini himself in 1923 and by other Fascist ideologues as late as 1932.[102]
The seemingly paradoxical association of Fascism with the very movement the threat of which drew so many to the Fascist cause can be
explained by a common contempt and hatred for liberal ideology. As
Eugen Weber says, "All oppositional movements of the 20th century
seem to have in common this opposition to a liberalism defined on the

economic plane as the application of competitive *laissez-faire* and on the political plane as the individualistic counterpart of *laissez-faire*. . . ."[103] The emergence of Mussolini from Italian socialism, the way he mingled statements of admiration with anti-Bolshevik propaganda once in power, and his bizarre return to quasi-socialist principles at Saló, all indicate the way that Fascism arose by diverging from an origin shared with the left. Zeev Sternhell contends that this drift from left to right is in fact constitutive of continental fascism.[104]

Pound's habit of lumping Lenin together with Mussolini and his overtures to the American left may therefore seem less confused than they appear on the surface. In *Jefferson and/or Mussolini* he attacks "the bourgeois demo-liberal anti-Marxian anti-fascist anti-Leninist system" (JM, p. 72). Even the ordering of this explosion of adjectives, inserting as it does the Fascist system into the hyphenated space of Marxism-Leninism, expresses the identity, in Pound's mind, of left and right in a common anti-liberalism. He sees these movements as challenges, from different directions but beginning with very similar criticisms, of the democratic status quo: "Damn the bolsheviki as much as you like, the Russian *projects* have served as stimuli BOTH to Italy and to America. Our democratic system is, for the first time, on trial against systems professing greater care for national welfare" (JM, p. 104). In other words, Fascism and communism both promise greater care for the collective good, ignored and even compromised in systems based on individualism.[105]

Pound's almost obsequious approach to the American left therefore makes a certain amount of sense, even if, as Nicholls shows, his specific attempts to define common ground became more and more incoherent.[106] As he put it himself in a radio speech in 1941, "Yes, we were once young or younger, and many of us fell for the Russian Red Revolution. Because the Marxist diagnosis was pretty near right." What went wrong, according to Pound, was the remedy: "The remedy did NOT work." But the Fascist revolution continues the common anti-liberal project, "moving toward what the decent Reds wanted" (EPS, p. 18). In 1943 he says, "I don't know that I should have any difficulties accepting a REAL Bolshevik program" (EPS, p. 294). Pound apparently sensed some such program among the so-called Fascist left, left-over syndicalists such as Edmondo Rossoni, whom Pound came to revere only after his fall from real power.[107]

The fact is, however, that Pound could not remain interested in any program because his politics were essentially anti-programmatic. He tended to rest his hopes instead on individuals. Real Bolshevism meant Lenin, just as real Fascism meant Mussolini.[108] Pound tended to see both politicians as anti-political, anti-bureaucratic, and anti-theoretical. He praised Lenin for seeing that "bureaucracy was an evil" (SP, p. 217). He praised Lenin and Mussolini together as "practical men" who could see through the cant of ideologies and theories to manifest realities.[109] In this, Pound implicitly follows a line laid down by Por, who interpreted the apparent similarities between Lenin and Mussolini to mean that theoretical differences matter little where practical men are concerned.[110] Pound's admiration for Mussolini certainly amounted to irrational hero-worship, but the irrationality was in a sense willed. The practical individual became for him the embodiment of a revolution against abstraction, theory, ideology, against everything represented by liberalism. Mussolini represented for Pound the revolt and potential triumph of the particular.

How could Pound criticize liberal individualism and at the same time incarnate his opposition in a single individual? The fact that Fascism allowed him to take such seemingly incompatible positions accounts in large part for its appeal. For Fascism, like Marxism, promised to dissolve the liberal opposition between individual and community. As J. S. Barnes put it in *The Criterion*, "Fascism, in contrast to exponents of Italian Nationalism, regards man, not in the now old-fashioned, rationalistic abstract manner of the majority of post-Renaissance philosophies, but as a concrete being compounded of both the individual and the member of society, who, in order to be in harmony with himself, must make his interests one with those of the society to which he belongs. . . ."[111] Barnes repeats a critique begun by Mussolini when he was still a socialist, a critique mounted against social contract theories and other political doctrines that postulate an abstract individual logically or ethically prior to any society.[112] Sounding the Fascist slogan that "Liberty is not a right but a duty," Pound enlists himself in this effort to see individual freedom not in opposition to social claims but rather in harmony with them (EPS, p. 313). Pound thought he had found in Fascism what Lukács thought he had found in communism, a solution to the common concern they shared over the split in liberal society of individual from collective.

It was quite possible for Fascism to offer itself to an unsuspecting world as a movement to foster individual initiative and fulfillment. Por quotes the comforting words of Francesco Meriano to the effect that "the State is not that terrible thing one learns to hate in schools, the State of stamped official forms, of examinations, and all sorts of worries, but the promoter of individual initiative. . . ."[113] How soothing such words must have been to Pound, who never stopped confronting the world of authority like a brilliant but uncontrollable schoolboy. Before assuming power, Mussolini was apt to make equally attractive statements: "We return to the individual. We support everything that exalts and amplifies the individual, that increases his liberty, well-being, and latitude of life. We oppose everything that oppresses and mortifies the individual."[114] Even under the achieved Fascist state, individual fulfillment became part of the dogma enunciated by Gentile. The state, he said, "provides the necessary . . . conditions for the existence and development of the moral personality of the individual. . . . [It] conforms to the natural end of man, that of actuating his essential personality. . . ."[115] Thus Pound, like Yeats, could take Fascism as a movement toward greater self-realization.

Gentile meant to realize the individual by dissolving what he saw as the artificial opposition between individual and community, an opposition that arose in the first place through a wholly artificial notion of the individual. Once it is understood that man is a social animal, inconceivable outside of association with other human beings, then this artificial notion falls of its own weight. According to Gentile, "Liberalism negated the state in the interests of the particular individual; Fascism reaffirms the state as the true reality of the individual. And if liberty is to be attributed to real man, and not to that abstraction of individualistic liberalism, then Fascism is for liberty."[116] Thus Fascism could present itself as favoring freedom, democracy, even egalitarianism, without any of the centrifugal forces then tearing at most European nations. It claimed to resolve the tension between freedom and community, *homme* and *citoyen,* by what P. Vita-Finzi calls "a brilliant philosophical riddle." In Gentile's words, "the only freedom that can be taken seriously is that of the State and of the individual within the State."[117]

Pound was thoroughly bemused by this riddle, almost as if he had been provided with a solution too elegant for his uses. When he calls in *Guide to Kulchur* for an individualism "without any theoretical and ideological bulwarks" (GK, p. 52), he is apparently calling, like Gentile, for an antiliberal individualism, one founded on a particular historical context and not on ahistorical abstractions. Thus he includes in *Guide* a virtual paraphrase of Gentile's dictum: "The state exists for the individual, but in our time the individual who does not deem his own acts and thought in certain ways and degrees up and down as to their use to the state . . . is an inferior individual" (GK, p. 190). In "A Visiting Card," written in Italian in 1942, he provides a visual image of this ideal relationship: "A thousand candles together blaze with intense brightness. No one candle's light damages another's. So is the liberty of the individual in the ideal and fascist state" (SP, p. 306).

Yet Pound continued in these same years to write as if Fascism had merely achieved in a perfected form the very individualism postulated by the liberal governments. Throughout *Jefferson and/or Mussolini* he praises Italian Fascism for liberating the individual from excessive government interference: "Mussolini is NOT a fanatical statalist wanting the state to blow the citizen's nose and monkey with the individual's diet" (JM, p. 69).[118] He refers quite positively in the radio speeches to "the ole Rights of Man," and even suggests that the Fascist regime "is the continuation of the strife for the rights of man" (EPS, pp. 32, 316). And he complains, in the same book in which he says that the state and individual are interdependent, that American politics ignores "the demarcation between state and individual" (GK, p. 156). In fact, Pound proclaimed in 1933 that "*the problem of our time is to find the border between public and private affairs*" (SP, p. 240). It seems as if Pound had heard and absorbed Gentile's beautiful riddle, but that it was impossible for him to phrase the claims of the individual in any way that did not reestablish its opposition to the community. These inconsistencies might be explained by Pound's lack of interest in intellectual consistency or by his political innocence, but it might also be that he unwittingly exposes the shallowness of Gentile's solution, for Fascism in practice proved rather different from the paradise of freedom he offered.

One of the practical measures by which Fascism promised to resolve the liberal opposition of individual and community was a change in representation. According to Por, "Parliamentary rule, as we know it, based on universal suffrage, is democratic in theory only. . . ." Since there is no essential similarity between the people and their representative, representation becomes a matter of mere mathematics and government is estranged from the governed. Thus, according to Por, one of the most important reforms proposed by Fascism is the institution of "Vocational Parliaments," which will "represent all functions in the country" *as* functions.[119] In this way, a synecdochal form of representation replaces the purely metonymic one characteristic of liberal democracy, and an organic organization supplants a mechanical one. Pound very strongly favored such a change. He says of Mussolini, "He wants a council where *every kind* of man will be represented by some bloke of his own profession, by some deputy who has identical interests and a direct knowledge of the needs and temptations of a given profession" (JM, p. v).[120]

In principle, Pound finds in Fascist plans for vocational representation the sort of mediation Hegel hoped to interpose between the individual and the state. In this, Fascism evinced its debt to guild socialism, a debt that allowed Pound to see in Fascism a plan to decentralize society, organizing it laterally by vocation rather than vertically by abstract suffrage. Understood in this way, Fascism may have seemed the actualization of the hopes of Major Douglas, who taught Pound to oppose concentrations of economic power and to favor "decentralised local authority" (SP, p. 208).[121] But in practice, of course, Fascism accomplished just the opposite, and Pound accommodated himself by seeing the central authority as a kind of coordinator: "GUILD organization, coordinated at the top, that being the only place you CAN correlate . . ." (EPS, p. 112).[122] Such statements seem particularly disingenuous, because it must have been quite clear even to someone as isolated by geography and armored by preconception as Pound that Mussolini was rather more than a coordinator. The very vagueness of the authority Pound grants to "the top" frees it to exercise power to almost any degree.

Fascism appealed to Pound precisely because it made such intellectual inconsistency painlessly easy. There was a time, early on to be sure, when Mussolini presented himself as the advocate of a minimal state, even of a laissez-faire state.[123] Pound clung to these early pretensions for years, announcing in 1933 that Fascism envisioned "the day when the state could sit back and do nothing" (JM, p. vii). For him, the essential principle on which Fascism organized society was that "everything that can be done by informal and individual effort should be so done and that the state should govern only where and when necessary" (JM, p. 115).[124] Even as late as 1943, he continued to claim that Fascism had realized the "professed Jeffersonian ideal. That of governing LEAST" (EPS, p. 287). One of the cant slogans of the radio speeches is local control, which Pound presents as if it were a Fascist principle opposed by the Allies (EPS, p. 369).

At such times, Pound seems pathetically deluded, and yet he cannot have been unaware of the totalitarian nature of the Fascist regime because he specifically praised it, sometimes almost in the same breath in which he called for decentralization and local control. In *Guide to Kulchur,* he says, "In Italy the trouble is not too much statal authority but too little" (GK, p. 254). This book, published in 1938, is full of attacks on schismatics who prevent the state from becoming "an organism capable of containing all faith, or the constructive urges of all" (GK, p. 332). This is what Pound means when he calls this book totalitarian, that it is dedicated to a conception of "the whole people" (GK, p. 29). Within a year of its publication, he was quoting Hitler on the importance of "INTERNAL coherence."[125] This conception of the state is not just different from but is actively opposed to that of the minimal state. Mussolini himself coined the chillingly apt aphorism: "Everything within the state, nothing outside the state, and nothing against the state." This means, as Mussolini says, that the state "is not the night watchman," not merely the passive guarantor of the rights of its citizens.[126] It is instead, the "ethical state," the embodiment of all the means and ends of the individuals within it. The contrast could not be stronger between this sort of "positive freedom" and the negative freedom Pound praises elsewhere.

Revulsion against fascism now runs so strong that it is almost impossible to recall why it was once so seductive. Hindsight into its internal contradictions makes it seem intellectually as well as morally shameful. And so it was. But allowing men like Pound to avoid contradiction was the source of its power. Fascism promised to fulfill the individual and to restrain individualism, to set free localities and professions and to meld every group into one great whole, to liberate the particular from iron abstractions and to find one great abstraction to fulfill every particular. In practice, of course, Mussolini had to make choices, which tended as time went on to resolve these contradictions in favor of totalitarian centralization. Pound managed to preserve his contradictions far longer, in part by studiously avoiding the practical and in part by idolizing Mussolini as the epitome of practical efficiency. Pound focused such intense regard on Mussolini because it was only in this man that the contradictory promises of fascism retained their illusory balance.

Gentile took Hegel's notion of the nation as a "spiritual totality" constituted in a "single being" to mean that a single individual might incarnate the nation. In Italy, this individual was Mussolini, to whom the crowds proclaimed, "You are Italy."[127] Thus the Fascist state did in fact reconcile individual and community, but only in a curiously restricted way. For there was really only one individual with whom the state was in full agreement and that was Mussolini. All other individuals had to subordinate themselves in some way in order to join in the great spiritual individual that was Fascist Italy. Mussolini resolved in himself, on a metaphorical level, what could not be resolved in reality. Thus the Fascist state had all the hallmarks of an individual – it was capricious and temperamental – while also representing to the country an impersonal order. That Mussolini was clearly one – one man – allowed him to represent the organic unity many in Italy longed for.[128] That he was famously mercurial and inconsistent allowed Mussolini to present his regime as anti-theoretical, pragmatic, open to the individual instance as against abstract generalities. Pound idolized Mussolini because he represented both romantic individualism and impersonal order, thus allowing an indefinite postponement of the inevitable clash between them.[129]

Yeats had been attracted to Mussolini for precisely the same reasons, and, though Eliot always disdained Mussolini, probably because of those very personal qualities that attracted Pound, the dictator represents a logical realization of his desire to incarnate a whole culture in the few. Yeats and Eliot came close to fascism because it represents one very prominent exponent of their program to rejoin the individual and the collective in a historically determined union. But there were other, quite different exponents of the same ambition, socialism among them. European history of the time provides a number of examples of socialists who became fascist sympathizers, like Henri de Man, and of cultural reactionaries like the young Lukács, who became communists.[130] Pound left his ambiguous beginnings to become one of the period's most notorious fascist sympathizers, whereas Yeats and Eliot did not, for reasons that may say a good deal about both Pound and fascism.

Yeats and Eliot, for all their dissatisfactions, were solidly rooted in a particular society in a way that Pound was not. His relationship to Italy differs from Yeats's ancestral tie to Ireland and Eliot's no less ancestral tie to England in obvious ways. Pound was the ultimate freebooter, personally wilder and politically more eclectic than his friends. He was far more the rambunctious individual, as Eliot learned over and over in the 1930s while trying to manage his friend's erratic contributions to the *Criterion*. Where Yeats serves in Ireland's Senate, Pound was politely patronized in America's. It may be for this very reason, because of the very extremity of Pound's individualism, that he required a correspondingly more extreme authority and came to idolize the conflation of individual and authority in Mussolini.

Just as Eliot and Yeats were in some ways too conservative to become fascists, Pound became one precisely because he was a modernist and because he needed a system that promised to back modernism with a strong set of eternal values that would somehow leave modernism untouched. Sternhell, among others, has argued that fascism triumphs where the more traditional forces of reaction are weak, not where they are strong, and he shows how there can be deep antipathy between conservatism and fascism.[131] Pound is, in a sense, a personal embodiment of the same principle. It was because he had shed most of the traditional ties to his own country, because he lived in defiance of all conventional conservative values, that his search for authority took him to such extremes. This might, at some risk, be rephrased in a positive way, to say that Pound became a fascist where Yeats and Eliot did not because he was a more uncompromising, though perhaps less intellectually rigorous, critic of his own society.

Pound was certainly the only one of the three to take economics at all seriously. Yet the contradictions in Pound's appreciation for fascism appear most obviously where he expended the most effort, in his attempts to conceive a modern political economy. Pound was, at least in one sense, profoundly anti-capitalistic. Beginning with the "effects of capitalism on art and letters" (SP, p. 232), which, needless to say, he found deleterious, Pound proceeded to the conclusion that the capitalist system was nothing more or less than "black death" (JM, p. 128).[132] Yet Pound defines capitalism in such a way as to minimize the effect even of such shrill condemnations as these. The mere emphasis on finance capital as opposed to industrial capital exempts a good deal of the system Marx sought to change,[133] but Pound distinguishes further between capital and property, which, he claims, does not oppress. "Therefore: it would be possible to attack the 'rights' or 'privileges' of capital without attacking the rights or privileges of property" (SP, p. 233). In other words, Pound wants to own things himself while attacking the system built on the principle of private ownership.

The most revealing of these distinctions is the one Pound draws between capitalists and producers. History, as Pound sees it in 1944, is a "struggle between the Producers and the Falsifiers of Bookkeeping . . ." (SP, p. 173). Such falsification is the work of capitalist monopolizers, who produce nothing but gain all their lucre by siphoning off what is produced by others. In 1941, he challenged his American listeners to "separate the starvers from the producers, the growers, the makers," among which he naturally included artists and writers (EPS, pp. 17, 294). This distinction is an old one for Pound, but the terminology of these wartime statements clearly betrays Mussolini's influence. In the radio speeches, Pound uses the concept of producers in the same way Mussolini did to coopt the communist attack on capital. According to Mussolini, producers were all those who were economically useful regardless of class; it was therefore in the worker's interest to cooperate with capital, the captains of which were also producers.[134] Pound draws a factual and a moral distinction between mercantilist capitalism and industrial capitalism, which produces. The moral distinction rests on the primitive ethic that the fruits belong to the producer.[135]

How can this strong moral emphasis on productivity be squared with the common charge in recent criticism that Pound ignores the issue of production?[136] It is hard to argue with the essential point made in such criticisms, that Pound sees as distributional problems that are in reality imbalances created by a particular mode of production.[137] It also seems true that, for all his talk of revolution, Pound criticizes capitalism from a point of view so limited as to make revolution unnecessary. But this does not mean, as some critics have argued, that Pound ignores production because his ideal society is static and agrarian.[138] For Pound was capable of at least mouthing the essentials of Marxist analysis: "Any set of social doctrines is valid only *in relation* to modes of production (communication, distribution)."[139] And, as Jean-Michel Rabaté says, he is quite comfortable with the idea that the "production of ideas" is economically related to other kinds of production.[140] Pound's manifest attention to production, even his moral valuation of it, biases him toward an open-ended, developmental model of history and a kind of society quite at odds with his equally strong conservatism. Here the conflict between revolution and reaction emerges in terms of political economy.

These terms are Italy's as much as they are Pound's. It is just as difficult to separate Pound from Italy as it is to separate Yeats from Ireland, and, in many ways, the two countries act out the same political drama. At the advent of Fascism, Italy was only thinly industrialized, and it had been independent for only a relatively short time. It was a country, like Ireland, for which "the shift from non-modern to modern status is the central issue."[141] A.F.K. Organski says in his analysis of Italian modernization that only fully industrialized countries can turn their attention to problems of distribution, whereas countries like Italy must concentrate on production, otherwise there is simply nothing to distribute.[142] Whether Organski's model represents an ineluctable reality or not, it does correspond to the situation in Italy as the Fascists saw it. Even the earliest proto-fascists had argued against socialist programs of redistribution in favor of increased production, and Mussolini was to make production a basic Fascist article of faith.[143] In 1919, he coined the term "productive socialism," which was to become in fact the earliest version of Italian Fascism. At the inaugural meeting of the movement, Mussolini made equal claims for "the reality of production and the reality of the nation," suggesting a parallel between productivity and national self-realization. This emphasis did not diminish when Fascism achieved its domination. As Gregor puts it, "Fascist insistence on the primacy of production was constant throughout the Fascist period."[144]

Greater productivity could only be realized through modernization, which meant, according to Gregor, "an industrialized Italy, with flourishing urban centers, secular political control of community life . . . and a rationalized bureaucratic infrastructure."[145] Productivity, in other words, meant progress, which is, as Nolte suggests, inherently revolutionary: "Does not the 'developmental dictatorship' itself, with its eyes on the future, its irreverence for the past, and its concern with practical tasks, stand to some extent 'to the Left'?"[146] Even if the glorification of productivity tended to legitimate capitalism, it could hardly do so without also unleashing all the other energies and expectations that Marx says it is the role of capitalism to free from the structures of feudalism.[147] But this is exactly where Fascism confronted its contradictions. As Alan Cassels puts it, Fascism wanted "modernization but without the attendant evils of liberalism, democracy, and even socialism."[148] In attempting to modernize while leaving traditional class structures in place, Fascism took on incompatible tasks. It promised to the country the fruits of capitalism while depending heavily on a class, the petit bourgeoisie, traditionally mistrustful of big capital.[149] It glorified the producer, the man of action and energy, while bringing to Italian society a greater rigidity than it had ever known. In doing so, it acted out on a broad scale the political economy of modern anti-modernism.

Pound tried desperately to perfect the same economy on a smaller scale. The very figures of speech he uses to praise Mussolini betray his delight in the energy of modernization: "There are no brakes on the engine" (JM, p. 24). He lauds the Russians for knowing "enough to WANT factories and to want 'em in a hurry" (JM, p. 39). And he continued to justify the Fascist regime on the grounds of progress and efficiency, for having electrified the trains, drained swamps, and increased grain yields.[150] At the very same time, however, he tried to enlist Mus-

solini in a project of reactionary anti-modernism. He compared Mussolini to Jefferson in that they both "hate machinery or at any rate the idea
of cooping up men and making 'em all into UNITS, unit production. . ." (JM, p. 63). And he emphasized, especially in the radio
speeches, the moral value of the "homestead" and the rural life continuous with it.[151] One of the attractions of Fascism for Pound was obviously
the way it allowed him to take up such inconsistent positions, to be very
loud on both sides of a question.

For Pound, a golden moment in the story of Fascism came in 1934
when Mussolini declared "that the problem of production was solved,
and that they could now turn their minds to distribution" (JM, p. vii).[152]
Pound may be referring to grain production, the "battle for grain" having been won by 1934, when Italy became self-sufficient in this respect,
or to industrial production, which had by 1935 finally recovered from the
Depression.[153] In either case, Mussolini's declaration becomes so important to Pound because it allows him to resolve, at least in appearance, the
contradictions in his own political economy. For the shift to distribution
is not primarily a reactionary shift away from industrial production. It
represents instead the triumphant arrival of Italy at a stage of tech-
nological and industrial modernism. It is science, according to Pound's
account of Mussolini's speech, that "has multiplied the means of producing plenty" (JM, p. viii). "Sane engineers," Pound says in *ABC of Economics*, "tell us that the question of production is solved" (SP, p. 234). The
turn to distribution, in Pound's mind, is made possible by the accomplishments of modern industrial technology, which Italy did not possess
until 1934.[154]

According to Organski, distribution is the concern of societies in
which capitalism is an achieved fact and of stable pre-capitalist societies.[155] Pound's vision of Italy fuses these two types so as to suggest
that the productive forces of capitalism achieve a stable, even closed,
society in which distribution is the only remaining concern. He often
celebrates the explosive changes brought by technology: "During the
past twenty years the fundamental capacities of humanity for supplying
itself with everything it wants have changed at a geometrical ratio out-
soaring anything previous man had guessed at" (JM, p. 76). But the result
of this power is not, in Pound's mind, incessant change. Instead, Pound
foresees a life of increased leisure, as if capitalism had made its feverish
efforts only so as to offer its workers a few more days off: "Now-a-days,
in normal times, the necessity of working as formerly does not exist"
(SP, p. 178). Curiously, Pound usually envisioned this happy, stable life
in agrarian terms: "As long as men face the responsibility of feeding
themselves and their families from what they can get from the earth, by
planting seed, reaping crops, raising cattle, there is NOT any great con-

fusion" (EPS, p. 176). Fascist Italy became such a persuasive example for Pound because it seemed to fuse the incompatible parts of his social vision, combining vigorous industrialism with an agrarian ethos. For Pound wanted to believe that modernization would cancel itself out, that industrial development would bring into being a society resembling the closed societies of the feudal agrarian past.[156]

Pound seizes on Mussolini's 1934 declaration because it seems to him to represent a historical fulcrum at which production tips and gives way to distribution. Production, in this sense, cancels itself out, making further advances unnecessary. This curious political economy represents a developed version of Pound's earliest historical theories in which he saw historical change as achieving its own end. In 1934, Mussolini succeeds, through a campaign of modernization, in bringing history to a successful conclusion.[157] The version of history at work here resembles Eliot's in "The Metaphysical Poets," where the modernization of poetry returns it to an eternal standard.

The inherent instability of this vision of a self-canceling modernity emerges in Pound's attempts to define money. Pound lavished his most vituperative language on monopolists and hoarders, real and imaginary, the worst of which were, he felt, the monopolists of money (SP, p. 182).[158] In Pound's opinion, money had but one purpose, to circulate and thus to increase prosperity. The faster it circulated, the better.[159] He thus cast about for a kind of money that could not be hoarded, money that would observe a minimum speed limit, "money that cries to be spent within a given period of time" (SP, p. 277). If, as many recent considerations of Pound have suggested, money is a society's most fundamental sign system, then perishable money would provide society with a constant demonstration of the production and decay of signs. There can be no motivated signs in such a system because the link between sign and referent is in constant jeopardy. In fact, Pound celebrates a purely conventional semiosis of money, and he condemns attempts to conceive of money as anything more than a momentary representation of value.[160]

The economy implied by such a theory of money is developmental, productive, and open-ended. Pound's theories imply that the economy of his perfect state would thrive on constant change and on the free expression of the will of individuals. Such an economy might even be called inherently democratic, because the free circulation of money and the impossibility of hoarding would theoretically break down stratified social relationships and feudal bonds.[161] It would certainly be an economy of incessant modernization. Paradoxically, this is just what Pound feared. He covered this "open" economy with another, closed, economy, whose stability was guaranteed by a monetary unit with a truly motivated relationship to the goods it represented.

The inconsistencies in Pound's concept of historical value reappear in his attempts to find a basis for the value of money. The idea that value is conventional, determined by and limited to a particular society, is one of the bases of historicism. If money is "a symbol of collaboration . . . of work done within a system" (SP, p. 311), then its value rests on the strength of the agreement behind that collaboration. In other words, money gets its value "Not by nature, but by custom," in Pound's crucial paraphrase of Aristotle (SP, p. 329). Like all other values, according to historicism, it is contingent and specific.[162] But Pound recoiled from the obvious implications of this definition of money, as he had from the similar definition of historical value in general. Making money dependent on the agreement of a society seemed fine when that agreement was itself historically conditioned, the expression of centuries of tradition. In the present, however, political agreement is often arrived at quite differently, sometimes by mere vote, which would leave the value of money and of the goods it buys open to the sort of market Pound had always hated and feared.

For Pound, letting the market determine value was to slide into contradiction. Value in his mind was qualitative, whereas the market measured mere quantities. Like Lukács, he saw industrial capitalism as the degradation of quality to the level of quantity.[163] Thus there had to be some external guarantor of value beyond the votes of the mob of consumers. At times, Pound chose nature as this basis: "With her wonderful efficiency nature sees to it that the circulation of material capital and its fruits is maintained, and that what comes out of the soil goes back into the soil with majestic rhythm, despite human interference" (SP, p. 346). Thus Pound describes an ideal closed economy without the instability that accompanies human political agreements.

Pound's most common definition of monetary value superimposes this closed economy on the open one. Money, he says in 1942, "is a symbol of a collaboration between nature, the state, and an industrious populace" (SP, p. 327). As Nicholls says, this superimposition works for Pound because he does not see the actual order and the social order in essential conflict.[164] But he was certainly prescient enough to see that the political order often diverged from what he felt was natural and that a modern industrial workforce was not always industrious in the sense he meant. What guaranteed the congruence of nature and society was the firm direction of "the few": "It is nature, the actual existence of goods, or the possibility of producing them, that really determines the capacity of the state. Yet it resides above all in the will and the physical force of the people. And the will becomes concentrated in the few" (SP, p. 312). The few mediate between nature and society, making possible the coordination of the open and the closed economies. Ultimately, the few came to mean Mussolini alone, whose sovereign word guaranteed the lira: "The lira is not based on gold but is at the discretion of His Excellency, the Leader of the government."[165] An originally historicist definition of value has come to rest in total despotism. Though Pound sees Mussolini as the mediator between nature and his people, he in fact betrays the gap between them, between the two definitions of value and the two economies, a gap that could only be closed by executive fiat.

The open economy, with its appeals and its threats, has a racial counterpart. Rabaté points out the connection between economics and race in the ancient pun on the term *tokos,* which means offspring both financially and biologically.[166] An unrestrained economy is one that allows free circulation, even free reproduction, which has grave implications for a historical conservatism. For the open economy would be racially modern, that is to say, heterogeneous and in constant flux, whereas the closed economy would be racist in its exclusivity. Pound's glorification of productivity could not escape these implications, though he covered it with a racism uncommonly severe.

According to Hyam Maccoby, "Ideological fallacies have an uncanny way of showing themselves in the form of anti-Semitism."[167] For Pound, as for many anti-Semites, the Jews represent both capitalism and its opponents. Of course, Pound adds his voice to the endless Western vendetta against the "Hebraic money system" (SP, p. 351), by which he means both usury in particular and capitalism in general. But Pound also indulges in another caricature, that of the Jew as revolutionary anti-capitalist. He says that "Communism with its dictatorship of the proletariat is merely barbarous and Hebrew" (GK, p. 270). During the war this strain became especially shrill: "The Bolshevik anti-morale comes out of the Talmud, which is the dirtiest teaching that any race ever codified. The Talmud is the one and only begetter of the Bolshevik system" (EPS, p. 117).[168] Finally, Pound collapses capitalism and communism together as dual aspects of the international Jewish conspiracy. He argues in a radio speech of 1942 "that Bolshevism pretended to be an attack on capital, that it was financed by New York Jew millionaires, and that it, in effect, attacked private ownership of land and of living space" (EPS, pp. 175–176). According to Nolte, Mussolini had made the same fantastic charge, accusing Lenin "of reintroducing capitalism into Russia" and of being part of the "joint efforts of Jewish bankers in London and New York."[169]

The Jewish figment makes possible a critique so illogical that it would otherwise evaporate of its own. Capitalism is blamed for dominating society, but also for having brought the proletariat into being as a threat against the stability of society. The uncomfortable position of fascism, both capitalistic and anti-capitalistic, is exposed here. But it is also true that fascism uses the specter of the Jew to obscure a contradiction it was itself exacerbating. The dual critique against modern society as regimented and centralized but also fragmented and anarchistic does rest on some basis in actuality. Fascism came to power in part by claiming to resolve this contradiction, but the anti-Semitic campaigns of such as Pound confess its inability to do so. Anti-Semitism allows such as Pound to continue to criticize modernity from incompatible points of view without making good on fascism's claim to resolve them into one.

The relationship of modernity and race is, at the most basic level, full of conflicts that Pound's own position made unavoidable. As Casillo shows, Pound excoriates the Jews both as atavistic, unchanging traditionalists and as carriers of the bacillus of modernity.[170] The inconsistency rests on a more basic contradiction. Gregor maintains that racial determinism "ran counter to Fascism's philosophy of ethical voluntarism and personal heroism."[171] In other words, racism, resting as it does on a belief in unchanging characteristics determined by biology, is fundamentally anti-modern, because it would prohibit individually willed change. Perhaps for this reason, among others, Mussolini resisted German theories of racial homogeneity, advertising Italy as the "product of diverse ethnic fusions."[172] Mussolini may have been uneasy about German racial theories because Italy was always a potential target of them.[173] On the other hand, it was hard to seriously propose a totalitarian system, unified in a single will, that had any room for what Paolo Orano called "self-regarding sects."[174] The record of Italian Fascism on this subject is markedly inconsistent because race exposed general inconsistencies in a regime that promised both rapid advancement into the future and quasi-religious reliance on tradition.

Pound himself was even more confused than the regime he admired. A passage in one of the radio speeches shows, in its tortured logic and syntax, the difficulty of his position: "Time, geography, history, that is, the age old conditioning of a place and a people, affected by TRUTH, by natural forces, made by Human WILL directed on forces" (EPS, p. 152). Here he makes racial character the result of nature and of human will somehow exerted on nature. In doing so, he exposes his own divided allegiance to traditions rooted in genes and soil and to a modernity that would have to be made by individual exertion. The radio speeches expose another, much older, contradiction, that between identity and difference: "You make a race by homogeneity and by avoiding INbreeding" (EPS, p. 132). Pound does not tell his listeners how to accomplish this neat trick because he could not. And his own position in Italy held him poised on the very edge of the contradiction.

Except for the years in St. Elizabeth's, Pound lived his entire life in rented quarters far from his ancestral homeland. He supported himself in

Italy on money received from abroad.[175] The very fact of the radio broadcasts, which were motivated at least in part by financial considerations, betrayed the thinness of Pound's connection with Italy, for he had no other way to make his living except by telling the country of his birth fantastic stories about his country of adoption. In this situation, Pound could have only one consistent position on the issue of race and tradition. The very existence of the broadcasts implies that isolation is bad for a society, and Pound made this point explicitly many times: "isolations of this kind are BAD for a nation" (EPS, p. 114). One of the most amazing sub-themes running through these quintessentially intolerant speeches is the necessity of racial tolerance: "What races can dwell together without constantly inciting other races to start fraternal slaughter, and civil assassination?" (EPS, p. 173). In many of the broadcasts, Pound clucks his tongue over the way "people pick on minorities" (EPS, p. 387). In a truly sadistic reversal, he blames racial intolerance on those he was doing his best to make its victims: "So the BBC says you must hate the Germans, that is regular Semite logic" (EPS, p. 295).[176]

Pound's own life as a cosmopolitan enabled him to see the advantages of a tolerant, heterogeneous society. Yet, at the same time, he rails against cosmopolitanism. "Breed GOOD, and preserve the race," he says is the first point of a Nazi program he entirely supports (EPS, p. 140). The melting pot, he tells his American audience, "may have been a noble experiment. I very much doubt it. At any rate it has flopped, it is a failure" (EPS, p. 157). When political policies come, not out of ideologies but out of "blood, bone and endocrines," then racial homogeneity becomes necessary to political coherence.[177] Thus, according to Nicholls, "Pound welcomed the Italian Race Laws of 1938 because these seemed to him necessary to protect Mussolini's achievement from alien and subversive elements."[178] There is no explanation as to why Pound himself was not an alien element. In fact, his pathetic attempts to appear American, the cracker-barrel wisdom and the exaggerated American drawl of his speeches on Italian radio, only dramatized the painful fact of his isolation. Pound preached the wisdom of the homestead to a population of listeners who were defending his ancestral homeland from the country of his allegiance.

These contradictions show how little able Pound was to solve the problem he had taken up many years before in "Provincialism the Enemy." For thirty years he remained caught between the same alternatives of identity and difference and his virulent anti-Semitism is an index of how completely Fascism had failed to resolve the dichotomy. On one hand, Pound represents the Jews as invasive and disintegrative, the epitome of the rootless cosmopolitan. He warns his American listeners, "The danger is not that you WILL BE invaded, it is that you HAVE BEEN invaded" (EPS, p. 86) by "4 to 8 million invaders, all part of a widely distributed RACE" (EPS, p. 100). The Jew, in such speeches, is a parasite, a poison, a contamination: "Not a jot or tittle of the hebraic alphabet can pass into the text without danger of contaminating it" (SP, p. 320).[179] On the other hand, Pound sees the Jews as too cohesive, as "HIGHLY organized" (EPS, p. 100) and threatening to the rugged individual: "I dunno where the rugged American INDIVIDUAL is going to git FUNDS to combat 'em" (EPS, p. 4). As Rabaté says, the Jews are criticized in *The Cantos* as incestuous, dominated by the family, a very odd criticism coming from the champion of the homestead.[180] Such inconsistencies show the burden the Jews are called upon to bear in this analysis as carriers of all the unresolved contradictions left by fascism. Every problem that fascism purported to solve simply by shirking it reappears in the anti-Semitism of such as Pound.

The virulence of the radio speeches can be partially explained (it can never perhaps be fully explained) by the fact that Pound comes to blame the Jews both for making the speeches necessary and for making them fail. This is to say that the Jews are to blame for Pound's own isolation, which is emblematic of the lack of a cohesive tradition in England or America, but also for the conformist indifference that drove him from those countries in the first place. By all rights, the speeches should be unnecessary. If nations are motivated by racial agreements embedded in blood and bone then speeches over the radio could have no real effect and no real purpose. The very fact that Pound must hector his overseas listeners means that they do not now enjoy the conditions that would make agreement with him possible. This, Pound claims, is the fault of the Jews: "Their kike postal spies and obstructors, kikarian and/or others annoy me by cuttin' off my normal mental intercourse with my colleagues" (EPS, p. 7). With Jews in charge of all organs of communication "what chance of gettin' together or agreein' on any policy?" (EPS, p. 159). The pointless rhetorical violence and the deadening repetitiousness of the radio speeches come from this double bind. If the speeches are necessary, then they can hardly have any effect, because the sort of commonalty they demand could only precede agreement and not result from it. Thus Pound puts verbal genocide where argumentation should be. The result is a massive, if veiled, confession of political and intellectual failure.

Violence, even if it is only verbal, becomes an essential component of Pound's fascism. The unstable nature of the fascist compromise is expressed in violence. As Eugen Weber puts it, "The Fascist must move forward all the time; but just because precise objectives are lacking he can never stop. . . ."[181] An anti-theoretical, anti-ideological movement finally makes an ideology out of dynamism, which then rigidifies in paradox. Constant movement, tumult, conflict, keep the ideological contradictions of the movement obscure, postponing resolution for an indeterminate future. For the revolutionary and modernizing aspects of fascism always threaten to open up just what the movement most wants to close, so that there is an endless escalating process of conflict and deferral.

Pound's poetry drove him forward toward the same dilemma. Brooker claims that "the completion of both Pound's poem and Italian Fascism manifestly require a similarly unqualified faith in the driving will towards order of the constructive simple personalities at their centres."[182] But the "driving will" is by definition disruptive of the very "order" it seeks. Will makes individual and dynamic what order rigidifies as stable and impersonal. The Cantos, according to Sieburth, divide in the same way, between "excess, expenditure, and intertextual dispersion" and an order "that seeks to contain and chasten this anarchic or nomadic proliferation through an authoritarian and didactic reduction of diversity to a single truth."[183] The Cantos must keep going in part because they cannot resolve this tension, which is political as well as formal.

Pound had begun The Cantos with two rather different models of history, one open, sequential, perhaps even aleatory, the other closed, static, and symmetrical. The early portions of this poem written in installments were called "drafts," yet the drafts gradually became finished texts by default. For many years, the poem depended on a gigantic gamble, on Pound's faith that he could "get down all the colours or elements I want for the poem" and then "bring them into some sort of design and architecture later."[184] Pound would forestall inquisitive readers by warning them to wait until the whole was done, but as late as 1960 he was still groping: "I must clarify obscurities; I must make clearer definite ideas or dissociations."[185] His indecision did, however, pay a valuable dividend. It allowed him to poise The Cantos between a radically disordered method and the promise of final order and thus to compromise for a time between two different models of his own history, one progressive and modern, based on constant change and contingency, the other stable and ancient.[186]

Pound certainly felt that the two methods would meet someday in a perfect Paradiso. But his belief was, as Rabaté says, "savagely rebutted by a history whose evolution was dramatically ironic."[187] Having made the poem an all-purpose repository for his constantly developing interests, Pound could hardly close it off from a life that became more and more disordered. It seems only appropriate that, having tied his poem to the tail of the Axis powers, in an obvious hope for the order it could not achieve on its own, Pound should have had to suffer the utter wreck of these regimes, which might also have wrecked his poem. That the defeat of his side instead saved the poem is the final political paradox of Pound's life.

4. THE PISAN CANTOS

In 1944, Pound wrote, "For forty years I have schooled myself, not to write an economic history of the U.S. or any other country, but to write an epic poem which begins 'In the Dark Forest' crosses the Purgatory of human error, and ends in the light. . ." (SP, p. 167). This plan, as Chace succinctly puts it, was "overwhelmed by events."[188] Pound's poem, which had been growing more and more totalitarian in its form, was suddenly stopped short of its goal. The theory of history on which it depended, a theory in which history has an essential continuity, an equilibrium that simply rinses out error, was subjected to a ruthless test.

The Cantos would almost certainly have faced such a crisis even without the war as Pound's omnivorous literary appetite, his desire to explain everything, brought him nearer and nearer to the law enunciated by Adorno: "Works of art become relative precisely because they cannot help pretending to absolute."[189] But the circumstances in which the poet was forced to redirect his poem give the crisis a political as well as a poetic significance. The *Pisan Cantos* are so various and contradictory, so open, in a way, precisely because Pound does not repent, because he attempts to keep in play the fascist balance of contraries, assimilating even the defeat into its dialectic of freedom and discipline, chance and necessity. Yet in his very attempt to learn as little as possible from defeat, Pound confesses its most significant lessons.

Like much of Pound's earlier work, these cantos are explicitly concerned with the relation of particulars to generalities. In Canto 74, he quotes Aristotle's dictum that philosophy is not for young men because "their generalities cannot be born from a sufficient phalanx of particulars" (74/441).[190] At times, these cantos seem to long for a relationship of general and particular that goes "past metaphor" (82/526) to identity, as in the passage borrowed from Whitman where he links humankind and the earth sexually – "lie into the earth to the breast bone, to the left shoulder" – and then historically: "man, earth : two halves of the tally" (82/526). This physical conjuncture represents a relationship of the individual to the vast and ancient earth that is so close metaphor is no longer necessary. The conjuncture has a political dimension as well. The one who "joins with the process" is, like the struggling ant he sees near his tent in the DTC, a "boon companion to equity" (83/531). "When all the equities are gathered together," he says, "it springeth up vital," but "if deed be not ensheaved and garnered in the heart / there is inanition" (83/531). Unity among companions, like unity of human faculties within the individual, means political health. The image of the sheaves is one of individuals gathered into a greater strength and health than they can have alone. Though the image need not evoke the fascist bundle of sticks or rods, it should indicate the essential political doctrine of fascism, which Pound repeats in Canto 78: "not a right but a duty" (78/479). Against the liberal doctrine of individual rights, Pound poses the fascist principle of collective duty.

The fall of Mussolini is the breaking of this relationship between particular and general or individual and community. Pound's image for this reversal, the head down crucifixion of Mussolini, is also one of the many usurping the power of the one: "That maggots shd / eat the dead bullock" (74/425). The beautiful passage on the same page in which Pound asks "what whiteness will you add to this whiteness, what candor?" is a hymn to the metaphysical perfection suggested by Mussolini's "candor." This becomes clear when Pound quotes himself several cantos later: "'What shall add to this whiteness?' / and as to poor old Benito / one had a safety-pin / one had a bit of string, one had a button / all of them so far beneath him" (80/495). Mussolini is the whole of which the lower orders, the underlings, can only possess the bits and pieces. He is one of the "authenticities disputed by parasites" (74/448), dispute being by its very nature divisive, whereas Pound sees Mussolini's authenticity as a physical attribute, the strength of the ox, the perfection of whiteness as a color, which are joined a few pages into Canto 74 in the white ox he sees on the road to Pisa (74/428).

The bovine imagery has a cruel return when Pound uses it against the Jews: "The yidd is a stimulant, and the goyim are cattle / in gt / proportion and go to saleable slaughter" (74/439). Here the metaphor has a double edge, because it criticizes both the Christian mob for letting itself be duped by the Jews and the Jews themselves, who are now placed in the role of the maggots of the first page of Canto 74. They have that paradoxical nature that Pound ascribes to them in his radio speeches in that they divide and also drive their victims as a herd. The culprit within the individual is that "pusillanimous wanting all men cut down to worm size. / Wops, maggots, crumbled from simple dishonesty" (87/570). The cowardice that cuts a great man like Mussolini (or Pound?) down to the size of everyone else makes for uniformity but also for disintegration, crumbling, as the uniform atoms lose their direction. If Mussolini is the incarnation of a perfect union of individual and community, the Jews are his antithesis, divisive and conformist at the same time.

For Pound, therefore, "collaboration" has the same peculiar double meaning that Rodolphe Gasché has recently discovered in the wartime writings of Paul de Man: "Collaboration at creating a Europe where 'a free contact between peoples that know themselves as different and insist on difference, but also hold each other mutually in high esteem, secures political peace and stability.'" Collaboration means the mutual relationship of different entities in a unity.[191] In Canto 80, in a passage where with obvious self-interest Pound wonders "will they shoot" Quisling, he also determines not "to lose faith in a possible collaboration" (80/494). On the surface, Pound uses the word "collaboration" to mean community effort, but the proximity of the reference to Quisling obviously exposes the less savory meaning just under the surface. The oddity of Pound's peculiar obliquity here is that he manages to identify Quisling's treason, and by implication his own, with community effort. Elsewhere he defends Laval and Petain, identified only by their initials, as "gli onesti" (76/460) and Mussolini, Laval, Quisling, and perhaps Alessandro Pavolini as "full of humanitas" (84/539). These references conspire to create a community of collaborators, a group defined by treason but proposed here as a brotherhood of honest men. The paradox is that in order to commit this collaboration each man had to turn against and reject collaboration with his own country. In this way, the contradiction of Pound's position emerges despite him.

Just as Mussolini appears as a principle of unity sullied by the maggots below him, fascism itself is figured as a lost metaphysical perfection now enshrined in the mind. "Italia tradita," Pound insists, is "now in the mind indestructible" (74/430). The story of the city of Wagadu, resurrected four times, serves as evidence that enables Pound to say "I believe in the resurrection of Italy" (74/442). These references are perhaps the best evidence that the *Pisan Cantos* depend on a kind of memory that is not weakened but paradoxically strengthened by defeat in the practical world.[192] But a few pages later, Pound mocks the idea of resurrection by quoting from his own early poetry: "'ghosts move about me' . . . but as Mead said: if they were, / *what have* they done in the interval" (74/446). Pound seems to mock both memory and resurrection, because his own past poetry is brought in only for the sake of a joke and his own past doctrine that all experience is in principle available to the present is submitted to Mead's searching irony. Yet, a few lines further, Pound reverts to praise of "resurgent ΕΙΚΟΝΕΣ."

The layers of irony and reverence on this page betray a deeper strain in Pound's ideas about time. Early in the canto, he insists that "il tempo rivolge" (74/428), but even here there is a confession of the contingency and arbitrariness of the return: "We will see the old roads again, question, possibly / but nothing appears much less likely." This canto is full of the pathos of "the white wings of time passing" (74/437), but it also includes such meager jokes as "Amber Rives is dead, the end of that chapter / see Time for June 25th" (74/434). As Kenner says, the beautiful image of the white wings allows us to see time as it passes, but so does the bleak metonymy by which the popular magazine becomes associated with the force behind the deaths it chronicles.[193] There is another such joke in Canto 81 when "the egg broke in Cabranez' pocket / thus making history" (81/518). If history is made of such lowly accidents, how can the poet plan on a resurrection of the perfect Italy now lost?

Such jokes indicate that Pound could welcome the accidental, even as he was using it to define the eternal, and there are many passages in which the contingent and the accidental are given a valuation that is not merely negative: "it exists only in fragments unexpected excellent sausage" (74/438). In a passage that bears obvious reference to Pound's plans for his own poem, he seems to welcome the accident that has diverted him: "By no means an orderly Dantescan rising / but as the winds veer" (74/443). There is even an instance in which Pound speaks negatively of "centuries hoarded" (80/498) as if memory were a kind of usurer. In such passages it becomes clear that Pound constantly pits two contrasting temporal values against one another: eternity against vitality; stillness against movement. "The stillness outlasting all wars" (74/427) has an obvious appeal for the poet who bet on the losing side of this war, but elsewhere Pound sanctifies the fluid instead: "The sphere moving crystal, fluid"; "no dolphin faster in moving / nor the flying azure of the wing'd fish under Zoagli" (86/457,459).

The standard way of understanding this dichotomy is not to see it as a dichotomy at all, to merge stillness and movement, as Pound certainly does at times, in images such as that of the fountain at the end of Canto 74, or in heuristic metaphors like Kenner's knot.[194] De Man calls this "the most demanding of reconciliations, that of motion and stasis. . . ."[195] In a sense, everything depends on this reconciliation, because it is the very basis of the wager Pound makes on fascism, that tradition and modernity can be reconciled, that there can be a revolution that will return humankind to a prehistory of perfect stability. It is the issue that jeopardizes the very existence of the *Pisan Cantos,* which occupies the space that was to have included Pound's Paradiso with an antiparadise based on an accident of history. That Pound continues in these poems his polemic on behalf of the modern (74/445,448) while also virtually drowning in nostalgia, and sputtering "b . . . . h yr/progress" (76/453), indicates that he has not stopped trying to effect this reconciliation.

The temporal nature of the poems themselves, the relation in them of language to time, indicates how paradoxical this reconciliation can be. Early in Canto 74, Pound relates the story of Ouan Jin, who "spoke and thereby created the named / thereby making clutter / the bane of men moving / and so his mouth was removed / as you will find it removed in his pictures" (74/427). Here the two possible meanings of "stillness" in phrases like "the stillness outlasting all wars" play against one another. Ouan Jin's stillness, his silence, is necessary to avoid stillness, to allow a nomadic people to move freely about the landscape. Names, on the other hand, slow a people down. The passage thus contains in embryo a paradox the *Pisan Cantos* work out at length: Language is necessary to memory, to the stillness that will outlast the temporary setback represented by the defeat of Mussolini, but, on the other hand, the same quality in language will impede the swiftness, the fluidity, that the poem also sacralizes. The language of the passage itself creates some of the tension between these two possibilities. To allow men to move, Ouan Jin's mouth must be removed, and the pun suggests an intricate reversal in which to remove is not to move again but to stop moving. Pound twists the pun again with his assurance that "you will find it removed in his pictures." How can one find something that has been removed? What would it mean to remove a mouth in any case, because a mouth is already a hole? In these twists and turns, Pound pokes at the word *move* hidden within *remove* and at the paradox that joins them. The poem itself moves by contiguity, identifying what seem to be opposites through an accident of sound. That Pound conflates Wanjina, from Australian folklore, with Ouan Jin, identified by Terrell as a writer[196] and by Pound as "the man with an education" (74/426), indicates the relevance of this paradox to his own project in the DTC.

Naming and remembering are obviously associated in this poem that relies so much on Pound's own memories and on the names from his past and present. The comic demand to the weirdly named Snag to name the books of the Bible is perhaps one version of the poet's charge to himself: "Name 'em, don't bullshit ME" (74/430). Over and over Pound gives names and poses the named against the unnamed as if this relationship were parallel to that between the defined and the undefined. Names, that is, stand against bullshit. But on the other hand, names are, in the Ouan Jin passage and elsewhere, synonymous with bullshit. A reverent passage in Canto 78 draws on Gavin Douglas's translation of the Aeneid: "the lateyn peopil taken has their name / bringing his gods into Latium" (78/478). The passage associates the taking of names and the preservation of gods with what seems to be real reverence until Pound adds the line "saving the bricabrac."[197] The Latin people thus seem to have made the mistake feared by the Australians, having cluttered themselves with names. They have moved, but in so doing have neglected to remove.

Rabaté notes the relationship between the Ouan Jin passage, with its fear of clutter, and a passage in Canto 14, which stigmatizes the "clatter of presses" (14/61).[198] The clatter of language is its clutter, the capacity of language to proliferate sounds and meanings like those that link "move" and "remove" until definition disappears. But if Pound clearly hates and fears this clatter at times, he also, at other times, positively solicits it. He is amused by visual-verbal puns like the "two red cans labeled 'FIRE'" (74/443), which might also contain a verbal pun between the indicative and the imperative, considering that this *is* the army. He plays this way with the names of guards and prisoners in the DTC: "'Steele that is one awful name' . . . Blood and Slaughter to help him" (78/479). When Whiteside settles down to wash a dog (79/485) or Talbot is rhymed with a dog that is "tall but / not so tall as all that" (80/515), we see some of the humor that made Pound sign some of his money pamphlets with the British pound sign. There are quite a few such moments in these cantos, not all of them associated with proper names: "I wonder what Tsu Tsze's calligraphy looked like / they say she could draw down birds from the trees" (80/495). Here Pound succinctly summarizes the ancient story of a drawing so realistic it could lure real birds to marvel at it.

A pun is perhaps economical in that it combines two meanings into one word, but it also advertises the slippage between sound and meaning. Rabaté is certainly right when he insists on the importance of ploce in the *Pisan Cantos*: "Pound all the time asserts that he only says what he says."[199] But, on the other hand, Pound also shows constantly that he says something other than what he says. The poems are full of loose improvisations like "this grass or whatever here under the tentflaps" (74/446) and of lapses like the one that transpires in Canto 79 when the poem spins its wheels for almost thirty lines while Pound tries to come up with the name of Gui d'Arezzo (79/486–487). In such instances, the relationship between time and language becomes palpable and it becomes clear that at least some of the poem exists in the gap between intention and name. The lapse in memory lets time into the poem and also advertises the temporal gap between what the poet wants to say and what is said, which is in fact a temporal gap within what is said. An essentially metonymical relationship between names and things appears even as Pound is trying to assert their identity.

The roll call is perhaps the best representation of this relationship, a string of names that appears from time to time in the *Pisan Cantos*, breaking whatever continuity they have. Pound's almost happy-go-lucky attitude to these breaks coincides with the more serious assertion of the value of the fluid, even the contingent. The passage that proclaims that paradise is available only in fragments is broken by a snappy "(Hullo Corporal Casey)" (74/438). The breathless mood is broken, but the break illustrates in a way what the poetry was trying to say. Earlier in the same canto, in the midst of a string of quotes from his fellow prisoners, Pound gives what almost might be a confession: "'the things I saye an' dooo'" (74/436). The speaker admits that he does not understand himself, that he says and does things that surprise even him, and in so admitting he suggests a purely contingent relationship between intention and language that often obtains in these poems. Though Pound may not be quoting this fellow prisoner with approval, he is himself in a position where improvisation is the only possibility and he does not reject its gifts.

What appears here is the result of a bargain Pound began to make with himself long before Pisa. In *Guide to Kulchur,* he quotes Confucius's dictum "To call people and things by their names, that is by the correct denominations, to see that the terminology is exact" (GK, p. 16). But the *Guide* is also an improvisation: "I am to put down so far as possible only what has resisted the erosion of time, and forgetfulness" (GK, p. 33). Pound had been preparing for Pisa for years, working by memory in the faith that improvisation and correct naming would coincide. This procedure is his own practical version of the coalescence of stasis and speed, stillness and fluidity, and of the fascist combination of order and constant revolution. The *Pisan Cantos* demonstrate the instability of this compromise, but at the same time they show Pound to be as much amused as he is shocked by its breakdown.

At the same time, by the same means, Pound violates the boundaries between his poem and the outside world. As he said to the camp censor, "The form of the poem and main progress is conditioned by its own inner shape, but the life of the DTC passing OUTSIDE cannot but impinge, or break into the main flow."[200] In other words, the random events of the present day, which break the "flow" of the poem, also break through the boundary between the poem and the world. This means that in allowing poetic contingency to rule over the poem, even if only at times, Pound also admits the contingent relationship between his poem and the political realities outside it. Once the poet gives himself up to chance, he also gives up the autonomy of his poetic form. Formally, the *Pisan Cantos* thus suggest a rather more complicated relationship between part and whole, individual and community, than the one with which they begin. Rather than proposing an organic interdependence, Pound proposes a relation in which chance links part to part and the poem to the world in a relationship that is based on difference and inconsistency but which is ineluctable nonetheless.

The relationship between the different parts of the *Pisan Cantos* bears these same characteristics. The most common connective is, of course, *and,* one of Pound's favorite poetic devices almost from the beginning. But Pound also makes effective use of *but.* In Canto 74, he begins an anecdote about Tangier with "but in Tangier I saw from dead straw ignition" (74/432). The implied contrast remains unclear, because the previous lines are not in any way antithetical to these. In Canto 76, Pound quotes two discontinuous lines from *Aucassin and Nicolette,* one in quotation marks, one not, as if they were in opposition: "'in heaven have I to make?' // but all the vair and fair women" (76/455). The quotation marks and the double space between the lines make it seem as if these lines have nothing to do with one another, whereas the conjunction seems to suggest a contrast between them. Pound uses the same technique to comic effect in Canto 77: "So Miscio sat in the dark lacking the

gasometer penny / but then said: 'Do you speak German?'" (77/469). It
appears that Ito in fact delivered the second line some time after lacking
the penny. The collapse of time in Pound's account makes it appear that
Ito speaks fluent non sequitur if not German.

In these instances the conjunction suggests that individual lines of the
poems exist in a relationship of undefined tension with one another. Ito's
seeming non sequitur and Pound's own elision of passing time produce
the same sort of metonymy in which chance links things necessarily but
not harmoniously. De Man suggests that the difference between "necessity and chance" is "a legitimate way to distinguish between analogy and
contiguity," metaphor and metonymy.[201] If so, then Pound's submission
of his poem to the rule of chance means a stylistic submission to
metonymy, to an arrangement in which contiguity takes precedence over
analogy. This is not to contradict the more common reading of the *Pisan
Cantos,* which favors analogy, seeing in it a triumph over the contingency
of history. But Pound qualifies this valuation of analogy himself with an
equal and opposite emphasis on the value of accidents and mistakes.

As a whole the *Pisan Cantos* suggest one part-whole relationship based
on necessity and another quite different one based on contingency. To do
so is not in itself to depart from fascist philosophy, which was quite
capable of accommodating a theory of stable order and one of revolutionary breaks. Before Pisa, however, there was in Pound's mind a confidence
that revolutionary breaks would return society to a stable order, that
modernization would restore a traditional society. Movement, contingency, accident are folded back into a vision of continuous unity. In
the *Pisan Cantos,* on the other hand, Pound begins to dismantle this
solution even as he advances it, or rather he allows a dissolution to occur
that he is in any case powerless to prevent. In these cantos, there is a
formal relationship of particular to general, chance to necessity, just the
opposite of that to which the poem had been proceeding, at which it had
tediously arrived in the *China Cantos.* There an emphasis on the particular had gradually blown itself into a bloated dogma of the eternal; in the
Pisan Cantos this dogma still exists, but the air is beginning to leak out
through little holes made by the accidents of camp life.

On the other hand, couldn't such an admission of the power of accident serve as an excuse, a diminution of Pound's personal responsibility
in the fiasco of fascism? There is some evidence that Pound believed
something like this at Pisa and later. But the *Pisan Cantos* also begin
sketchily to suggest that there *is* a relation between particulars that is not
merely accidental, but which is not that of identity either. In this "definition," contingency links individuals together as it does individual moments, in a relation of necessity but not of similarity. Human beings
belong together not because they are the same, and not because they share

certain cultural presumptions, but because they suffer a shared subjection to the necessities of history. Responsibility therefore comes to rest on contingency, metaphor on metonymy, not because the former transcends and resolves the latter, but because the very strength of the latter cannot be escaped, as its very necessity links together in the great DTC of modern society what has otherwise no commonality.

An example of this sort of unity, and of its limitations, appears in Canto 74. In a passage that veers characteristically back and forth between self-pity and false bravado, Pound names his *comes miseriae:* "Comites Kernes, Green and Tom Wilson / God's messenger Whiteside . . ." (74/436). The passage positively bursts with grandiloquent metaphors for Pound's imprisonment: He is Christ between the thieves, Ulysses in the pigsty, even, it seems at one point, a slave trapped in the Middle Passage. All these pocket dramas inflate Pound and denigrate his fellow prisoners even as he calls them companions. But, at the same time, this passage represents a rewriting of the earlier literary roll-call that begins: "Lordly men are to earth o'ergiven / these the companions . . ." (74/432). In its first form, the roll call represents a recapturing of Pound's past history, an insertion of Ford, Yeats, Joyce and others into a timeless pantheon that mocks their recapture by the earth. In its second form, the roll call of the companions Kernes, Green, and Wilson represents no such thing. The gathering unity is that of the coincidence of imprisonment, the commonality nothing more than subjection to the Army and its "g.d.m.f. generals all of 'em fascists."

Pound can hardly escape his bondage to fascism with such a gratuitous gesture, and it is easy to overemphasize the degree of self-conscious repentance in such moments. But it is also impossible to ignore the immense differences between the *Pisan Cantos* and the cantos immediately preceding them and to deny that this difference is accounted for by a change in Pound's view of history. In this way, the *Pisan Cantos* join *The Tower* and *The Waste Land* as modernist masterworks that conceive a formal and social unity by accepting the contingencies of history. In none of these cases does the poem represent the final words of the author, and Pound was the most conspicuous backslider, both in poetry and in politics. But the three works do represent an alternative conception huddled within the massive authoritarian fantasies of these three writers, an alternative that, paradoxically, could not have existed without those fantasies.

Conclusion

Much of modern politics and aesthetics can be traced to the philosophical problem Hegel identified with modernity itself: "When the might of union vanishes from the life of men and the antitheses lose their living connection and reciprocity and gain independence, the need of philosophy arises."[1] From a desire like Hegel's to reconnect the antitheses without losing any of their newly won independence come the most radical movements of modern politics – fascism and communism – as well as a newly militant conservatism and even a chastened liberalism that has spurned laissez-faire. From the same sense of disconnection there arises an aesthetic tradition, the English version of which Raymond Williams has traced back through Ruskin and Morris to Pugin.[2] Yeats, Eliot, and Pound are heirs of both traditions, and their work constantly illustrates the many connections between the two. Since Schiller, the political project of reconciling the antitheses has naturally had recourse to the aesthetic, and the aesthetic has in its turn always contained political implications.

The experience of Yeats, Eliot, and Pound also shows, however, that this relationship harbors certain paradoxes. The aesthetic can complete its assigned task and reconcile social and political contradictions only by remaining aloofly aesthetic; its political power rests in a way on its power to resist politics. The three poets make this claim for their own work in many different ways. Yeats's aristocrat, Eliot's man of letters, Pound's scholar of the luminous detail – all achieve political relevance by asserting and maintaining their difference from the mundanely political. Yet the three were so steeped in the politics of their time that they could hardly resist applying their solutions, which then shattered in their hands. Yeats, Eliot, and Pound were, therefore, political failures, men whose lives veered back and forth between grandiose authoritarian fantasies and abject isolation, the very antitheses they had hoped to join. Though their critical and polemical prose often promises that aesthetic modernism will

187

resolve the problems left by social and political modernism, the poetry confesses line by line its inability to do so.

Because modern literary criticism has had the same program as literary modernism, it has had in a sense too high a stake in the outcome. From Richards through Abrams to Levenson, critics have found in literary modernism precisely the reconciliation it promised. If nothing else, contemporary attacks on conventional literary criticism have exposed it as an interested party in the modernist project. In fact, it sometimes seems as if literary criticism has a greater interest in reconciliation than the poets themselves. From the very beginning, New Criticism, in the person of John Crowe Ransom, patronized Eliot as an unsystematic critic, insufficiently absolute in his standards, even while turning his poetry into a justification for its own absolutes.[3] Ever since, literary criticism has repaired the fragmentary, discontinuous material left to it by modern poetry so as to produce at last the solutions modernism itself had only promised.

It is no wonder, then, that post-structuralism, which advanced in the United States by flogging New Criticism even after it was nearly dead, should have rejected both modernism and the larger aesthetic project of reconciliation. In the early 1950s, Paul de Man was able to attack New Criticism, Marxism, and the structuralism of Roland Barthes at once for "the tendency to expect a reconciliation from poetry. . . ." The mistake, or rather the philosophical vulgarity, in each case is to treat as historical a rupture that is in fact ontological: "The problem of separation inheres in Being, which means that social forms of separation derive from ontological and metasocial attitudes. For poetry, the divide exists forever." De Man thus rules out of court any attempt to date the crisis that Hegel identifies with modernity and also any dreams of resolving it. Therefore, modernism's most egregious error is to believe in its own existence, a fond dream de Man rudely interrupts in "Literary History and Literary Modernity." But modernism also errs even more fundamentally in believing in the aesthetic, in cherishing the dream of reconciliation that de Man calls "the desire that haunts modern thought." Thus de Man's final work was to be a ruthless expose of the aesthetic ideology as a cowardly attempt to shrink to manageable size the cleavage in the very being of humankind.[4]

De Man's has been an influential attack, specifically in that its terms are repeated by other critics such as J. Hillis Miller and Perry Meisel, and generally in that any aesthetic that hankers after identity or that projects a reconciliation of any tensions whatever is now commonly reprehended.[5] But it is now possible to see that this rejection of the aesthetic and of the theory of history that contains it has a history of its own. One might apply to de Man himself the statement in "Literary History and Literary

Modernity" that "The more radical the rejection of anything that came before, the greater the dependence on the past."[6] This might be read as a suggestion, even a confession, that the attempt to decouple literature and history, to define Hegel's antitheses as permanently divided aspects of being, is itself part of a specific history.

That history was obscured until late in 1987, when it was revealed that in 1941 and 1942 de Man had contributed articles to two Belgian newspapers controlled by the Nazis. One of the many ironies attendant upon this disclosure was the resemblance it suggested between de Man and the very modernists he had helped to dethrone.[7] The same tired arguments about the relationship between the artist's opinions and his work, between aesthetics and politics, were rehearsed again, as if the Bollingen Prize controversy had erupted from the past to be ritually reenacted. A deeper irony comes from the fact that de Man, like Pound, had been attracted to fascism in the first place because it seemed to answer the very questions raised in the controversy over his collaboration: the relationship of particular to general, of one aspect of a life to the rest of that life, of a writer's opinions to his creative work, of art to politics, of the individual to the community. In fact, it can be argued that, like Yeats, Eliot, and Pound, de Man dedicates himself in his wartime articles to what Cynthia Chase calls, in a distinctly Hegelian context, "the problem of modernity" (R, p. 51).

As Els de Bens says, the large-scale political problem to which de Man's articles devote themselves is that of finding "an intermediate way in between individualism and commitment to solidarity" (R, p. 91).[8] That these are separate is due, de Man suggests, to the decadence of liberal democracy. Even as a young socialist writing in *Jeudi* and *Cahiers du Libre Examen*, de Man argued that the war was in part due to a moral collapse of the democracies of Europe, a collapse he said later could be seen in the "cultural division that governed these last years of the liberalist era" (WJ, p. 309).[9] The most logical explanation for de Man's collaboration is that he felt, as Ortwin de Graef says, "that collaboration would remove the obstacles formed by decaying, decadent democracies and would thus lead to a better world" (R, p. 105).[10] In other words, fascism promised to resolve the split between individual and collective, to connect, as John Brenkman puts it, "private experience . . . to values that would orient his active participation in a public world" (R, p. 34).

De Man therefore contrasts, in a number of instances, though not everywhere in these articles, French theorizing with its political individualism to German intuition with its emphasis on solidarity: "To the extent that in France man is being considered and analyzed only as an isolated individual, in Germany attempts are being made to use the subtle connections between the individual and the community as mainsprings for novelistic fiction" (WJ, p. 332). For this reason, de Man often criticizes the French and praises Germany as a model: "The problem that presents itself is no longer that of knowing what political forms the sacred laws of the individual will dictate to the reigning power, but indeed of elucidating the considerably more modest question: how to insert the human person into a highly centralized and disciplined order" (WJ, p. 185).[11]

Perhaps the most revealing moment in all the wartime articles comes in the late contribution called "Literature and Sociology," in which de Man criticizes the French practice of considering human beings only as individuals and also suggests that there must be certain sociological laws. Without such laws, he exclaims, "we are forever condemned to live in the arbitrary" (WJ, p. 332).[12] This is clearly the fear that motivates most of this journalism, the fear of social chaos, which is at bottom a fear of the metaphysically arbitrary, of a world without relations. But, as Sandor Goodhart shows, it is just such a world that de Man presents in his mature work, a world of pure contingency and "random event." De Man's project was at least to propose the unthinkable, the "irreducible singularity" of phenomena (R, p. 218). As he says in *The Rhetoric of Romanticism*, "Nothing, whether deed, word, thought, or text, ever happens in relation, positive or negative, to anything that precedes, follows, or exists elsewhere but only as a random event whose power, like the power of death, is due to the randomness of its occurrence."[13]

De Man's mature criticism is most obviously at odds with his wartime journalism in its utter rejection of any scheme of reconciliation. His antipathy to the aesthetic in general and to literary modernism in particular may therefore imply a rejection of the political movements that had promised reconciliation. And, in large part, literary criticism in the United States has followed de Man's lead: Having wasted its youth in misguided dreams of balancing out the particular and the general, the one and the many, it now settles into the mature, if somewhat chilled, embrace of the metaphysically singular. Given the politics attendant upon de Man's youthful dreams, it is hard to argue that this is a change for the worse.

De Man himself shows, however, how impossible it is to abide in pure singularity, and he does so, appropriately, in an analysis of literary modernism. Any literature with a pretense to originality and independence "cannot assert itself without at once being swallowed up and reintegrated into a regressive historical process."[14] Claims of singularity, that is to say, remain blind to the ineluctable identity containing them, a theoretical principle de Man instances against modernism's pretenses to novelty but one which might as easily illuminate the inescapably historical nature of his own project. As he shows himself in his analysis of Rousseau, assertions of difference, independence, novelty, singularity, are subject to "the inevitable relapse into patterns of totalization."[15] Though de Man insisted to the end that this duplicity is not historical and therefore not open to solution, political or literary, his own theories suggest that such an insistence must itself mask a subjection to history. Surely de Man discovered something of this subjection as a young journalist defending the autonomy of literature in publications controlled by the Nazis.

This historical reading of de Man is not offered as a genealogical explanation. On the contrary, the only way to avoid a naively genealogical explanation of de Man's mature work is to see that the apparent distance between the young man's projects of reconciliation and the mature critic's insistence on singularity cannot be mapped out neatly over time but must be collapsed so that each is implicit in the other. As Peter Dews argues in another context, "Pure singularity is itself an abstraction, the waste-product of identity-thinking. . . ." Though this statement might be applied to de Man in a purely historical and biographical way, so that singularity becomes nothing more than a reflex of "identity-thinking," born out of revulsion from it, it can also be applied theoretically: "If every moment is prized purely for its uniqueness, without reference to a purpose or a meaning, to a before or an after, without reference to anything which goes beyond itself, then what is enjoyed in each moment becomes paradoxically and monotonously the same. . . ."[16] The very insistence on singularity produces a totality just as undifferentiated as any implied by the desire for reconciliation.

Thus the temptation to follow de Man's revulsion against his own youthful enthusiasm for the dark forces of social reconciliation is a misleading and delusive one. As Dews puts it, paraphrasing Adorno, "Non-identity cannot be respected by abandoning completely the principle of identity."[17] Adorno himself steers between the positions taken up by New Criticism and post-structuralism. What Adorno says about "the official curators of culture" could be said with equal justice of conventional literary criticism: Their "assertion that there is an undifferentiated unity in classical-traditional works of art can be refuted by looking more closely at any single one of them: They all reveal the illusion of unity to be the result of conceptual mediation."[18] The great works of literary modernism do not manage to reconcile unity and difference, the singular and the identical, the one and the many. To pretend that they do is at once to falsify the works, to recapitulate their collusion in the politics of repression, and to remove from the works the only saving remnant of critical power in them.

That remnant, Adorno argues, is precisely art's failure to produce reconciliation in a society that everywhere prevents it. But this critical remnant cannot be preserved if reconciliation is abandoned or rejected as hopelessly tainted. Art preserves reconciliation as an ethical indictment of the status quo in failing to achieve reconciliation. Assumed as fact, reconciliation serves the most repressive forces in politics and aesthetics, because it pretends that real differences no longer exist. Preserved as an indictment of the society in which it manifestly does not exist, reconciliation remains an ethical standard that could motivate change. As Adorno puts it, "While firmly rejecting the appearance of reconciliation, art none the less holds fast to the idea of reconciliation in an antagonistic world."[19]

It can hardly be argued that Yeats, Eliot, and Pound "firmly reject the appearance of reconciliation" or that theirs is the sort of principled, conscious refusal that Adorno associates with Beckett. But Adorno's position does suggest that something of value remains in the reactionary modernism of these three poets. Their desire to close the gap between individual and community, fact and value, freedom and necessity, remains a legitimate indictment of the status quo, but only insofar as their own schemes of reconciliation collapse and in so doing demonstrate the fundamental contradictions of modern society.

If modernism fails to achieve the social miracles it promises, if it even fails to resolve in aesthetic terms the social problems it attacks, then critics should not be reluctant to admit it, because this failure is hardly peculiar to aesthetic modernism. Moreover, it was this very failure that preserved within modernism an alternative to its overt political fantasies. To rightly appreciate these writers is therefore to insist on the gaps left in their work. To reject the work in toto, however, is in a sense to ignore the social problematic from which it suffers and to banish from literature as irresolvable a problem whose very promise lies in our inability to solve it.

Notes

Introduction

1 Several recent studies have refused to shirk this responsibility. Sympathetic attempts to deal with these issues include Elizabeth Cullingford, *Yeats, Ireland and Fascism* (London: Macmillan, 1981) and Christopher Ricks, *Eliot and Prejudice* (Berkeley: University of California Press, 1989). The most thoroughly hostile is Robert Casillo, *The Genealogy of Demons: Anti-Semitism, Fascism, and the Myths of Ezra Pound* (Evanston: Northwestern University Press, 1988). See Casillo, pp. 9–16, for a discussion of the ways that Pound critics have avoided the subject of politics or, on the other hand, used politics to condemn Pound out of hand. The best and most balanced study of the politics of Eliot and Pound remains William Chace, *The Political Identities of Ezra Pound and T. S. Eliot* (Stanford: Stanford University Press, 1973). The only book-length discussion of the politics of all three published since John Harrison's rather preliminary *The Reactionaries* (New York: Schocken, 1967) is Cairns Craig, *Yeats, Eliot, Pound and the Politics of Poetry* (Pittsburgh: University of Pittsburgh Press, 1982). The many useful aspects of Craig's study are diminished by the eccentric thesis linking the three poets to associationist psychology.

2 For example, Cullingford takes issue point by point with the famous denunciation of Yeats by Conor Cruise O'Brien, "Passion and Cunning: An Essay on the Politics of W. B. Yeats" (in *In Excited Reverie,* ed. A. Norman Jeffares and K.G.W. Cross [New York: St. Martin's Press, 1960]), as if the only alternative to blanket condemnation were complete exculpation. Apparently for Cullingford to succeed in her own terms, Yeats must not only not be a fascist but must instead be a liberal democrat. See also the blithe assertion of Ricardo Quinones that "From the Modernists discussed in this book, from the values and aesthetic modes of which their works are made up, it would not be possible to derive any code largely conformable to that of fascism. In fact, they are polar opposites." *Mapping Literary Modernism* (Princeton: Princeton University Press, 1985), p. 119. Quinones immensely simplifies his task by not including Pound among the modernists discussed.

3 "Modernity – An Incomplete Project" is the title of a talk delivered by

Jürgen Habermas in 1980 and published under that title in *The Anti-Aesthetic: Essays on Postmodern Culture,* ed. Hal Foster (Port Townsend, Wash.: Bay Press, 1983), pp. 3–15, and as "Modernity versus Postmodernity," *New German Critique* 22 (1981): 3–14. See also the lectures collected as *The Philosophical Discourse of Modernity,* tr. Frederick Lawrence (Cambridge: MIT Press, 1987) and *Habermas and Modernity,* ed. Richard J. Bernstein (Cambridge: Polity Press, 1985) in which Habermas is quoted as taking "the pathology of modernity" as *his* philosophical problem (p. 4).

4   The most thorough criticism of enlightenment and the self-betrayal of modernity is, of course, Max Horkheimer and Theodor W. Adorno, *Dialectic of Enlightenment* (1944), tr. John Cumming (1972; rpt., New York: Continuum, 1987). The opposite point of view, that cultural modernism has infected enlightenment rationalism with hedonistic irresponsibility, is advanced by Daniel Bell, *The Cultural Contradictions of Capitalism* (New York: Basic Books, 1976) and "Modernism and Capitalism," *Partisan Review* 65 (1978): 206–222. A whole political spectrum could perhaps be sketched in the space between these views. Another important discussion of enlightenment, modernity, and countermodernity is Michel Foucault, "What Is Enlightenment," in *The Foucault Reader,* ed. Paul Rabinow (New York: Pantheon, 1984), pp. 32–50. For the idea that modernity harbored anti-modernism from the very beginning, see Marshall Berman, *All That is Solid Melts into Air* (New York: Simon and Schuster, 1982).

5   E.J. Hobsbawm, *The Age of Empire 1875–1914* (New York: Pantheon, 1987), pp. 227–228.

6   For discussions of aesthetic modernism that stress these antagonisms, see Matei Calinescu, *Faces of Modernity* (Bloomington, Ind.: Indiana University Press, 1977), T.J. Jackson Lears, *No Place of Grace: Antimodernism and the Transformation of American Culture 1880–1920* (New York: Pantheon, 1981), Jochen Schulte-Sasse, "Modernity and Modernism, Postmodernity and Postmodernism: Framing the Issue," *Cultural Critique* 5 (Winter 1986–1987): 5–22, and Russell A. Berman, "The Routinization of Charismatic Modernism and the Problem of Post-Modernity," *Cultural Critique* 5 (Winter 1986–1987): 49–68 and reprinted with other relevant essays in *Modern Culture and Critical Theory: Art, Politics, and the Legacy of the Frankfurt School* (Madison: University of Wisconsin Press, 1989), pp. 118–135.

7   W.H. Auden, "The Public v. the Late Mr. William Butler Yeats," in *The English Auden,* ed. Edward Mendelson (London: Faber and Faber, 1977), pp. 392–393.

8   Irving Howe calls this situation "the collapse of traditional liberalism, its lapse into a formalism ignoring both the possibilities of human grandeur and the needs of human survival." "Introduction," *The Idea of the Modern* (New York: Horizon Press, 1967), p. 25.

9   R. Berman, *Modern Culture and Critical Theory,* p. 121. See also pp. 46–47 ("the avant-garde protests against the manner in which bourgeois culture has insufficiently realized its own values"). See also Lears, p. 7.

10   Ezra Pound, *Guide to Kulchur* (1938; rpt. New York: New Directions, 1970), p. 254; T.S. Eliot, *After Strange Gods* (New York: Harcourt, Brace, 1933), p. 12.

11 See Jürgen Habermas, *Theory and Practice*, tr. John Viertel (Boston: Beacon Press, 1973), p. 42, and Richard Mulgan, "Liberty in Ancient Greece," and Charles Taylor, "Kant's Theory of Freedom," in *Conceptions of Liberty in Political Philosophy*, ed. Zbigniew Pelczynski and John Gray (New York: St. Martin's, 1984). Isaiah Berlin's *Four Essays on Liberty* (New York: Oxford University Press, 1970) provides the currently standard explanation of what is called "negative freedom." See the essays in Pelczynski and Gray for discussions of this work.

12 See Mulgan, pp. 9 and 11, Taylor, p. 101, and Ronald Dworkin, "Liberalism," and Michael J. Sandel, "Introduction," in *Liberalism and its Critics*, ed. Michael J. Sandel (Oxford: Basil Blackwell, 1984).

13 G.W.F. Hegel, *Lectures on the Philosophy of World History, Introduction: Reason in History*, tr. H.B. Nisbet (Cambridge: Cambridge University Press, 1975), pp. 204–205, and *Hegel's Philosophy of Right*, tr. T.M. Knox (Oxford: Clarendon Press, 1942), p. 229. See also William E. Connolly, *Political Theory and Modernity* (Oxford: Basil Blackwell, 1988), pp. 40–41.

14 Habermas, *Theory and Practice*, p. 85.

15 Karl Marx, *Critique of Hegel's Philosophy of Right*, tr. Annette Jolin and Joseph O'Malley (Cambridge: Cambridge University Press, 1970), pp. 32 and 117. See the discussion of this point in Terry Eagleton, *The Ideology of the Aesthetic* (London: Basil Blackwell, 1990), pp. 209–211.

16 Horkheimer and Adorno, *Dialectic of Enlightenment*, p. 13. Another analysis of the relationship of liberalism and totalitarianism is Herbert Marcuse's "The Struggle Against Liberalism in the Totalitarian View of the State," *Negations*, tr. Jeremy J. Shapiro (Boston: Beacon Press, 1968), pp. 3–42. The essay was originally published in 1934. For a penetrating discussion of the possibility that oppositional critique may reinforce the very system it seeks to call into question, see Vincent P. Pecora, "Adversarial Culture and the Fate of Dialectics," *Cultural Critique* 8 (Winter 1987–1988): 197–216. For an application of this idea to modern fiction, see Pecora's *Self and Form in Modern Narrative* (Baltimore: Johns Hopkins University Press, 1989).

17 See Charles Taylor, *Hegel and Modern Society* (Cambridge: Cambridge University Press, 1979), p. 118. The classic account of the connection between liberalism and capitalism is C.B. Macpherson, *The Political Theory of Possessive Individualism* (Oxford: Clarendon Press, 1962). Of course, liberalism has changed quite a bit from the time of Mill, in part by recognizing the justice of criticisms like those mentioned earlier. Because of the ideas of late nineteenth-century liberals like Hobhouse and Green, the original emphasis on negative freedom has been compromised a good deal to accommodate certain aspirations to social justice. See John Roberts, "T.H. Green," in Pelczynski and Gray, pp. 243–262, and Guido de Ruggiero, *The History of European Liberalism*, tr. R.G. Collingwood (1927; Boston: Beacon, 1959), pp. 148–149 and 156.

18 See W.B. Yeats, *Explorations* (1962: rpt., New York: Collier, 1973), pp. 22 and 43, and Ezra Pound, *Guide to Kulchur*, p. 43 and *Selected Prose, 1901–1965*, ed. William Cookson (New York: New Directions, 1973), p. 33.

19 T.S. Eliot, "Literature and the Modern World," *American Prefaces* 1 (1935): 20 and quoted in Lewis Freed, *T.S. Eliot: The Critic as Philosopher* (W. Lafayette,

Ind.: Purdue University Press, 1979), p. 108. Pound, *Guide to Kulchur,* p. 52. Eliot, *The Idea of a Christian Society* (New York: Harcourt, Brace and Co., 1940), p. 13.

20 From a 1930 notebook quoted in Donald T. Torchiana, *W.B. Yeats and Georgian Ireland* (Evanston: Northwestern University Press, 1966), p. 255, and *Explorations,* p. 316.

21 Yeats, *Explorations,* p. 268.

22 R. Berman, *Modern Culture and Critical Theory,* p. 121.

23 Karl Mannheim, *Conservatism,* ed. and tr. David Kettler et al (London: Routledge & Kegan Paul, 1986), p. 67. That the influence might also run in the other direction is shown by Roger Scruton's attempt to adapt Marx's analysis of alienation to a modern conservatism: *The Meaning of Conservatism* (London: Macmillan; Totowa, N.J.: Barnes & Noble, 1980), p. 122. See also Robert Nisbet, *Conservatism: Dream and Reality* (Milton Keynes: Open University Press, 1986), p. 49.

24 Raymond Williams, *Culture and Society 1780–1950* (1958; rpt. New York: Columbia University Press, 1983), p. 140. For a similar assertion by another Marxist scholar, see Fredric Jameson, *The Ideologies of Theory* (Minneapolis: University of Minnesota Press, 1988), 1: 134. On the other hand, a number of essays asserting the compatibility of Marxism and liberal values are to be found in *Marxism and Liberalism* ed. Ellen Frankel Paul et al (Oxford: Basil Blackwell, 1986) and *Marxism and the Good Society,* ed. John P. Burke, Lawrence Crocker, and Lymand H. Letgers (Cambridge: Cambridge University Press, 1981). Those who assert that Marxism is in fact a realization of the promise of liberalism generally differentiate between merely "procedural" liberalism and the values that are its essence. See, for example, Lawrence Crocker, "Marx, Liberty, and Democracy," in Burke.

25 Zeev Sternhell, *Neither Right nor Left: Fascist Ideology in France,* tr. David Maisell (Berkeley: University of California Press, 1986), p. 14. See also Sternhell's contribution, "Fascist Ideology," in *Fascism: A Reader's Guide,* ed. Walter Laqueur (Berkeley: University of California Press, 1976), pp. 327–329.

26 For the convergence of left and right in Italian Fascism, see A. James Gregor, *The Ideology of Fascism* (New York: Free Press, 1969). For their convergence in proto-fascism and Nazism in Germany, see Jeffrey Herf, *Reactionary Modernism: Technology, Culture, and Politics in Weimar and the Third Reich* (Cambridge: Cambridge University Press, 1984). Spengler is quoted on p. 50. See also Hugh Seton-Watson, "Fascism, Right and Left," *Journal of Contemporary History* 1 (1966): 187.

27 See Herf, pp. 27 and 37.

28 For a discussion of the common genealogy of right-wing culturalism and left-wing ideology critique, see Nicholas Abercrombie, Stephen Hill, Bryan S. Turner, *The Dominant Ideology Thesis* (London: Allen & Unwin, 1980).

29 Williams, p. 328. See the distinction between culture and totality drawn in Herbert Marcuse, "The Affirmative Character of Culture," in *Negations,* pp. 94–95. The most complete discussion of such theories is Martin Jay's *Marxism and Totality* (Berkeley: University of California Press, 1984). The issue of materialism would seem to separate these two theories and camps definitively. As Sternhell shows, it was Marxist materialism that repelled right-wing socialism and helped to turn it into fascism. On the other hand, many conservatives share with the left the project for a fusion of theory and praxis, which does bias them in favor of the concrete and practical.

30 Peter Stansky, *Redesigning the World: William Morris, the 1880s, and the Arts and Crafts* (Princeton: Princeton University Press, 1985), p. 37. The presiding geniuses of this movement, Ruskin and Morris, illustrate in themselves its potential for both conservatism and socialism.

31 Joan Campbell, *The German Werkbund: The Politics of Reform in the Applied Arts* (Princeton: Princeton University Press, 1978), p. 204.

32 Sternhell, p. 203.

33 Cullingford, p. 16.

34 T.S. Eliot, "Tradition and the Practice of Poetry," *Southern Review* 21 (1985): 878.

35 See his letter to *New Masses* 2 (December 1926): 3.

36 Quoted in George Watson, *Politics and Literature in Modern Britain* (London: Macmillan, 1977), pp. 71–72.

37 Stephen Spender, "Writers and Politics," *Partisan Review* 34 (Summer 1967): 378. Spender no doubt speaks mostly for himself, but he also reports that John Cornford was led to communism by reading *The Waste Land*. See the similar reaction of A.L. Morton, as reported after the fact in "T.S. Eliot – A Personal View," *Zeitschrift für Anglistik und Amerikanistik* 14 (1966): 284.

38 Georg Lukács, *History and Class Consciousness*, tr. Rodney Livingstone (1971; rpt., Cambridge: MIT Press, 1985), pp. 134, 155, 156, and 91–92. See Eagleton's discussion, *Ideology*, pp. 322–324, and the analysis of *History and Class Consciousness* in Martin Jay's *Marxism and Totality*, especially pp. 110–111. Jay also includes a useful bibliography of studies of Lukács on pp. 81–82.

39 Eugene Lunn, *Marxism and Modernism* (Berkeley: University of California Press, 1982), p. 65. See also pp. 38–40, 97, and 106. For other arguments along the same lines, see Douglas Kellner, *Critical Theory, Marxism and Modernity* (Cambridge: Polity Press, 1989), pp. 9–12, and Andrew Feenberg, "Reification and the Antinomies of Socialist Thought," *Telos* 10 (Winter 1971): 93–118.

40 T.S. Eliot, *Knowledge and Experience in the Philosophy of F.H. Bradley* (London: Faber, 1964), p. 22; "The Origins: What Is Romanticism?" (lecture outline, reprinted in A.D. Moody, *Thomas Stearns Eliot Poet* [Cambridge: Cambridge University Press, 1979], p. 43). The rest of the lecture outlines show in a number of places his feeling that "contemporary socialism has much in common with royalism" (p. 47). See Chapter 2 for a discussion of this affinity. See also the discussions in A. Gelpi, *A Coherent Splendor: The American Poetic Renaissance, 1910–1950* (Cambridge: Cambridge University Press, 1987), p. 6, and Franco Moretti, *Signs Taken For Wonders*, rev. ed. (London: Verso, 1988), p. 220. Moretti draws a specific connection between Eliot's attempt to reconnect fact and value and that of Lukács.

41 Pound, *Selected Prose*, p. 197. For the very similar criticism of Lukács, see *History and Class Consciousness*, pp. 113 and 131.

42 Ezra Pound, *Selected Prose*, p. 192; W.B. Yeats, *A Critical Edition of Yeats's A Vision* (1925), ed. George Mills Harper and Walter Kelly Hood (London: Macmillan, 1978), pp. 130–131; *A Vision* (1937; rpt. New York: Collier, 1966), p. 72; George Mills Harper, *The Making of Yeats's A Vision: A Study of the Automatic*

Script (London: Macmillan, 1987), 1: 83. A. Norman Jeffares, *W.B. Yeats: Man and Poet,* 2nd ed. (1962; rpt., London: Routledge & Kegan Paul, 1978), pp. 351–352.

43 The classic attack is Lukács's "The Ideology of Modernism," *The Meaning of Contemporary Realism,* tr. John and Necke Mander (London: Merlin, 1963). As a young man, however, Lukács had phrased his rebellion against official Hungarian culture as "a glorification of the international modern movement as against what I looked on as boundless Hungarian conservatism." In fact, the literary enthusiasms of the young Lukács reproduce in uncanny ways those of the major Irish, English, and American modernists: Ibsen, Hauptmann, the French up to Verlaine, Swinburne, Shelley, and Keats. Ferenc Tökei, "Lukács and Hungarian Culture," *New Hungarian Quarterly* 13 (Autumn 1972): 110. For a fuller discussion of specific resemblances between Lukács and Eliot, see my essay, "Eliot, Lukács, and the Politics of Modernism," in *T.S. Eliot: The Modernist in History,* ed. Ronald Bush (Cambridge: Cambridge University Press, 1991), pp. 169–189. There was among the other major theorists of Western Marxism as well an "aristocratic-socialist anti-capitalism" that resembled in significant ways the anti-capitalism of purer reactionaries like Yeats, Eliot, and Pound. The two groups shared antipathies and also certain paradoxical projects, not the least of which was the desire to redeem culture by attacking official *Kultur.* See Lunn, p. 212 and Martin Jay, *The Dialectical Imagination: A History of the Frankfurt School and the Institute of Social Research, 1923–1950* (Boston: Little, Brown, 1973), pp. 294–295. For a brief argument for the similarity of these two movements as movements, see Jay, *Marxism and Totality,* pp. 10–11. For a specific comparison of Lukács to the aesthetic modernism of Joyce, Pound, and Eliot, see Eagleton, *Ideology,* pp. 316–325.

44 F.O. Mathiessen, *The Achievement of T.S. Eliot* (1935; 2nd ed. New York: Oxford University Press, 1947), p. 144.

45 There are a number of discussions of Lukács's romantic anti-capitalism, including Mary Gluck, *Georg Lukács and His Generation 1900–1918* (Cambridge: Harvard University Press, 1985), Michael Löwy, *Georg Lukács – From Romanticism to Bolshevism,* tr. Patrick Camiller (London: NLB, 1979) and "Naphta or Settembrini? Lukács and Romantic Anticapitalism," *New German Critique* 42 (Fall 1987): 17–32, and Andrew Arato and Paul Breines, *The Young Lukács and the Origins of Western Marxism* (New York: Seabury Press, 1979). For a detailed definition and typology of romantic anti-capitalism, see Michael Löwy and Robert Sayre, "Figures of Romantic Anti-Capitalism," *New German Critique* 32 (Spring-Summer 1984): 42–92. Paul Breines, in "Marxism, Romanticism, and the Case of Georg Lukács," *Studies in Romanticism* 16 (Fall 1977): 473–489, argues that the importance of Lukács "is to have *sought* to restore to Marxism its lost Romantic dimension" (p. 479).

46 Lunn, p. 89; Lukács, *History and Class Consciousness,* pp. 237 and 137. For Lukács's particular definition of history, see pp. 143 and 151–152.

47 Richard Shusterman, *T.S. Eliot and the Philosophy of Composition* (London: Duckworth, 1988), p. 9; Lee Congdon, *The Young Lukács* (Chapel Hill: University of North Carolina Press, 1983), p. 178. Gareth Steadman Jones confirms this association in a negative way when he criticizes Lukács by saying that "the metaphors of *Capital* are never those of the *Wasteland* (sic)." "The Marxism of the Early Lukács: an Evaluation," *New Left Review* 70 (November–December 1971): 45.

48 W.B. Yeats, *Letters*, ed. Allan Wade (London: R. Hart-Davis, 1954), p. 693. For Pound's attack on *Kultur*, see Chapter 3. Moretti says of modernism that its "extensive range of political choices can be explained only by its basic political indifference" (p. 247). I am arguing just the opposite, that the affinities of modernism with the left as well as the right come from its intense concern for politics.

49 Though a number of recent studies, among the many devoted to modernism and literary history, have argued that literary modernism is historicist in nature, none has discussed the political implications of that term. There is now a rather long list of recent critical works discussing the role of historical understanding and investigation in literary modernism. These include Gregory Jay, *T.S. Eliot and the Poetics of Literary History* (Baton Rouge: Louisiana State University Press, 1984), Joseph G. Kronick, *American Poetics of History: Emerson to the Moderns* (Baton Rouge: Louisiana State University Press, 1984), and Jeffrey M. Perl, *The Tradition of Return: The Implicit History of Modern Literature* (Princeton: Princeton University Press, 1984). The idea that modernism is historicist by nature has been advanced by Perl (p. 278), David Lodge, "Historicism and Literary History: Mapping the Modern Period," *New Literary History* 10 (Spring 1979): 547–555, Harvey Gross, *The Contrived Corridor* (Ann Arbor: University of Michigan Press, 1971), and James Longenbach, *Modernist Poetics of History* (Princeton: Princeton University Press, 1986). See also Wendy Steiner, "Collage or Miracle: Historicism in a Deconstructed World," in *Reconstructing American Literary History*, ed. Sacvan Bercovitch (Cambridge: Harvard University Press, 1986) and Malcolm Bradbury and James McFarlane, "The Name and Nature of Modernism," in *Modernism 1890–1930*, ed. Malcolm Bradbury and James McFarlane (Harmondsworth, Middlesex: Penguin, 1976), p. 20.

50 Isaiah Berlin, *Vico and Herder: Two Studies in the History of Ideas* (London: Hogarth, 1976), p. 34.

51 G.W.F. Hegel, *Natural Law*, tr. T.M. Knox (Philadelphia: University of Pennsylvania Press, 1975), p. 65. For a discussion of this point, see Seyla Benhabib, *Critique, Norm, and Utopia: A Study of the Foundations of Critical Theory* (New York: Columbia University Press, 1986), p. 26.

52 For Marx, see, for example, "The Communist Manifesto," *Selected Writings*, ed. David McLellan (Oxford: Oxford University Press, 1977), p. 234; for Croce, see Pietro Rossi, "The Ideological Valences of Twentieth-Century Historicism," *History and Theory*, Beiheft 14 (1975): 20. For useful general discussions, see Berlin, *Vico and Herder*, Karl Mannheim, "Historicism," in *Essays on the Sociology of Knowledge*, ed. Paul Kecskemeti (London: Routledge & Kegan Paul, 1952), Friedrich Meinecke, *Historism*, tr. J.E. Anderson (London: Routledge & Kegan Paul, 1972), and H. Stuart Hughes, *Consciousness and Society: The Reorientation of European Social Thought 1890–1930* (1958; rpt., New York: Octagon, 1976). This kind of historicism is obviously different from that attacked in Karl Popper's *The Poverty of Historicism*.

53 See, for example, Fredric Jameson, *Marxism and Form* (Princeton: Princeton University Press, 1971), pp. 6 and 324–325. Jameson is, of course, concerned to separate a Marxist historicism from other, less liberating varieties. In this context, see his essay, "Marxism and Historicism," in *Ideologies*. Terry Eagleton argues that Jameson fails in this attempt, that Jameson's historicism ignores the pressure of "the Althusserian critique of Marxist historicism." *Against the Grain* (London: Verso, 1986), p. 73. Arguments like this one, in which Marxism is progressively purified of ideas bearing a reactionary taint, illustrate the general point to be made here, that there is an affinity between Marxism and what seems its opposite.

54   Hans Robert Jauss, *Toward an Aesthetic of Reception,* tr. Timothy Bahti (Minneapolis: University of Minnesota Press, 1982), p. 6. See also Maurice Mandelbaum, *History, Man, and Reason* (Baltimore: Johns Hopkins, 1971), p. 42. Mandelbaum's book is particularly interesting in showing the currency of historicist ideas among even the least likely thinkers, such as John Stuart Mill (pp. 51, 165, 168).

55   Georg G. Iggers, *The German Conception of History: The National Tradition of Historical Thought from Herder to the Present* (Middletown: Wesleyan University Press, 1968), p. 6.

56   Mannheim, *Conservatism,* p. 35.

57   Rossi, p. 22. From the time of Vico, historicism opposed natural law. See Berlin, *Vico and Herder,* p. 34. One of the most interesting conservative attacks on natural law is contained in Henry Sumner Maine's *Ancient Law* (1864; rpt., Tucson: University of Arizona Press, 1986).

58   See, for example, Edmund Burke's differentiation between the rights of man and a people: "For to be a people, and to have these rights, are things incompatible." *An Appeal from the New to the Old Whigs* (London: Dodsley, 1791), p. 119. See also Maine's contrast between rights based on the individual and those derived from kinship in the family (p. 163).

59   Abdallah Laroui, *The Crisis of the Arab Intellectual: Traditionalism or Historicism?,* tr. Diarmid Cammell (Berkeley: University of California Press, 1976), p. 100. See also the discussion in Arif Dirlik, "Culturalism as Hegemonic Ideology and Liberating Practice," *Cultural Critique* 6 (Spring 1987): 32–43. Even Althusser is willing to admit the limited value of historicism in such contexts. See *Reading Capital,* tr. Ben Brewster (London: NLB, 1970), p. 141.

60   Karl Löwith, *From Hegel to Nietzsche,* tr. David E. Greene (New York: Doubleday Anchor, 1967), p. 216.

61   As Tzvetan Todorov says, paraphrasing Friedrich Schlegel, "Periods are like the citizens of a republic . . . The time of despotic monarchies has passed, the spirit of the bourgeois revolution breathes on the arts as on the sciences, and along with it comes history, that is, the recognition of irreducible differences." *Theories of the Symbol,* tr. Catherine Porter (Ithaca: Cornell University Press, 1982), p. 287. Rolf Gruner contends that historicism is progressive per se because it judges the past instead of simply abiding by it and also establishes the right of the present to its own standards. "Progressivism and Historicism," *Clio* 10 (Spring 1981): 279–290.

62   Hegel, *Reason in History,* p. 46, and *Philosophy of Right,* p. 11.

63   Habermas, *Philosophical Discourse of Modernity,* p. 73.

64   Scruton, p. 191.

65   Historicism has also been accused from outside of sapping Germany's moral strength and leading the way to Hitler. See Theodor Schieder, "The Role of Historical Consciousness in Political Action," *History and Theory,* Beiheft 17 (1978): 5–6. Note that this accusation differs from the similar one leveled by Popper against philosophies of history.

66 Jauss, p. 50; Iggers, p. 38; Wilhelm Dilthey, "The Rise of Hermeneutics," tr. Fredric Jameson, *New Literary History* 3 (Winter 1972): 243. In the later part of his career, Dilthey explored the much more promising possibility that language, as objectified meaning, could serve as a stable standard. See Paul Ricoeur, *Hermeneutics and the Human Sciences,* tr. John B. Thompson (Cambridge: Cambridge University Press, 1981), pp. 49–53. This is the possibility now pursued by Habermas.

67 See, for example, Hans-Georg Gadamer, *Truth and Method* (New York: Crossroad, 1985), p. 198 and Ricoeur, p. 53.

68 Leszek Kolakowski, *Main Currents of Marxism,* tr. P.S. Falla (Oxford: Clarendon Press, 1978), 1:77.

69 Kolakowski, 1:265. See also Benhabib, pp. 54, 61, and 69.

70 Marx, *Selected Writings,* p. 83.

71 See, for example, Ernst Bloch, *Natural Law and Human Dignity,* tr. Dennis J. Schmidt (Cambridge: MIT Press, 1986), pp. 191–192. This argument is also often advanced by Eagleton.

72 Benhabib, p. 69. See also Habermas's contention, quoted in Benhabib, that "From the beginning there was a lack of clarity concerning the normative foundation of Marxian social theory" (p. 8). Contemporary disciples of Lukács like Agnes Heller can quite unselfconsciously refer to the "human cause" as if there were only one. "Lukács' Aesthetics," *New Hungarian Quarterly* 7.24 (Winter, 1966): 90. In "Marxian Freedom, Individual Liberty, and the End of Alienation," John Gray asserts that "Marx writes out conflict and divergence from the human essence." Paul, p. 185.

73 The danger is identified by Berlin in his consideration of positive freedom, a conception by which a true humanity is distinguished from empirical human beings, who may thus be coerced in the interests of their better selves. Berlin, *Four Essays,* pp. 132–133. See as well the entry on "human nature" in *A Dictionary of Marxist Thought,* ed. Tom Bottomore et al (Cambridge: Harvard University Press, 1983), pp. 214–215.

74 See Benhabib, p. 29.

75 Ezra Pound, *The Cantos* (New York: New Directions, 1982), 53/265 and 82/526. Though the two instances are separated by quite a bit in *The Cantos,* Pound was quoting the "two halves of the tally" motto as early as 1938, about the time Canto 53 was written.

76 Cullingford, p. viii. T.S. Eliot, *Notes towards the Definition of Culture* (New York: Harcourt, Brace and Co., 1949), p. 62.

77 Herf, p. 207.

78 Sanford Schwartz, *The Matrix of Modernism* (Princeton: Princeton University Press, 1985), p. 115. Michael Levenson, *A Genealogy of Modernism* (Cambridge: Cambridge University Press, 1984), p. 186. Schwartz also draws a brief comparison between Eliot and Lukács (p. 162).

79 Eagleton, *Ideology,* p. 25.

80   Friedrich Schiller, *On the Aesthetic Education of Man,* ed. Elizabeth M. Wilkinson and L.A. Willoughby (Oxford: Clarendon Press, 1967), p. 151. See also M.H. Abrams, *Natural Supernaturalism* (New York: Norton, 1971), pp. 209–213, Todorov, pp. 154–160 and 279–280, and Eagleton, *Ideology,* p. 99.

81   See Paul de Man's attack on this assumption: "The Dead-End of Formalist Criticism," *Blindness and Insight: Essays in the Rhetoric of Contemporary Criticism,* 2nd ed. (Minneapolis: University of Minnesota Press, 1983), p. 237.

82   M.H. Abrams, "Structure and Style in the Greater Romantic Lyric," in *From Sensibility to Romanticism,* ed. Frederick W. Hilles and Harold Bloom (New York: Oxford University Press, 1965), pp. 206, 220, 218. The Coleridge passage is quoted from *Collected Letters,* ed. Earl Leslie Griggs (Oxford: Oxford University Press, 1956), 4:545. See also Abrams' *Natural Supernaturalism.*

83   Two particular sides can be represented by Marjorie Levinson, "Wordsworth's Intimations Ode: A Timely Utterance," in *Historical Studies and Literary Criticism* (Madison: University of Wisconsin Press, 1985), ed. Jerome J. McGann, pp. 48–75, which attacks from a New Historicist angle, and J. Hillis Miller, "Tradition and Difference," *Diacritics* 2 (1972): 6–13, which attacks from a deconstructionist point of view.

84   Schwartz, p. 73. For a discussion of various theories of "two modernisms," see Stanley Sultan, *Eliot, Joyce and Company* (New York: Oxford University Press, 1987), pp. 102–115, especially p. 106 where Sultan says, "the modernists' successful syncretism of the contraries was the radical source of the newness that distinguished their art." A hostile separation of modernism into two different types is that of Perry Meisel, *The Myth of the Modern: A Study in British Literature and Criticism after 1850* (New Haven: Yale University Press, 1987).

85   Levenson, p. 186. The same point is made, in a negative way, by Moretti, who argues that, reconciliation being impossible in a radically divided society, the "modern lyric" now devotes itself to "compromise" so as to temper and even legitimate conflicts that cannot be resolved (pp. 33–34). Eliot then becomes, in some sense, the villain of Moretti's book, for precisely the same reasons that Levenson makes him a hero, for offering new and powerful means of bringing equilibrium to basic philosophical, political, and poetic conflicts (pp. 219–220).

86   Levenson, p. 189.

87   The most persuasive discussions of this aspect of Pound's work are to be found in Marjorie Perloff, *The Poetics of Indeterminacy: Rimbaud to Cage* (1981; rpt., Evanston: Northwestern University Press, 1983) and *The Dance of the Intellect: Studies in the Poetry of the Pound Tradition* (Cambridge: Cambridge University Press, 1985).

88   See Yeats, *Explorations,* pp. 193 and 313 and Eliot, *Selected Essays 1917–1932* (New York: Harcourt, Brace, 1932), p. 117. There is a substantial debate on the subject of modernism and autonomy. The basic text is probably Peter Bürger, *Theory of the Avant-Garde,* tr. Michael Shaw (Minneapolis: University of Minnesota Press, 1984). Bürger argues that the avant-garde negates the autonomy of art by highlighting the institutional nature of art and the art work. As Berman says, discussions following Bürger usually separate modernism from the avant garde. I agree with Berman's contention that this unacceptably conflates modernism with the nineteenth-century art forms it particularly challenged. See *Modern*

Culture and Critical Theory, pp. 72–73, and p. 253, n. 4. For Berman, modernism also subverts the autonomy of the work of art, but, in a way that follows Adorno, he argues that this reduces its critical power. See pp. 42–53 and 70–98. For many other critics, modernism falls into a recapitulation of the very autonomy it tries to undermine. See, for example, Terry Eagleton, *Against the Grain,* p. 140. Moretti also sees modernism as longing for conventional autonomy and thus turning its back on public issues and political responsibility (pp. 210, 246–247). The constant here is the critical standpoint toward modernism. If autonomy is seen as providing an independent vantage point from which to criticize society, then modernism is said to abandon autonomy. If, on the other hand, autonomy is seen as part of bourgeois ideology, then modernism is said to favor it. It may be that modernism has in fact an ambivalent or contradictory attitude toward this question that mirrors its ambivalent position in society itself.

89   Theodor Adorno, "Reconciliation under Duress," in *Aesthetics and Politics,* by Ernst Bloch et al (London: NLB, 1977), p. 171. See also Lunn, pp. 83 and 118.

90   Horkheimer and Adorno, *Dialectic of Enlightenment,* pp. 130–131. See the commentary on this passage in Habermas, *Modernity,* p. 112.

Chapter 1

1   The following abbreviations will be used in the text to identify quotations from the works of Yeats: A, *The Autobiography of William Butler Yeats* (New York: Collier, 1965); CL, *Collected Letters of W.B. Yeats,* ed. John Kelly (Oxford: Clarendon Press, 1986–), v. 1; E, *Essays* (New York: Macmillan, 1924); EI, *Essays and Introductions* (New York: Macmillan Collier, 1961); EX, *Explorations* (New York: Macmillan Collier, 1962); L, *Letters,* ed. Allan Wade (London: R. Hart-Davis, 1954); M, *Memoirs,* ed. Denis Donoghue (New York: Macmillan, 1973); OTB, *On the Boiler* (Dublin: Cuala Press, 1938); SS, *Senate Speeches,* ed. Donald R. Pearce (Bloomington, Ind: Indiana University Press, 1960); UP, *Uncollected Prose,* ed. John P. Frayne and Colton Johnson (New York: Columbia University Press, 1970), 2 vols.; VP, *The Variorum Edition of the Poems of W.B. Yeats,* ed. Peter Allt and Russell K. Alspach (New York: Macmillan, 1957). Thomas Parkinson states received opinion on Yeats quite succinctly: "Yeats was a modern poet but not a modernist." "Yeats and the Limits of Modernity," *Yeats: An Annual of Critical and Textual Studies* 3 (1985): 60.

2   For a disparaging use of the term "modern," see UP, 1:113. But Yeats was also capable of taking up quite the opposite position if goaded to it. In 1889, he insisted, "The people of my own age are in the long run the most important. They are the future" (CL, p. 142). Opposing Edward Dowden in 1895, he declared, "It does not seem to me a question for us whether this literature be important or unimportant, but only whether it be new or not new. If it be new no man living can measure its importance, or say what sails may be filled by it in the future. . ." (CL, p. 430).

3   W.J. McCormack, *Ascendancy and Tradition in Anglo-Irish Literary History From 1789 to 1939* (Oxford: Clarendon Press, 1985), pp. 296–297.

4   W.J. McCormack, "'The Protestant Strain': Or, A Short History of Anglo-Irish Literature from S.T. Coleridge to Thomas Mann," in *Across a Roar-*

ing Hill: The Protestant Imagination in Modern Ireland, ed. Gerald Dawe and Edna Longley (Belfast and Dover, NH: Blackstaff Press, 1985), p. 60.

5 "Equality, it seemed," according to F.S.L. Lyons, "was no substitute for nationality." F.S.L. Lyons, *Ireland Since the Famine* (London: Weidenfeld and Nicolson, 1971), p. 563.

6 Elizabeth Cullingford, *Yeats, Ireland and Fascism* (London: Macmillan, 1981), p. viii.

7 See Charles Taylor, *Hegel and Modern Society* (Cambridge: Cambridge University Press, 1979), p. 51 and Shlomo Avineri, *Hegel's Theory of the Modern State* (Cambridge: Cambridge University Press, 1972), p. 99.

8 A. Norman Jeffares, *A New Commentary on the Poems of W.B. Yeats* (Stanford: Stanford University Press, 1984), p. 31.

9 Henry David Thoreau, *A Week, Walden, Maine Woods, Cape Cod* (New York: Library of America, 1985), p. 331.

10 William Butler Yeats, *John Sherman & Dhoya,* ed. Richard J. Finneran (Detroit: Wayne State University, 1969), p. 47. See p. 92 for the "Innisfree" incident.

11 Fredric Jameson, *The Political Unconscious: Narrative as a Socially Symbolic Act* (Ithaca, NY: Cornell University Press, 1981), p. 249. For Simmel's similar analysis, see Georg Simmel, *On Individuality and Social Forms,* ed. Donald N. Levine (Chicago: University of Chicago Press, 1971), p. 257.

12 Isaiah Berlin, *Four Essays on Liberty* (New York: Oxford University Press, 1970), p. 123.

13 See also Guido de Ruggiero, *The History of European Liberalism,* tr. R.G. Collingwood (1927; rpt., Boston: Beacon, 1959), p. 350. Berlin's association of negative freedom with liberalism has been challenged, though it remains the starting point of nearly every such discussion. See John Gray, "On Negative and Positive Liberty," in *Conceptions of Liberty in Political Philosophy,* ed. Zbigniew Pelczynski and John Gray (New York: St. Martin's, 1984), pp. 321-348.

14 Michael J. Sandel, "Introduction," in *Liberalism and its Critics,* ed. Michael J. Sandel (Oxford: Basil Blackwell, 1984), p. 5.

15 As Gray says, "there is an important sense in which negative freedom (as Berlin originally conceives of it) is consistent with the presence and absence of any conditions whatsoever" (p. 339).

16 *Hegel's Philosophy of Right,* tr. T.M. Knox (Oxford: Clarendon Press, 1942), p. 33.

17 Seamus Deane, *Celtic Revivals* (London: Faber & Faber, 1985), p. 15.

18 The importance of the distinction between negative and positive freedom to Irish politics is indicated by R.L. McCartney's Field Day pamphlet, which bases its defense of continued partition on Berlin's essay. McCartney's assertion that traditional liberal notions of negative freedom are the best guarantee of minority rights is weakened by bland assertions such as this: "The United Kingdom of Great Britain and Northern Ireland is, with all its faults, a pluralist state. Its catholic millions and their Irish co-religionists who have chosen to live there find no oppression, nor in real terms do they suffer any social or political disadvantage." R.L. McCartney, *Liberty and Authority in Ireland* (Derry: Field Day Theatre Co., 1985), p. 25.

19 Jeffares, p. 31.

20 McCormack, *Ascendancy and Tradition*, p. 295. See also p. 346.

21 Hugh Kenner, *A Colder Eye: The Modern Irish Writers* (New York: Penguin, 1983), p. 75. Kenner also produces a much more elaborate pattern of stress on p. 74.

22 Oliver MacDonagh, *States of Mind: A Study of Anglo-Irish Conflict 1780–1980* (London: Allen & Unwin, 1983), p. 16.

23 Malcolm Brown, *The Politics of Irish Literature From Thomas Davis to W.B. Yeats* (London: Allen & Unwin, 1972), p. 46.

24 MacDonagh, p. 110.

25 Brown, pp. 50–55.

26 Quoted in Nicholas Mansergh, *The Irish Question 1840–1921*, 3rd ed. (London: Allen & Unwin, 1975), p. 96.

27 Yeats's earliest poetry shows a distinct tension between liberal and historical versions of nationalism. "The Two Titans," subtitled, "A Political Poem," depicts Ireland as a young country straining at its bonds, robbed of its right of self-assertion and freedom (VP, p. 687). A slightly later but more characteristic poem, "The Celtic Twilight," depicts Ireland as an old mother, whose glory lies in the past. Her strength comes from the way she repudiates the concept of right and wrong, subordinating such arguments to the truth of mood (VP, p. 147). For a more psychological interpretation of "The Two Titans," see Richard Ellmann, *Yeats: The Man and the Masks* (1948; rpt., New York: Norton, 1979), p. 49.

28 John O'Leary, *Recollections of Fenians and Fenianism* (London: Downey and Co., 1896), 2:160.

29 Marcus Bourke, *John O'Leary: A Study in Irish Separatism* (Tralee: Anvil Books, 1967), p. 189. See also p. 187, where Bourke derives Yeats's oligarchical principles from O'Leary.

30 See, on the other hand, Yeats's complaint that with Parnell's fall "Irish imagination fled the sordid scene" (EX, p. 372). See also Lyons's discussion of this historical juncture, *Ireland Since the Famine*, pp. 18 and 232. In this turn to culture after political disappointment, Yeats and the Revival reenact the original turn of nineteenth century German Romanticism. See Taylor, p. 6.

31 In *Culture and Society*, Raymond Williams traces the English influence of this doctrine back as far as Pugin. *Culture and Society: 1780–1950* (1958; rpt., New York: Columbia University Press, 1983). E.H. Gombrich has frequently described its beginnings in Hegel, who says, "All the features which stand out in the history of a nation are intimately connected with one another." G.W.F. Hegel, *Lectures on the Philosophy of World History, Introduction: Reason in History*, tr. H.B. Nisbet (Cambridge: Cambridge University Press, 1975), p. 101. Hegel credits Montesquieu with originating this idea.

32 Berlin, pp. 5 and 12.

33 Cullingford, p. 9.

34 Quoted in Philip L. Marcus, *Yeats and the Beginning of the Irish Renaissance* (Ithaca, NY: Cornell University Press, 1970), p. 2. See Marcus' discussion, pp. 1–34.

35 F.S.L. Lyons, *Culture and Anarchy in Ireland: 1890–1939* (Oxford: Clarendon Press, 1979), p. 2.

36 Lyons, *Culture and Anarchy*, p. 39.

37 Marcus, p. 15.

38 George Watson, *Irish Identity and the Literary Revival* (London: Croom Helm, 1979), p. 96.

39 See Marcus, p. 25.

40 Watson, p. 32.

41 Denis Donoghue, *We Irish: Essays on Irish Literature and Society* (New York: Knopf, 1986), p. 16.

42 Mansergh, p. 23.

43 J.C. Beckett, *The Anglo-Irish Tradition* (London: Faber and Faber, 1976), p. 101.

44 Marcus, p. 21.

45 Beckett, pp. 102–103. See also Watson, p. 95, where this passage is quoted and commented on.

46 John Hutchinson, *The Dynamics of Cultural Nationalism: The Gaelic Revival and the Creation of the Irish Nation State* (London: Allen & Unwin, 1987), p. 140.

47 See Watson, p. 98.

48 Seamus Deane, "The Literary Myths of the Revival: A Case for their Abandonment," in *Myth and Reality in Irish Literature,* ed. Joseph Ronsley (Waterloo: Wilfred Laurie University Press, 1977), p. 320.

49 Watson, pp. 71–72.

50 Conor Cruise O'Brien, *States of Ireland* (London: Hutchinson, 1972), p. 73.

51 John Kelly, "Choosing and Inventing: Yeats and Ireland," in *Across A Roaring Hill: The Protestant Imagination in Ireland,* eds. Gerald Dawe and Edna Longley (Belfast and Dover, N.H.: Blackstaff, 1985), p. 20.

52 De Ruggiero, p. 5.

53 Paul de Man, *The Rhetoric of Romanticism* (New York: Columbia University Press, 1984), p. 146.

54 For a discussion of the relationship between aristocratic "Wealth of Being" and the aesthetic, see Terry Eagleton, *The Ideology of the Aesthetic* (London: Basil Blackwell, 1990), p. 36. As Eagleton points out, this ideal descends through Arnold, Ruskin and Morris to become "a powerful critique of middle-class individualism." The list might, of course, have been extended to include Yeats.

55 As Eagleton puts it in his discussion of Schiller, "The aesthetic is whatever is the other of any specific social interest; it is without bias to any definite activity, but precisely on that account a general activating capacity. Culture is the negation of all concrete claims and commitments in the name of totality . . ." (p. 109).

56 T.R. Whitaker, *Swan and Shadow: Yeats's Dialogue with History* (Chapel Hill: University of North Carolina Press, 1964), p. 170. See also Daniel A. Harris, *Yeats, Coole Park and Ballylee* (Baltimore: John Hopkins University Press, 1974), p. 91.

57 Whitaker, p. 169.

58 Frank Kermode, *Romantic Image* (1957; rpt., New York: Vintage, 1964), p. 34.

59 See, in particular, Marjorie Perloff, "The Consolation Theme in Yeats's 'In Memory of Major Robert Gregory'" *Modern Language Quarterly* 27 (1966): 306–322.

60 Bernard G. Krimm, *Yeats and the Emergence of the Irish Free State 1918–1939* (Troy, NY: Whitston, 1981), p. 95.

61 See Harris, p. 49.

62 Harris, p. 129.

63 According to Randolph Quirk et al, *A Comprehensive Grammar of the English Language* (London: Longman, 1986), *would* in such cases is equivalent to *used to* (pp. 228–229).

64 See Perloff, p. 319.

65 Elizabeth M. Wilkinson and L.A. Willoughby, eds., *On the Aesthetic Education of Man,* by Friedrich Schiller (Oxford: Clarendon Press, 1967), p. xxxix.

66 Wilkinson and Willoughby, p. cxcii.

67 D.J. Gordon and Ian Fletcher, *W.B. Yeats: Images of a Poet* (1961; rpt., Westport, Conn.: Greenwood Press, 1979), p. 33.

68 Harris, p. 136.

69 Kenneth Burke, *A Grammar of Motives* (1945; rpt., Berkeley: University of California Press, 1969), pp. 35–38.

70 Richard Ellmann, *The Identity of Yeats* (New York: Oxford University Press, 1964), p. 138.

71 Perloff's is the most intricate account of these relationships.

72 See Peter Sacks, *The English Elegy: Studies in the Genre from Spenser to Yeats* (Baltimore: John Hopkins University Press, 1985), p. 274.

73 Sacks, p. 293.

74 De Man, p. 146.

75 Homi K. Bhabha, "Signs Taken for Wonders: Questions of Ambivalence and Authority under a Tree outside Delhi, May 1817," in *"Race," Writing, and Difference,* ed. Henry Louis Gates, Jr. (Chicago: University of Chicago Press, 1986), p. 172.

76 For Eliot's views on the responsibility of the elite, see "Responsibility and Power," *Christian News-Letter,* Dec. 1, 1943, pp. 1–4.

77 Paul de Man, *Allegories of Reading* (New Haven: Yale University Press, 1979), p. 261. See also Karl Mannheim's analysis of the "conservative experience of property" in which there is "a definite, vital, and reciprocal relationship between the owner and his property" quite different from the sort of relationship that can be altered by legal documents. *Conservatism,* tr. David Kettler and Volker Meja (London and New York: Routledge & Kegan Paul, 1986), pp. 89–90.

78 See EI, p. 526 and EX, p. 312. In *Yeats and Politics in the 1930s* (London: Macmillan, 1988), Paul Scott Stanfield traces Yeats's preoccupation with family to Balzac. See p. 122, however, where Stanfield justly observes that Yeats found in Balzac what he already believed. There is also a useful discussion of the term "kindred" in Stanfield's chapter on eugenics (p. 156). See also Cullingford, p. 132.

79 Yeats argued at one time that "if your family have lived in Ireland for generations, you may be certain in your mind that you are, whether you like it or not, a Celt. . . . No matter what our names testify we are predominantly Celtic." Quoted, with no date, in Kelly, p. 17.

80 Henry Sumner Maine, *Ancient Law: Its Connection with the Early History of*

Society, and Its Relation to Modern Ideas (1864; rpt., Tucson: University of Arizona Press, 1986), pp. 127, 126. Maine's analysis might lend a historical dimension to the argument advanced by Mark Taylor in *Death Is the Mother of Beauty* (Chicago: University of Chicago Press, 1987) that metaphor per se is founded on concepts of kinship.

81   Maine, pp. 165, 128.

82   McCormack, "The Protestant Strain," p. 73.

83   MacDonagh, p. 38.

84   MacDonagh, Chapter 3.

85   Ronald Bush, "Yeats, Spooks, Nursery Rhymes, and the Vicissitudes of Late Modernism," *Yeats: An Annual of Critical and Textual Studies* 3 (1985): 23.

86   *Criterion*, 5 (June 1927): 283.

87   Quoted in Kelly, p. 1.

88   In *The Permanence of Yeats*, ed. James Hall and Martin Steinmann (New York: Collier, 1961), p. 235. See also Ellmann, *The Man and the Masks*, p. 243.

89   Harold Bloom, *Yeats* (New York: Oxford University Press, 1970), pp. 360–361.

90   Quoted in Mansergh, p. 138.

91   See Donald T. Torchiana, *W.B. Yeats and Georgian Ireland* (Evanston: Northwestern University Press, 1966), p. 201.

92   See the discussion of these issues in Krimm, pp. 72–73. Note, however, that Krimm seems to have missed the speech on the Public Safety Bill, SS, p. 60.

93   Cullingford, p. 183.

94   Harris, pp. 161–162.

95   For an account of this change, see Peter Faulkner, *Yeats and the Irish Eighteenth Century* (Dublin: Dolmen Press, 1965), and Torchiana.

96   Harris, p. 160.

97   McCormack, *Ascendancy and Tradition*, p. 358.

98   See O'Brien, Chapter 6, "The Catholic State."

99   Seamus Deane, "Heroic Styles: The Tradition of an Idea," in *Ireland's Field Day*, Field Day Theatre Company (London: Hutchinson, 1985), p. 49.

100   Quoted in Deane, *Celtic Revivals*, p. 23. Yeats took much comfort from Burke's general emphasis on the necessity of an aristocracy to a healthy state, especially in *An Appeal from the New to the Old Whigs* (1791). But he neglected Burke's contention that the Anglo-Irish were not fitted by circumstances to play such a role. See *A Letter from the right Hon. Edmund Burke to Sir Hercules Langrishe . . .* (London: Debrett, 1792), especially p. 15.

101   Quoted in Torchiana, p. 193. See also Williams, p. 11.

102   Cullingford, p. 132. On the same page Cullingford describes "kindred" as gradually incorporating all of Ireland, even including those outside Yeats's own tradition. Here, she drastically undervalues the oppositional nature of the term as Yeats used it in political controversy.

103   Quoted in Torchiana, p. 162.

104   Quoted in Lyons, *Ireland Since the Famine*, p. 540. The form of property ownership characteristic of the new state also fits Yeats's ideology. MacDonagh notes that it has been called "familialism." Whether Yeats would approve of the particular families now in hereditary possession of the land is hard to tell. See MacDonagh, p. 50.

105 Odon Por, *Fascism,* tr. E. Townshend (London: Labour Publishing, 1923), pp. 149–152. For the relationship between Pound and Por, see Chapter 3.
106 Quoted in Cullingford, p. 148.
107 Quoted in A. James Gregor, *The Ideology of Fascism* (New York: The Free Press, 1969), p. 156.
108 Quoted in Cullingford, p. 204.
109 Stanfield, pp. 70–71 and 76.
110 The table is to be found in A. Norman Jeffares, *W.B. Yeats: Man and Poet,* 2nd ed. (London: Routledge & Kegan Paul, 1962), pp. 351–352. It is discussed by Cullingford on p. 216 and by Stanfield on pp. 72–74.
111 See Eagleton's *The Ideology of the Aesthetic* for a modern elaboration of this idea, especially p. 369, where Eagleton juxtaposes the "left-aesthetic tradition, from Schiller and Marx to Morris and Marcuse" to the right-wing tradition that ends in aesthetic modernism.

Chapter 2

1 T.S. Eliot, *After Strange Gods* (New York: Harcourt, Brace, 1933), p. 53. This work will be referred to hereafter in the text as ASG. The following abbreviations will be used to identify other citations in the text: NDC, *Notes towards the Definition of Culture* (New York: Harcourt, Brace, 1949); OPP, *On Poetry and Poets* (London: Faber and Faber, 1957); SE, *Selected Essays 1917–1932* (New York: Harcourt, Brace, 1932); UOM, "*Ulysses,* Order, and Myth," *The Dial* 75 (November 1923): 480–483; UPUC, *The Use of Poetry and the Use of Criticism* (1933; rpt., London: Faber and Faber, 1980).
2 Irving Babbitt, *Rousseau and Romanticism* (Boston: Houghton Mifflin, 1919), p. xv. See also the work of another of Eliot's early teachers, Josiah Royce, *The World and the Individual* (1899; rpt., New York: Macmillan, 1923). See especially the supplementary essay entitled "The One, the Many, and the Infinite," which attacks Bradley. That these matters were discussed by Eliot is made evident in Harry T. Costello's *Josiah Royce's Seminar,* ed. Grover Smith (New Brunswick, NJ: Rutgers University Press, 1963), pp. 167–169.
3 Richard Wollheim, *F.H. Bradley* (Harmondsworth, Middlesex: Penguin, 1959), p. 233.
4 G.W.F. Hegel, *Natural Law,* ed. H.B. Acton (Philadelphia: University of Pennsylvania Press, 1975), p. 46, n. 40.
5 Hegel, *Natural Law,* p. 65. In *The Philosophy of History,* Hegel insists that individuals exist "in a particular country with a particular religion, and in a particular constellation of knowledge and attitudes. . . ." *Lectures in the Philosophy of World History, Introduction: Reason in History,* tr. H.B. Nisbet (Cambridge: Cambridge University Press, 1975), p. 46.
6 See also *Philosophy of Right,* tr. T.M. Knox (Oxford: Clarendon Press, 1942), p. 33 and p. 157, and *Reason in History,* p. 98. Hegel does not dispute the idea that individuals have fundamental rights, only the derivation of these rights

from quasi-historical theories of what is "natural." See for discussion of this distinction, Lewis P. Hinchman, *Hegel's Critique of the Enlightenment* (Tampa/Gainesville: University Presses of Florida, 1984), p. 105, and Jürgen Habermas, *Theory and Practice,* tr. John Viertel (Boston: Beacon Press, 1973), pp. 121–141. See also the discussion of the natural law essay in Shlomo Avineri, *Hegel's Theory of the Modern State* (Cambridge: Cambridge University Press, 1972), pp. 82–86, and Seyla Benhabib, *Critique, Norm, and Utopia: A Study of the Foundations of Critical Theory* (New York: Columbia University Press, 1981), especially p. 28.

7 Hegel uses the phrase "duty for duty's sake" when discussing Kant in *The Philosophy of Right,* p. 90.

8 See the discussion of the argument in David Bell, "The Insufficiency of Ethics," in *The Philosophy of F.H. Bradley,* ed. Anthony Mansur and Guy Stock (Oxford: Clarendon Press, 1984), pp. 64–65. See also Pamela McCallum, *Literature and Method: Towards a Critique of I.A. Richards, T.S. Eliot and F.R. Leavis* (Dublin; Atlantic Highlands, NJ: Gill and Macmillan; Humanities Press, 1983), p. 111.

9 F.H. Bradley, *Ethical Studies* (1876; rpt., New York: Stechert, 1927), p. 150.

10 Bradley, *Ethical Studies,* pp. 150–151.

11 R.G. Collingwood, *The Idea of History* (1946; rpt., New York: Oxford University Press, 1956), p. 141. It is important to note that Bradley criticizes and attempts to transcend the formula he offers in "My Station and its Duties." These criticisms are aptly summarized by Wollheim, pp. 247–251. See also Peter Nicholson, "Bradley as a Political Philosopher," in Mansur and Stock, pp. 122–124. In Bradley's final "ideal" morality, however, the "first and still most important contribution comes from one's station and its duties" (Wollheim, p. 251).

12 Bruce Robbins, "Modernism in History, Modernism in Power," in *Modernism Reconsidered,* ed. Robert Kiely (Cambridge: Harvard University Press, 1983), p. 244. For an interpretation of "Prufrock" that sees it as accomplishing a reconciliation of identity and difference, see Sanford Schwartz, *The Matrix of Modernism* (Princeton: Princeton University Press, 1985), pp. 96 and 100–101.

13 Terry Eagleton, *Walter Benjamin: or Towards a Revolutionary Criticism* (London: Verso, 1981), p. 31.

14 T.S. Eliot, *The Complete Poems and Plays 1909–1950* (New York: Harcourt, Brace & World, 1971), p. 5. All subsequent quotations in the text will be taken from this volume. Because there are only a few poems in question, no further page numbers will be given. In the case of *The Waste Land,* parenthetical line numbers will be provided, because these are present in most printings of the poem. Passages from *Four Quartets* will be identified parenthetically by poem (BN, etc.) and section number.

15 Kenneth Burke, *A Grammar of Motives* (1945; rpt. Berkeley: University of California Press, 1969), p. 506.

16 See the struggle between the will and the will of the "unclean members" in the *Confessions* 4.11. See also 8.11. In Neo-Platonic terms, Augustine sees lust as a fall from unity into multiplicity.

17 Burke, p. 509.

18 Richard Ellmann, *The Identity of Yeats* (1954; rpt., New York: Oxford University Press, 1964), p. 139.

19 William Empson, *The Structure of Complex Words* (London: Chatto & Windus, 1951), p. 101.

20 In *He Do the Police in Different Voices: The Waste Land and its Protagonist* (Chicago: University of Chicago Press, 1986), Calvin Bedient uses the term "false plenitude," p. 56.

21 Roman Jakobson, *Selected Writings* (The Hague: Mouton, 1971), II:258–259.

22 A.D. Moody, *Thomas Stearns Eliot Poet* (Cambridge: Cambridge University Press, 1980), p. 33.

23 As Terry Eagleton puts it in another context, "freedom in these social conditions has lapsed into anarchy, and necessity into iron determinism." *The Ideology of the Aesthetic* (London: Basil Blackwell, 1990), p. 207.

24 For reproductions of the syllabi, see Moody, pp. 41–49, and Ronald Schuchard, "T.S. Eliot as an Extension Lecturer, 1916–1919," *Review of English Studies*, 25 (1974): 163–173 and 292–304. For discussions of the intellectual background of these lectures, see Schuchard and John D. Margolis, *T.S. Eliot's Intellectual Development 1922–1939* (Chicago: University of Chicago Press, 1972).

25 Moody, p. 44 and 47. Though such a convergence may now seem fantastic, Zeev Sternhell reports that there was a "socialist-monarchist" strain in the Action Française. Maurras himself used the term as did other conservatives and neo-fascists in France. Zeev Sternhell, *Neither Right nor Left: Fascist Ideology in France*, tr. David Maisel (Berkeley: University of California Press, 1986), pp. 57, 60, 63.

26 Georg Lukács, *The Meaning of Contemporary Realism*, tr. John and Necke Mander (London: Merlin Press, 1963), pp. 25–26. Eliot is mentioned four times in Lukács's massive *Die Eigenart des Ästhetischen*. In both works Lukács takes "The Hollow Men" as typical of Eliot's poetry.

27 See Eagleton's discussion in *Ideology*, pp. 322–325.

28 See Louis Menand, *Discovering Modernism: T.S. Eliot and His Context* (New York: Oxford University Press, 1987).

29 "In Memory of Henry James," *Egoist* 5 (Jan. 1918): 1. Quoted in Lyndall Gordon, *Eliot's New Life* (New York: Farrar, Straus, Giroux, 1988), p. 229.

30 Hegel, *Philosophy of Right*, p. 11. Bradley says, "Every man's present standpoint ought to determine his belief in respect to *all* past events." "Presuppositions of Critical History," in *Collected Essays*, v. 1 (Oxford: Clarendon Press, 1935), p. 2.

31 Quoted in Piers Gray, *T.S. Eliot's Intellectual and Poetic Development 1901–1922* (Brighton; Atlantic Highlands, NJ: Harvester; Humanities Press, 1982), p. 114.

32 This work is analyzed quite closely by Gray, Chapter 4.

33 T.S. Eliot, "A Commentary," *Criterion* 3 (January 1925): 163.

34 T.S. Eliot, "A Commentary," *Criterion* 17 (October 1937): 82.

35 Bradley, *Ethical Studies*, p. 171.

36 Jeffrey M. Perl and Andrew P. Tuck, "Foreign Metaphysics: The Significance of T.S. Eliot's Philosophical Notebooks," *Southern Review* 21 (Winter 1985): 84.

37   *The Letters of T.S. Eliot,* ed. Valerie Eliot, v. 1 (New York: Harcourt Brace Jovanovich, 1988), pp. 79–81. In 1916 he told Conrad Aiken, "I am still a relativist" (p. 146).

38   *A Garland for John Donne,* ed. Theodore Spencer (Cambridge: Harvard University Press, 1931), pp. 17–18.

39   See James Longenbach, *Modernist Poetics of History* (Princeton: Princeton University Press, 1986), p. 165; Michael Levenson, *A Genealogy of Modernism* (Cambridge: Cambridge University Press, 1984), pp. 184–185; and Gray, p. 170.

40   Bell, p. 54.

41   Longenbach, p. 165.

42   T.S. Eliot, *Knowledge and Experience in the Philosophy of F.H. Bradley* (London: Faber, 1964), p. 168.

43   Victor P.H. Li, "Theory and Therapy: The Case of T.S. Eliot," *Criticism* 25 (Fall 1983): 350. Li's argument might be summarized by this statement: "Eliot attacks theory as systematic analysis while aiming to achieve a *theoria* of immediate knowledge" (p. 349). In "Philosophy in Kinkanga: Eliot's Pragmatism," *Glyph* 8 (1981), Walter Benn Michaels offers an equally anti-systematic Eliot.

44   See also the reasoning in "Seneca in Translation" (1927). There Eliot compares Greek tragedy favorably to Roman on the grounds that it "is not the expression of a conscious 'system' of philosophy" (SE, p. 57). Criticism hostile to Eliot commonly takes it for granted that his desire to arrange particulars in a system is totalitarian. It should be noted, however, that "system" was a standard fascist term of contempt for bourgeois society. See Russell A. Berman, *Modern Culture and Critical Theory: Art, Politics, and the Legacy of the Frankfurt School* (Madison: University of Wisconsin Press, 1989), p. 102. Yeats also set himself against modern "systematising," even while creating a "system" of his own in *A Vision.*

45   In "The Philosophical Critic," William Righter says, "What at some moments looks as if it tends to the absolute, towards system and fixed standards, is from another point-of-view ready to accept a cultural relativism and the ambiguity of our position in the face of it." See *The Literary Criticism of T.S. Eliot,* ed. David Newton-De Molina (London: Athlone, 1977), p. 135. In his dissertation, Eliot takes up the question of cognitive relativism but leaves it hanging at the end. "Relativity," he says, "impels us toward the Absolute," but the Absolute can only be glimpsed beyond this, the last sentence of the published text because, as Eliot says at the outset, "the ultimate nature of the Absolute does not come within the scope of the present paper." *Knowledge and Experience,* pp. 169 and 31. The final effect of this circumspection is to leave the question eternally open, a result that can hardly solidify the claims of absolute knowledge.

46   Eliot, *Garland,* p. 5.

47   Patrick Gardiner, "German Philosophy and the Rise of Relativism," *Monist* 64 (1981): 139. The crisis of historicism suffered and described by Troeltsch and Meinecke had much to do with relativism, particularly with "the relativization of all values." Theodor Schieder, "The Role of Historical Consciousness in Political Action," *History and Theory,* Beiheft 17 (1978): 5. See also Georg Iggers, *The German Conception of History* (Middletown: Wesleyan University Press, 1968), p. 26.

48 Carl Wellman, "Ethical Implications of Cultural Relativity," *Journal of Philosophy* 60 (1963): 178.

49 See Philippa Foot, "Moral Relativism," in *Relativism: Cognitive and Moral,* ed. Jack W. Meiland and Michael Krausz (Notre Dame: University of Notre Dame Press, 1982), pp. 152–166.

50 Bernard Williams, "An Inconsistent Form of Relativism," in Meiland and Krausz, pp. 171, 173.

51 Note Jameson's confession: "Always historicize! This slogan – the one absolute and we may say 'transhistorical imperative' of all dialectical thought – . . . ." *The Political Unconscious* (Ithaca: Cornell University Press, 1981), p. 9.

52 Bernard Williams, p. 171.

53 As Perl says of Eliot, "His devotion to tradition and convention is not an expression of cultural absolutism but virtually the opposite: an expression of radical skepticism in regard to any one philosophical perspective." Perl and Tuck, p. 85. See also the much less sympathetic argument by Terry Eagleton, *Criticism and Ideology: A Study in Marxist Literary Theory* (London: NLB, 1976), p. 147.

54 "Milton II," in *Selected Prose of T.S. Eliot,* ed. Frank Kermode (New York: Harcourt Brace Jovanovich/Farrar, Straus and Giroux, 1975), p. 266. Originally published in *Proceedings of the British Academy* 33 (1947).

55 Frank Kermode, *Romantic Image* (1957; rpt., New York: Vintage, 1964), p. 145. Menand makes a similar argument, pp. 147–150. See also *Letters,* p. 460, where Eliot says that "any innuendos I make at the expense of Milton, Keats, Shelley and the nineteenth century in general are part of a plan to help us rectify, so far as *I* can, the immense skew in public opinion toward our pantheon of literature."

56 See Lewis Freed, *T.S. Eliot: The Critic as Philosopher* (W. Lafayette, Ind.: Purdue University Press, 1979), p. 132, and Andrew Ross, *The Failure of Modernism: Symptoms of American Poetry* (New York: Columbia University Press, 1986), p. 14.

57 Chris Baldick, *The Social Mission of English Criticism 1848–1932* (Oxford: Clarendon Press, 1983), p. 213. J. Hillis Miller says that the "ideal order" of "Tradition and the Individual Talent" is "much like a private ego enormously expanded." *Poets of Reality* (Cambridge: Harvard University Press, 1965), p. 158.

58 See the penetrating discussion of such elisions of the difference between description and prescription in Richard Wollheim, "Eliot and F.H. Bradley: an account," in *Eliot in Perspective,* ed. Graham Martin (London: Macmillan, 1970), pp. 187 and 189.

59 T.S. Eliot, *Selected Essays: New Edition* (New York: Harcourt, Brace & World, 1964), p. 346.

60 Murray Krieger, *The New Apologists for Poetry* (Minneapolis: University of Minnesota Press, 1956), p. 52. There is a similar objection in John Crowe Ransom's *The New Criticism* (Norfolk: New Directions, 1941), p. 147.

61 Ransom notes this inconsistency, p. 147.

62 Miller, p. 169.

63 Moody, p. 71.

64 Ransom, p. 152.

65 T.S. Eliot, *The Waste Land: A Facsimile,* ed. Valerie Eliot (New York: Harcourt Brace Jovanovich, 1971), p. 31. See Ronald Bush, *T.S. Eliot: A Study in Character and Style* (New York: Oxford University Press, 1984), pp. 56 and 69.

66 Hugh Kenner suggests that this vision of London was to have provided the poem "a sort of presiding personage, the original Fisher King as well as the original Waste Land." "The Urban Apocalypse," in *Eliot in His Time,* ed. A. Walton Litz (Princeton: Princeton University Press, 1973), p. 28.

67 See Eagleton's very similar description: "The division of labour maims and nourishes simultaneously, generating fresh skills and capacities but in a cripplingly one-sided way." *Ideology,* p. 219.

68 Quoted in Bush, p. 70.

69 Bush, p. 71.

70 For Babbitt, see Chapter 2.2. For Maurras, see 2.4. For Sorel, see Moody, p. 47. For Hulme, see Eliot's commentary, *Criterion* 2 (April 1924): 231 and William Chace, *The Political Identities of Ezra Pound and T.S. Eliot* (Stanford: Stanford University Press, 1973), p. 114.

71 *Facsimile,* p. 43.

72 *Facsimile,* p. 45.

73 Grover Smith, *T.S. Eliot's Poetry and Plays,* 2nd ed. (Chicago: University of Chicago Press, 1974), pp. 72–73. Perhaps the first attempt to take seriously Eliot's assertion that "What Tiresias *sees,* in fact, is the substance of the poem" is F.R. Leavis's in *New Bearings in English Poetry* (London: Chatto and Windus, 1932), p. 95. After Smith's rigid application have come some much more flexible attempts, including Michael Levenson's (pp. 186–193) and Calvin Bedient's. Bedient retains Leavis's idea that the poem is the work of an "inclusive human consciousness" but does not identify Tiresias as filling this role.

74 Levenson, p. 191.

75 Metonymy in this sense would contrast to metaphor in the way suggested by Paul de Man, where the "distinction between metonymic aggregates and metaphorical totalities" is "based on the presence, within the latter, of a 'necessary link' that is lacking in the former. . . ." *Allegories of Reading* (New Haven: Yale University Press, 1979), p. 259. To be metonymized would therefore be to be reduced to a mere part that represents only accidentally or contingently the whole from which it is taken or to be expanded by mere addition or aggregation without any necessary link between parts.

76 *The Education of Henry Adams* (Boston: Houghton Mifflin, 1918), p. 445. Quoted as epigraph to Sandra M. Gilbert and Susan Gubar, *No Man's Land: The Place of the Woman Writer in the Twentieth Century* (New Haven: Yale University Press, 1988), v. 1.

77 Theodor W. Adorno, *Prisms,* tr. Samuel and Shierry Weber (Cambridge: MIT Press, 1981), p. 263.

78 Hugh Kenner, *A Sinking Island: The Modern English Writers* (New York: Alfred A. Knopf, 1988), p. 188.

79 Stephen Spender, *T.S. Eliot* (New York: Viking, 1975), p. 112.

80 Adorno, *Prisms,* p. 252.

81 For a brief comparison of the two works, see Franco Moretti, *Signs Taken for Wonders: Essays in the Sociology of Literary Forms,* tr. Susan Fischer et al (London: Verso, 1983), pp. 212–213.

82   Georg Lukács, *The Theory of the Novel,* tr. Anna Bostock (Cambridge: MIT Press, 1971), p. 38. Subsequent citations will be identified in the text as TN.

83   See the explanation of this point in J.M. Bernstein, *The Philosophy of the Novel: Lukács, Marxism and the Dialectics of Form* (Brighton: Harvester Press, 1984), p. 192.

84   See Bernstein, p. 196. See also the excellent discussions by Andrew Feenberg, "Reification and the Antinomies of Socialist Thought," *Telos* 10 (Winter 1971): 101–102 and David Carroll, "Representation or the End(s) of History: Dialectics and Fiction," *Yale French Studies* 59 (1980): 213.

85   Paul de Man, "Georg Lukács's *Theory of the Novel,*" in *Blindness and Insight,* 2nd ed. (Minneapolis: University of Minnesota Press, 1983), p. 56.

86   *Knowledge and Experience,* p. 169.

87   Thus, it seems to me, Eloise Knapp Hay gives the wrong emphasis to the "delusion" of the explorers in Eliot's note. Christ *was* present on the road to Emmaus, but in a form that deluded his followers. Note how this interpretation of the negativity of "What the Thunder Says" differs from Hay's throughout. See *T.S. Eliot's Negative Way* (Cambridge: Harvard University Press, 1982), pp. 64–68.

88   Bernstein, p. 72. See Walter Benjamin, *Illuminations,* tr. Harry Zohn (New York: Schocken, 1969), p. 82.

89   The difference between this sort of irony and the kind made famous by Cleanth Brooks is that the latter is resolved within the text, which then becomes affirmative in character. Note, however, that Brooks ends his reading of *The Waste Land* by saying, "The statement of beliefs emerges *through* confusion and cynicism – not in spite of them." *Modern Poetry and the Tradition* (Chapel Hill: University of North Carolina Press, 1939), p. 172.

90   Adorno, *Prisms,* p. 164.

91   Bernstein, p. 205.

92   David Craig, "The Defeatism of *The Waste Land,*" *Critical Quarterly* 2 (1960): 241–252.

93   Stephen Spender, "Writers and Politics," *Partisan Review* 34 (Summer 1967): 378. A.L. Morton, "T.S. Eliot – A Personal View," *Zeitschrift für Anglistik und Amerikanistik* 14 (1966): 284, 291. For a detailed discussion of the debate in the 1930s on obscurity in poetry, see Valentine Cunningham, *British Writers of the Thirties* (Oxford: Oxford University Press, 1988), pp. 298–304.

94   See Francis Mulhern, *The Moment of Scrutiny* (London: NLB, 1979), p. 25, and Eric Bentley, ed., *The Importance of Scrutiny* (1948; rpt., New York: New York University Press, 1964), pp. 43 and 47.

95   Robert Graves, *Contemporary Techniques of Poetry* (London: Hogarth, 1925), pp. 6, 10.

96   Theodor Adorno, "Reconciliation under Duress," in *Aesthetics and Politics,* by Ernst Bloch et al (London: NLB, 1977), p. 166. In the same essay Adorno defends Eliot, along with Joyce, against Lukács's criticism (p. 162).

97   *For Lancelot Andrewes* (Garden City, NY: Doubleday Doran, 1929), p. vii. Morton knew Eliot, and he argues that Eliot was in fact more sympathetic to Marxism than he was to liberalism. A number of comments bear this out. In the *Criterion* for April 1932, Eliot said, "no one who is seriously concerned can fail to be impressed by the work of Karl Marx" (p. 468). In the *Criterion* for July 1933, he claimed that the reactionary "at this point feels a stronger sympathy with the communist" than with the "Liberal Reformer" (p. 643). In the same year, however, Eliot included in the "primer of heresy" at the end of *After Strange Gods* a quotation from John MacMurray's *The Philosophy of Communism* which declares "the rejection of idealism and the principle of the unity of theory and practice." Part of MacMurray's philosophy of praxis is the belief that "the validity of no belief whatever is capable of demonstration by argument" (p. 72). It is perhaps because Eliot suggested much the same thing himself so many times that he found this particular brand of heresy most "difficult to solve" (p. 69).

98   Nicholson, p. 119. See also the analysis of the British neo-Idealists given by Herbert Marcuse in *Reason and Revolution* (London: Oxford University Press, 1941), pp. 391, 395.

99   Roger Scruton, *The Meaning of Conservatism* (London: Macmillan, 1980), p. 52.

100   For the list of names Eliot gives to define his political position, see T.S. Eliot, "A Commentary," *Criterion* 4 (January 1926): 5. The list also includes Sorel, Benda, and Maritain. See Chace's discussion, pp. 126–132.

101   Richard Shusterman, *T.S. Eliot and the Philosophy of Composition* (London: Duckworth, 1988), p. 38. The relationship between Eliot and Hulme is a very complex one often touched on in the criticism. Levenson is concerned to show that Eliot misunderstood what Hulme brought back from Germany (pp. 208–209). That Eliot was influenced at all by Hulme before the *Criterion* days was first established by Ronald Schuchard, "Eliot and Hulme in 1916: Toward a Revaluation of Eliot's Critical and Spiritual Development," *PMLA* 88 (October 1973): 1083–1094. This is a particularly important achievement in that it demonstrates that Eliot's political and social interests were of long standing when he finally began to write polemically in the 1920s. See also Margolis, pp. 45–52.

102   Irving Babbitt, *Democracy and Leadership* (Boston: Houghton Mifflin, 1924), p. 44.

103   Babbitt, *Democracy*, p. 101. Bradley also seeks to rehabilitate prejudice, or prejudication, as does Gadamer.

104   Babbitt, *Democracy*, p. 104.

105   Chace, p. 129.

106   Eugen Weber, *Action Française* (Stanford: Stanford University Press, 1962), p. 29.

107   Robert Nisbet, *Conservatism: Dream and Reality* (Milton Keynes, England: Open University Press, 1986), p. 66.

108   Karl Mannheim, *Conservatism*, tr. David Kettler and Volker Meja (London: Routledge & Kegan Paul, 1986), p. 127.

109   Mannheim, *Conservatism*, p. 35.

110   Nisbet, pp. 23–29.

111   Pietro Rossi, "The Ideological Valences of Twentieth-Century Historicism," *History and Theory*, Beiheft 14 (1975): 23.

112   Michael Oakeshott, *Rationalism in Politics* (London: Methuen, 1962).

113   Thus I would differ with the position taken by Moody: "T.S. Eliot was not a political philosopher, and he had no political philosophy as such . . ." (p. 319).

The very diffidence and dilatoriness with which Eliot approached political questions are the result of a political philosophy no less distinct for being anti-systematic.

114 *Criterion* 10 (January 1931): 308; 11 (July 1932): 681.

115 *Criterion* 11 (July 1932): 681.

116 *Criterion* 8 (April 1929): 381.

117 Isaiah Berlin, *Four Essays on Liberty* (New York: Oxford University Press, 1970), pp. 132–133.

118 Oakeshott, pp. 21–22.

119 Scruton, p. 191.

120 See, for example, *Criterion* 7 (June 1928): 86.

121 See, for example, *Criterion* 8 (July 1929): 683; 10 (April 1931): 483; and 12 (July 1933): 642.

122 *Criterion* 10 (April 1931): 484.

123 T.S. Eliot, "The Man of Letters and the Future of Europe," *Sewanee Review* 53 (July–September 1945): 335. All subsequent quotations in this paragraph are from the same page.

124 T.S. Eliot, "In Memory of Henry James," *Egoist* 5 (January 1918): 1. Quoted in Gordon, p. 229.

125 *Criterion* 10 (January 1931): 314. For one of Eliot's most complete arguments to this effect, see "Literature and the Modern World," *American Prefaces* 1 (1935): 19–22.

126 Eliot's negative example is the United States, with its "plutocratic elite" and its "stream of mixed immigration" forming a rigid "*caste* system" (NDC, p. 44).

127 See, for example, Terry Eagleton, "Eliot and a Common Culture," in Martin, pp. 282–283.

128 Karl Marx and Friedrich Engels, *The German Ideology,* ed. C.S. Arthur (New York: International Publishers, 1970), pp. 65–66.

129 Benhabib, pp. 130–131.

130 Benhabib, p. 98.

131 T.S. Eliot, *The Idea of a Christian Society* (New York: Harcourt, Brace, 1940), p. 34.

132 Eliot, *Idea,* p. 43.

133 Shusterman, p. 3.

134 For a moderately positive comment on Mosley, see *Criterion* 10 (April 1931): 483. For Eliot's much more negative second thoughts, see *Criterion* 11 (January 1932): 269.

135 "Mr. Barnes and Mr. Rowse," *Criterion* 8 (July 1929): 690–691.

136 "The Literature of Fascism," *Criterion* 8 (September 1928): 288.

137 "The Literature of Fascism," p. 289.

138 T.S. Eliot, "Catholicism and International Order," in *Essays Ancient and Modern* (New York: Harcourt, Brace, 1936), p. 133.

139 T.S. Eliot, "A Commentary," *Criterion* 11 (October 1931): 72.

140 That the reorganization of the nation's economic life on centralized lines was an article of fascist faith is demonstrated in Sternhell, especially Chapter 6, and A. James Gregor, *The Ideology of Fascism* (New York: Free Press, 1969), pp. 292–308.

NOTES TO PP. 118-128

141   Drieu La Rochelle, quoted in Sternhell, p. 249. For the split between the Action Française and the neo-fascists, see also pp. 12, 25, 100, and 225. In *Yeats, Eliot, Pound and the Politics of Poetry* (Pittsburgh: University of Pittsburgh Press, 1982), Cairns Craig takes the manifest doctrinal similarities between the Action Française and neo-fascism to be definitive. He quotes Sternhell's shorter discussion of these similarities in *Fascism: A Reader's Guide* (Berkeley: University of California Press, 1976), ed. Walter Laqueur, but not the longer discussion, which was only published after Craig's own book. It seems to me that Craig's specific mistake, to equate monarchism with fascism when Drieu La Rochelle's comment makes clear the animosity between them, is only an index of a larger problem, the use of doctrinal similarities to measure political commitment. Though the Action Française shared many doctrines with the neo-fascists, so did anarcho-syndicalists and other leftists. Thus the practical division between the old conservatives and the new right seems far more important to me than their doctrinal similarities.

142   *Criterion* 10 (January 1931): 313-314.

143   Gordon, p. 98.

144   Terry Eagleton, *Exiles and Emigres* (New York: Schocken, 1970), p. 169.

145   M.H. Abrams, *Natural Supernaturalism: Tradition and Revolution in Romantic Literature* (New York: Norton, 1971), p. 319.

146   George Plimpton, ed., *Writers at Work: The Paris Review Interviews,* Second Series (New York: Viking, 1965), pp. 99-101. For another publication of this interview and a discussion of the circumstances surrounding it, see Donald Hall, *Remembering Poets: Reminiscences and Opinions* (New York: Harper & Row, 1978). See also the discussion of the growth of *Four Quartets* in Helen Gardner, *The Composition of Four Quartets* (London: Faber and Faber, 1978), pp. 14-28.

147   Angus Calder, *T.S. Eliot* (Brighton: Harvester Press, 1987), p. 145. For the topical background of the poems, see also Moody, p. 238.

148   Bush, p. 211.

149   William Spanos, "Hermeneutics and Memory: Destroying T.S. Eliot's *Four Quartets,*" *Genre* 11 (Winter 1978): 526.

150   Gordon, p. 114.

151   Quoted in Gardner, p. 157.

152   Gordon, p. 114; Moody, p. 254.

153   Gordon, p. 133.

154   Gordon, p. 136.

155   Eliot referred to himself as a metic in a letter of 1919. See *Letters,* p. 318. He was using the term as late as the Second World War. See Gordon, p. 208.

156   See Gordon, p. 137 and Moody, p. 2.

157   See Bush, p. 234.

158   Christopher Ricks, *T.S. Eliot and Prejudice* (Berkeley: University of California Press, 1988), pp. 260-261.

Chapter 3

1   The following abbreviations will be used to identify citations in the text: CEP, *Collected Early Poems of Ezra Pound,* ed. Michael John King (New York:

New Directions, 1976); EPS, *"Ezra Pound Speaking": Radio Speeches of World War II,* ed. Leonard W. Doob (Westport, Conn.: Greenwood Press, 1978); GK, *Guide to Kulchur* (1938; rpt., New York: New Directions, 1970); JM, *Jefferson and/or Mussolini* (1935; rpt., New York: Liveright, 1970); LE, *Literary Essays,* ed. T.S. Eliot (New York: New Directions, 1954); P, *Personae* (New York: New Directions, 1971); SP, *Selected Prose 1909–1965,* ed. William Cookson (New York: New Directions, 1973); SR, *The Spirit of Romance* (1910; rpt., New York: New Directions, 1968); TC, "Three Cantos," *Poetry* 10 (1917): 113–121, 180–188, 248–254.

2   "The fetishistic character of economic forms, the reification of all human relations, the constant expansion and extension of the division of labour which subjects the process of production to an abstract, rational analysis, without regard to the human potentialities and abilities of the immediate producers – all these things transform the phenomena of society and with them the way in which they are perceived. In this way arise the 'isolated' facts, 'isolated' complexes of facts, separate, specialist disciplines. . . ." Georg Lukács, *History and Class Consciousness,* tr. Rodney Livingstone (Cambridge: MIT Press, 1971), p. 6. This particular essay, "What Is Orthodox Marxism?" is dated March 1919.

3   George Mills Harper, *The Making of Yeats's A Vision: A Study of the Automatic Script* (London: Macmillan, 1987), II: 142.

4   For a different interpretation of these essays, see Sanford Schwartz, *The Matrix of Modernism* (Princeton: Princeton University Press, 1985), pp. 115–120.

5   Pound also attacks, in almost identical terms, the provincialism of modernists who are ignorant of the past. See "Pastiche. The Regional," *The New Age,* Aug. 28, 1919, p. 300.

6   "Pastiche. The Regional," *The New Age,* Sept. 11, 1919, p. 336.

7   "Pastiche, The Regional," *The New Age,* June 26, 1919, p. 156. These latter comments are in fact more characteristic of Pound even at this time. See "Patria Mia," *The New Age,* Oct. 31, 1912, p. 635, for the criticism that America lacks centralization (this line was removed from the text published in SP). See "The Renaissance" (1914) (LE, p. 220) for a similar criticism and a comment on "the value of centralization." Thirty years later, Pound was still making almost identical statements: "*Suburban minds* and sectarians fritter about with differences" (GK, p. 172).

8   Pound was attacking the industrial system in such terms as early as 1913. See SP, p. 111.

9   Lukács, p. 90.

10   Lukács, p. 137. As Pound says in "Pastiche, The Regional," "any sociological deduction from history must assemble a great number of such violently contrasted facts, if it is to be valid. It must not be a simple paradox, or a simple opposition of two terms." *The New Age,* Aug. 21, 1919, p. 284.

11   *The New Age,* Aug. 21, 1919, p. 284.

12   For an admirable discussion of "dissociation" in Pound, see Kathryne Lindberg, *Reading Pound Reading: Modernism after Nietzsche* (New York: Oxford University Press, 1987), especially pp. 117–121. In "Totalitarian Scholarship and the New Paideuma," *Germany and You,* 25 April 1937, Pound gives such inconsistencies a historical explanation. In the early part of the century, he says, it was necessary to be "disassociative" in talking about the various arts. In 1937 "we are concerned with the reintegration of the arts in totalitarian synthesis" (p. 96).

13 Pound evidently realized that part of the problem came from the adversarial nature of his writing. He wrote to Wyndham Lewis in 1931: "Anybody who rousts about in the unorthodox or uncodified constantly gets disparate stuff and lumps it together. (Fault in both our writings.)" *Pound/Lewis,* ed. Timothy Materer (New York: New Directions, 1985), p. 176.

14 Chris Baldick, *The Social Mission of English Criticism 1848–1932* (Oxford: Clarendon Press, 1983), pp. 87, 106.

15 Perhaps the most commonly accepted description of the Luminous Detail is that offered by Hugh Kenner, *The Pound Era* (Berkeley: University of California Press, 1971), pp. 152–153. Kenner sees the detail as a "patterned integrity" actually inherent in nature. Lately, a very different account has been offered by Joseph G. Kronick, who argues in *American Poetics of History* (Baton Rouge: Louisiana State University Press, 1984) that the detail both requires and resists interpretation (p. 180) and by Lindberg, who sees each detail as part of an endless chain of interpretation (pp. 98–99).

16 Ezra Pound, *ABC of Reading* (1934; rpt., New York: New Directions, 1960), p. 80.

17 For the original version of the anecdote see Jacob Burckhardt, *The Civilization of the Renaissance in Italy,* tr. S.G.C. Middlemore (New York: Random House, 1954), p. 58. Dennis Brown argues that Pound misinterprets Burckhardt. See "The Translation of History in the Early Cantos," in *Pound and History,* ed. Marianne Korn (Orono: National Poetry Foundation/University of Maine, 1985), p. 57.

18 Ezra Pound, *Gaudier-Brzeska* (1916; rpt., New York: New Directions, 1970), p. 111.

19 Burckhardt, *Civilization,* p. 265.

20 Jacob Burckhardt, *Force and Freedom: Reflections on History* (New York, Pantheon, 1943), p. 144. Hayden White says that Burckhardt presents the era of unity and wholeness as an accident, a brief inexplicable break in the general chaos of history. *Metahistory: The Historical Imagination in Nineteenth-Century Europe* (Baltimore: John Hopkins University Press, 1973), p. 250. Thus Burckhardt's method of writing history is, in White's words, a "stew or medley, fragments of objects detached from their original contexts. . . ." (p. 250). Works like *The Civilization of the Renaissance in Italy* defy the common expectation that history will appear as story. Instead, Burckhardt lumps details together in broad categories, a practice which, by replacing chronological with classificatory organization, emphasizes the idea of unity over that of development over time.

21 For another discussion of the influence of Burckhardt on Pound, see Michael André Bernstein, "Image, Word, and Sign: The Visual Arts as Evidence in Ezra Pound's *Cantos,*" *Critical Inquiry* 12 (Winter 1986): 352–353.

22 E.H. Gombrich, "In Search of Cultural History," in *Ideals and Idols: Essays on Values in History and in Art* (Oxford: Phaidon, 1979), pp. 38–40.

23 Gombrich, *Ideals and Idols,* p. 42.

24 Gombrich, *Ideals and Idols,* p. 43. See also Karl Löwith, *From Hegel to Nietzsche,* tr. David E. Greene (New York: Doubleday Anchor, 1967), pp. 33 and 226.

25 Joseph N. Riddel, "'Neo-Nietzschean Clatter' - Speculation and/on Pound's Poetic Image," in Ian F.A. Bell, ed., *Ezra Pound: Tactics for Reading* (London and New York: Vision and Barnes & Noble, 1982), p. 200.

26 Wilhelm Dilthey, "The Rise of Hermeneutics," tr. Fredric Jameson, *New Literary History* 3 (Winter 1972): 242–243. See also Jameson's discussion of what he calls "existential historicism," in "Marxism and Historicism," *New Literary History* 11 (Autumn 1979): 50–51 (rpt. in *The Ideologies of Theory* [Minneapolis: University of Minnesota Press, 1988], 2: 148–177) and the application of this term to Pound by James Longenbach, *Modernist Poetics of History* (Princeton: Princeton University Press, 1987), pp. 57–58, 101, and passim. See also the discussion in Schwartz, pp. 138–139.

27 Walter Pater, *Marius the Epicurean* (1885; London: Macmillan, 1985), I:109.

28 Walter Pater, *The Renaissance: Studies in Art and Poetry*, ed. Donald L. Hill (Berkeley: University of California Press, 1980), p. xxi.

29 Hugh Witemeyer, *The Poetry of Ezra Pound: Forms and Renewal, 1908–1920* (Berkeley: University of California Press, 1969), p. 9. See also Stuart Y. Mac-Dougal, *Ezra Pound and the Troubadour Tradition* (Princeton: Princeton University Press, 1972), pp. 90–91, Longenbach, pp. 55–56, and Ian F.A. Bell, *Critic as Scientist: The Modernist Poetics of Ezra Pound* (London: Methuen, 1981), p. 42. In the "Henry James" essay Pound speaks of James as working to isolate "these potent chemicals" that are "the nature of Frenchness, Englishness, Germanness, Americanness" (LE, pp. 300–301), or, in other words, the national personalities also named by the musical and artistic metaphors. Such chemicals are isolated by testing them against the artist's own personality.

30 Pater, *The Renaissance*, p. xx.

31 Longenbach makes much the same point: "As a transhistorical spiritual world, [*virtu*] links all particular individuals and makes understanding possible; in its specific manifestations, it is the essence of individuality" (p. 57). However, this formula elides too easily the difference between the transhistorical and suprapersonal and the specifically historical individual. The difficulties caused by doing so are discussed later. In fact, as Longenbach's analysis progresses, *virtu* comes to be "the essence of individuality" (p. 103) and as such is opposed to the national individuality Pound himself called *virtu*. See also p. 109. See also Schwartz's discussion on p. 140.

32 Longenbach, p. 80. It will become clear how my interpretation of "Near Perigord" and of Pound's career differs from Longenbach's.

33 As Ronald Bush puts it, "Browning makes us understand how a story teller uses the events of another poet's life for building blocks so that he can construct a satisfactory explanation of himself." Ronald Bush, *The Genesis of Ezra Pound's Cantos* (Princeton: Princeton University Press, 1976), p. 78.

34 Bush, p. 113.

35 Ezra Pound, *The Cantos* (New York: New Directions, 1972). Quotations from *The Cantos* will be identified in the text by canto and page number.

36 Lindberg concentrates instead on the affinities between Pound's emphasis on power and Nietzsche's, without mentioning Pater (p. 35).

37 Pater, *The Renaissance*, p. xx.

38 Pater, *The Renaissance*, p. xxi. Bell cites this statement from Pater's essay on Coleridge: "Modern thought is distinguished from ancient by its cultivation of the 'relative' spirit in place of the 'absolute'. . . . To the modern spirit, nothing is, or can be rightly known, except relatively" (*Critic as Scientist*, p. 191).

39   Hans-Georg Gadamer, *Truth and Method,* tr. Garrett Barden and John Cumming (New York: Crossroad, 1985), p. 176.

40   Quoted in Gadamer, p. 209.

41   One possible genesis for this solution lies in the Victorian background shared by these two writers. See Peter Dale, *The Victorian Critic and the Idea of History* (Cambridge: Harvard University Press, 1977), pp. 83–84.

42   Gadamer, p. 178.

43   Hans Robert Jauss, *Toward an Aesthetic of Reception,* tr. Timothy Bahti (Minneapolis: University of Minnesota Press, 1982), p. 50.

44   Wilhelm Dilthey, *Pattern and Meaning in History: Thoughts on History and Society,* tr. H.P. Rickman (New York: Harper, 1962), pp. 67–68.

45   See Moshe Barasch, *Theories of Art from Plato to Winckelmann* (New York: New York University Press, 1985), p. 216.

46   Barasch, pp. 287–288.

47   Gadamer, p. 205.

48   Dilthey, "Rise of Hermeneutics," 243.

49   Dilthey, *Pattern and Meaning,* pp. 123–124.

50   Gadamer, p. 264.

51   Longenbach assumes that Pound becomes a "positivist" historian in *The Cantos,* having "abandoned the principles of his early historicism" (p. 130). But in fact what looks like postivism is simply the logical extension of this historicism, which may begin in relativism but can end in the most rigid absolutism. See also p. 141. Michael F. Harper also asserts that Pound became a positivist historian in "Truth and Calliope: Ezra Pound's Malatesta," *PMLA* 96 (1981): 86–103.

52   Jeffrey Perl, *The Tradition of Return: The Implicit History of Modern Literature* (Princeton: Princeton University Press, 1980), p. 257.

53   White, p. 247.

54   Burckhardt, *Civilization,* pp. 225, 231, and 101.

55   In *The Historical Novel,* tr. Hannah and Stanley Mitchell (Lincoln: University of Nebraska Press, 1983), Georg Lukács discusses Burckhardt's mingled admiration for and horror of the great men of the Renaissance (pp. 178–179). There seems to be a similar mixture in Pound, rather than pure admiration or the disapproval found by Guy Davenport, *Cities on Hills: A Study of I-XXX of Ezra Pound's Cantos* (Ann Arbor, Mich.: UMI Press, 1983), p. 103.

56   Bush, p. 222.

57   T.S. Eliot, *Complete Poems and Plays, 1909–1950* (New York: Harcourt, Brace & World, 1971), p. 42.

58   See, for example, Thomas Jackson, "The Adventures of Messire Wrong-Head," *ELH* 32 (June 1965): 238–255.

59   Marjorie Perloff, *The Poetics of Indeterminacy: Rimbaud to Cage* (Princeton: Princeton University Press, 1981), p. 181.

60   Burckhardt, *Civilization,* pp. 104–105.

61   See also SP, p. 191.

62   It should be noted that Pound criticized this ideal on at least one occasion: "Entirely free from the renaissance humanist ideal of the complete man or from

Greek idealism, [Whitman] is content to be what he is, and he is his time and his people" (SP, p. 145). Perhaps the very early date of this statement (1909) and its polemical thrust against privileged standards of the past might help to explain it. On the other hand, Whitman does become a bit of a luminous detail himself, representing a whole age and people even in his differences from the Renaissance standard.

63 Fredric Jameson, *Fables of Aggression: Wyndham Lewis, the Modernist as Fascist* (Berkeley: University of California Press, 1979), p. 125.

64 For the terminology, see Roland Barthes, *Elements of Semiology,* tr. Annette Lavers and Colin Smith (New York: Hill & Wang, 1968).

65 Barthes, p. 59.

66 Michael André Bernstein, *The Tale of the Tribe: Ezra Pound and the Modern Verse Epic* (Princeton: Princeton University Press, 1980), p. 56.

67 Ezra Pound, *Confucius* (New York: New Directions, 1969), p. 53.

68 Peter Nicholls, *Ezra Pound: Politics, Economics, and Writing* (London: Macmillan, 1984), p. 156.

69 Jean-Michel Rabaté notes much the same dichotomy between order and chaos. See *Language, Sexuality, and Ideology in Ezra Pound's Cantos* (Albany: State University of New York Press, 1986), p. 114.

70 For a different view, see Matthew Little, "Pound's Use of the Word *Totalitarian,*" *Paideuma* 11 (1982): 147–156.

71 Nicholls, p. 116.

72 Gadamer, p. 481.

73 Jauss, p. 64.

74 Translated in Nicholls, p. 158.

75 For further instances, see LE, pp. 47, 298 and SP, pp. 51, 209–210. The most important of these passages is perhaps the one in which Pound denounces the tyranny that comes from "the dogma that the *theos* is one, or that there is a unity above the various strata of theos which imposes its will upon the sub-strata, and thence upon human individuals" (SP, p. 51). See also the discussion of several of these passages in a theological context in Robert A. Casillo, *The Genealogy of Demons: Anti-Semitism, Fascism, and the Myths of Ezra Pound* (Evanston: Northwestern University Press, 1988), pp. 30–31.

76 This sort of thing is now so universally reprehended that it is hard to see in it the germ of something more progressive. As Raymond Williams says of similar nineteenth century statements, "The element of professional protest is undoubtedly there, but the larger issue is the opposition on general human grounds to the kind of civilization that was being inaugurated." *Culture and Society 1780–1950* (1958; rpt., New York: Columbia University Press, 1983), p. 36. A similar argument underlies a good deal of Fredric Jameson's analysis of Lewis.

77 See the discussion of the contradiction between this belief and Pound's individualism in William M. Chace, *The Political Identities of Ezra Pound and T.S. Eliot* (Stanford: Stanford University Press, 1973), pp. 57 and 66.

78 See also Pound's criticism of the overly individualistic Greeks on p. 38. Some of the tension in Pound's thoughts on this subject is expressed in his contradictory statements on anonymous art. In *The Spirit of Romance,* Pound celebrates the signed arch of the Cathedral of Ferrara (p. 101) and in *Gaudier-*

Brzeska he says, "One has the tradition that columns should be hand-cut and signed" (p. 96). The most famous instance of this belief is the signature "Adamo me fecit" in Canto 45. But, at about the same time that he composed that canto, Pound also claimed that "the great mediaeval architects and stone-cutters refrained from signing their work. One of the great maladies of modern criticism is this first rush to look for the person. . . ." *ABC of Reading*, p. 147. He also praises "anonymous craftsmen" in *Jefferson and/or Mussolini*, p. 85. This contradiction exposes Pound's inconsistent beliefs in individual initiative and in collective achievement.

79   Thus it seems to me that Daniel Pearlman's assertion that Pound's "whole career exhibits an unflagging effort to deny the separation of the artist from society" must be severely qualified. "Ezra Pound: America's Wandering Jew," *Paideuma* 9 (Winter 1980): 476. So, too, would Hayden White's conception of aristocracy as synecdochal by nature. See *Tropics of Discourse* (Baltimore: Johns Hopkins University Press, 1978), p. 130. He sees the synecdochal nature of the aristocracy in a slightly restricted way, basing it only on resemblance. As these poets show, in political terms, synecdoche is often stronger when based on difference. This is but one of the many contradictions that Fascism papered over. When Mussolini invented the concept of the "proletarian elite," he joined mass politics and elitism in a way very similar to that imagined by Pound. See A. James Gregor, *The Ideology of Fascism* (New York: The Free Press, 1969), pp. 106, 116, and 175, and Ernst Nolte, *Three Faces of Fascism,* tr. Leila Vennewitz (New York: Holt, Rinehart and Winston, 1965), p. 158.

80   Thus Pound's very interesting claim that Britain "will have no 'new age of cathedrals' until it takes a chance on the 'maniacs.' " "The Curse," *Apple (of Beauty and Discord),* Jan. 1920, p. 23. Here he makes cathedrals, common symbols of collective achievement in an age of faith, the products of isolated "maniacs."

81   See the excellent discussions of this issue in Rabaté, pp. 41–42, and Nicholls, p. 15. Both scholars emphasize, quite rightly, Pound's constant contrast between speed and obstruction. But it should also be noted that, when opposition and delay are made indicative of an artist's truthfulness, the dichotomy between speed and obstruction becomes unstable.

82   See also SP, p. 262, JM, p. 18, and many other instances throughout the work. This belief made him well-disposed toward Fascist voluntarism when he encountered it in Italy. See Nolte, pp. 154–155 for a discussion of the role of voluntarism in Fascist thought.

83   See Chace's discussion of this problem, pp. 16–17.

84   Quoted in C. David Heymann, *Ezra Pound: The Last Rower* (New York: Seaver, 1976), p. 97. Por was a Hungarian-Italian syndicalist resident in Italy in the 1930s, a Fascist sympathizer and theoretician whom Pound came to admire and to translate. See GK, pp. 166–67 and 246.

85   Two books attempt to sum up divergent views of Fascism: Renzo de Felice, *Interpretations of Fascism,* tr. Brenda Huff Everett (Cambridge: Harvard University Press, 1977) and A. James Gregor, *Interpretations of Fascism* (Berkeley: University of California Press, 1974). The sameness of titles attests to Gregor's admiration for the controversial de Felice. See also the discussion in Cairns Craig, *Yeats, Eliot, Pound and the Politics of Poetry* (Pittsburgh: University of Pittsburgh Press,

1982), pp. 260–265. A minor aspect of this conceptual difficulty has to do with the capitalization of the term. In this chapter, I will try to differentiate between fascism as a doctrine diffused over the continent of Europe and Fascism as a regime in Italy by capitalizing only the latter. It will become clear that my analysis is specific to Italy, with certain implications for France, but that it may not be applicable to Germany. This limitation is both necessary, due to limitations of space, and preferable, considering Pound's close relationship to conditions in Italy.

86 For an example of such an analysis in Pound scholarship, see Peter Brooker, "The Lesson of Ezra Pound: An Essay in Poetry, Literary Ideology and Politics," in Bell, *Tactics for Reading,* especially p. 21. It is also sometimes argued, by writers of different persuasions, that Fascism represents the recapture of what was originally an anti-capitalist movement. See Jameson, *Lewis,* p. 15 and A. James Gregor, *Italian Fascism and Developmental Dictatorship* (Princeton: Princeton University Press, 1979), pp. 131, 142.

87 See the 1934 statement by Henri de Man, at that time in the Belgian Labor Party, quoted in Eugen Weber, *Varieties of Fascism* (1964; rpt., Malabar, Fla.: Krieger Publishing, 1982), p. 32, and the similar claims made by J.S. Barnes, in "Fascism," *Criterion* 8 (April 1929): 456. See, for a general discussion, Weber's Chapter 4.

88 Roland Sarti, *Fascism and the Industrial Leadership in Italy, 1919–1940* (Berkeley: University of California Press, 1971). A rather similar argument was advanced on the left by Ernst Bloch. See Martin Jay, *Marxism and Totality* (Berkeley: University of California Press, 1984), p. 188.

89 The issue of Fascism and modernization will be discussed in some detail below. For an argument that Fascism is a development from the liberal individualism associated with property see Brooker, pp. 14 and 16. See also Herbert Marcuse, "The Struggle Against Liberalism in the Totalitarian View of the State," in *Negations,* tr. Jeremy J. Shapiro (Boston: Beacon Press, 1968). The idea that Fascism is quintessentially anti-liberal is developed at length in the final chapter of Gregor's *Ideology of Fascism.*

90 George L. Mosse, "Fascism and the Intellectuals," in *The Nature of Fascism,* ed. S.J. Woolf (London: Weidenfeld and Nicolson, 1968), p. 207. See also Zeev Sternhell, "Fascist Ideology," in *Fascism: A Reader's Guide,* ed. Walter Laqueur (Berkeley: University of California Press, 1976), p. 321.

91 For a discussion of Fascism as a "melting pot" of ideas and interests, see Sarti, p. 134.

92 Odon Por, *Fascism,* tr. E. Townshend (London: Labour Publishing, 1923), p. 169. See also pp. 162, 170–171, and 204. For similar comments from British, Belgian, and French fascists, see Weber, pp. 28–29. Por's statement anticipates the more cannonical formulation of Gentile, enshrined in 1932 in the *Enciclopedia Italiana:* Fascism "is not an ideology, it is not a closed system, and it is not really even a programme, if by programme one means a plan conceived in advance and projected into the future. . . ." G. Gentile, *Fascismo e cultura* (Milan, 1928), p. 49, and quoted in Nicholls, p. 98. Nicholls says, correctly, that it is difficult to know whether Pound read this work, but there is a passage in JM that sounds like a virtual paraphrase: "The fascist revolution is infinitely more INTERESTING

than the Russian revolution because it is not a revolution according to a preconceived type" (p. 24).

93   Quoted in Roland Sarti, "Fascist Modernization in Italy: Traditional or Revolutionary?" *American Historical Review* 75 (April 1970): 1029.

94   Dennis Mack Smith, *Mussolini* (London: Weidenfeld and Nicolson, 1981), p. 188. For the background of Mussolini's intuitionism and anti-intellectualism, see Gregor, *Ideology*, pp. 114 and 123–124.

95   See also JM, p. 66 and Casillo, pp. 108–109.

96   But Pound was never to be entirely consistent on anything. On the same page of the same essay, he says, "What we have needed is not less theory but more theory." For the assertion that John Adams's experience was not theoretical, see SP, p. 168. See also his praise of Edmondo Rossoni, GK, pp. 166–167.

97   Quoted in Gregor, *Ideology*, p. 185. For a similar pronouncement from Gentile, see p. 216. See also Por, p. 19.

98   See also the statement that Mussolini writes law not "for an ideal republic situated in a platonic paradise but as an arrangement possible in Italy in the year VIII or IX of the Era Fascista . . ." (JM, p. 57). But, as Pound says at the very end of the book, if it is to spread, Fascism must study "not the advisabilities of particular time and place but the permanent elements of sane and responsible government" (JM, pp. 127–128). The movement of JM from its denunciation of all that is "anti-storico" to this invocation of "permanent elements" is characteristic of Pound.

99   Por, p. 173. These are Por's words. For the Mussolini article, "Forze e consenso," see pp. 173–176. See also Sternhell, "Fascist Ideology," pp. 325–337 and 347. There is a counter-argument, to the effect that "the 'seeds of fascism' can be seen in 'liberal' ideology," in Nicos Poulantzas' *Fascism and Dictatorship*, tr. Judith White (London: NLB, 1974), p. 128. The emphasis in this argument, derived in part from Gramsci, is, however, on liberal nationalism, which is clearly a different kind of liberalism from that attacked here by Mussolini.

100   Casillo, pp. 129–131. See also the letter reprinted in Heymann, p. 326. Chace suggests that in Pound's lexicon "liberalism" means tolerance, but *most* of the time it seems to stand for just the opposite (p. 41). See also the quite different point of view in Brooker, where liberalism and fascism are connected (pp. 14 and 16).

101   Por, p. 174. For a comparison between Lenin and Mussolini much like those to be found in Pound, see p. 5.

102   For similar statements by Enrico Corradini and Ugo Spirito, see Gregor, *Ideology*, pp. 296–297. For comments on "Forza e consenso," see p. 174. There is a running analysis in this book of the anti-liberal nature of fascism. For examples, see pp. 163, 168, 171, and 376. For similar statements from Sergio Panunzio, see Gregor's "Fascism and Modernization: Some Addenda," *World Politics* 26 (April 1974): 383.

103   Weber, p. 13.

104   Zeev Sternhell, *Neither Right nor Left: Fascist Ideology in France*, tr. David Maisel (Berkeley: University of California Press, 1986).

105   Pound did not retain this sense of the common anti-liberal project through the war. In 1944 he says, "Liberalism and Bolshevism are in intimate agreement in their fundamental contempt for the human personality" (SP, p. 342). He also speaks of "the Bolshevik-Liberal psychology" (SP, p. 348). The villain in this essay is Stalin, whom Pound sees as quite different from Lenin, and the critique works by linking Stalinism with the abstract approach to human problems Pound always criticized as liberal. For an analysis of Pound that begins with the idea of a common left-right anti-liberalism, see Burton Hatlen, "Ezra Pound and Fascism," in Korn, pp. 146–152.

106 Nicholls, pp. 79–87. Nicholls notes that as late as 1935 Pound had no objection to being defined as a communist (p. 81). For a discussion of Pound's growing anti-communism, see Casillo, pp. 193–194.

107 See Casillo, pp. 197–198. There is also the odd episode reported by Felice Chilanti, member of a group of dissident "leftist Fascists," who entertained Pound, considering him one of their group, during the war. See "Ezra Pound Among the Seditious in the 1940's," tr. David Anderson, *Paideuma* 6 (1977):235–250. The seriousness of Pound's contacts with this group seems best illustrated by his attempts to interest it in the peanut.

108 See the statement in JM that Pound does not think "fascism is possible in America without Mussolini, any more than I or any enlightened bolshevik thinks communism is possible in America without Lenin" (p. 98).

109 "Simplicities," *The Exile* 4 (Autumn 1928): 3.

110 Por, p. 5.

111 Barnes, p. 449. For very similar statements, see Por, pp. 149, 177. See also Sternhell, "Fascist Ideology," p. 345.

112 See Gregor, *Ideology,* p. 102. See also Gregor's discussion of Panunzio in *Italian Fascism,* p. 39 and Nolte's discussion of Gentile, p. 244, and Sternhell, "Fascist Ideology," p. 329.

113 Por, p. 179.

114 Quoted in Gregor, *Ideology,* p. 156.

115 Quoted in Gregor, *Ideology,* p. 231.

116 Quoted in Gregor, *Ideology,* p. 223. See the similar argument advanced by Barnes, p. 453. See also Sternhell, "Fascist Ideology," p. 346.

117 P. Vita-Finzi, "Italian fascism and the intellectuals," in Woolf, p. 232.

118 See also pp. 63, 74, 104, and 108.

119 Por, pp. 182 and 154. This is, of course, the sort of representation Hegel envisioned, not of "individuals or a conglomeration of them, but one of the essential spheres of society and its large-scale interests." *Hegel's Philosophy of Right,* tr. T.M. Knox (Oxford: Clarendon Press, 1942), p. 202.

120 See also EPS, pp. 102, 111, 204. But when the discussion shifts to trade unions, Pound discovers in himself a deep suspicion of organizations based on function: "Men of the same trade never meet without a conspiracy against the general public" (JM, p. 46). See also SP, p. 209, and Casillo, pp. 195–196.

121 In this early article (1920), Pound quotes Douglas. See also SP, p. 211. As will be seen shortly, the dates of these statements are important, for Pound gradually dropped or compromised his opposition to political centralization. There had always been something contradictory in his attitude toward cultural centralization, which he often favored as conducive to great artistic achievement. Pound managed this contradiction by an utterly empty ethical distinction between good centralization and bad. For Pound's involvement in Guild socialism, see Hatlen, p. 152.

122   See also the statement quoted by Nicholls that Italian Fascism "has evolved FROM guild socialism, curing *de facto,* the anarchic element in a mere congeries of non-correlated guilds" (p. 83). See also Casillo's discussion: "Thus, like the Guild Socialists and Fascists, Pound initially stressed localism and decentraliza-tion and ironically ended up by endowing the state with coercive, perhaps total-itarian powers" (p. 200). In *No Place of Grace* (New York: Pantheon, 1981), T.J. Jackson Lears argues that decentralist critiques are inherently totalitarian insofar as they oppose parliamentary representation (p. 308).

123   See Nolte, p. 212 and Gregor, *Italian Fascism,* p. 131. This was, of course, Mussolini's ploy to draw support from big business.

124   Pound began saying such things about the state at least as early as 1925. See SP, pp. 213–215. See similar statements elsewhere in JM, pp. 11, 15, and 45.

125   "Communications," *Townsman,* 6 April 1939, p. 12. Hitler is identified both by name and as "Der Führer."

126   Gregor, *Ideology,* p. 189. See also the discussion in Nolte, p. 218.

127   Hegel, p. 103. Gregor, *Ideology,* pp. 222, 196, 237.

128   See Nicholls's discussion of the "government of one man" in the late Can-tos (p. 253) and the discussion of Sartre in Fredric Jameson, *Marxism and Form* (Princeton: Princeton University Press, 1971), p. 271.

129   See Chace's discussion of Pound and Mussolini, p. 66.

130   For an illuminating discussion of one pair of such examples, Lukács and Paul Ernst, who became a proto-fascist, see Ferenc Fehér, "The Last Phase of Romantic Anti-Capitalism: Lukács' Response to the War," *New German Critique* 10 (Winter 1977): 139–154.

131   Sternhell, pp. 25–26, 100, 110, 118.

132   Pound made such comments as early as 1919. See Casillo, p. 191.

133   This is standard proto-fascist rhetoric. See Sternhell, *Neither Right nor Left,* pp. 164, 189.

134   Paraphrased from Mussolini in Sarti, "Fascist Modernization," p. 1037. For Pound's similar statements, see EPS, pp. 294 and 296.

135   See EPS, pp. 234 and 265. In "The Jew as Anti-Artist: The Anti-Semitism of Ezra Pound," *Midstream* 22 (March 1976), Hyam Maccoby argues that produc-tivity is the key term of Pound's life (p. 59).

136   See, for example, David Murray, "Pound-Signs: Money and Representa-tion in Ezra Pound," in Korn, p. 178 and Richard Sieburth, "In Pound We Trust: The Economy of Poetry/The Poetry of Economics," *Critical Inquiry* 14 (Autumn 1987): 166. The most fully nuanced of all such discussion is Rabaté's. See pp. 86, 187, and 201.

137   For a good summary of Marx's version of this distinction, see *A Dictionary of Marxist Thought,* ed. Tom Bottomore et al (Cambridge: Harvard University Press, 1983), p. 131.

138   Murray, p. 183; Nicholls, p. 59.

139   "Simplicities," *The Exile* 4 (Autumn 1928): 3.

140   Rabaté, p. 86.

141 A.F.K. Organski, "Fascism and Modernization," in Woolf, p. 22. Organski draws here on the general theory offered in *The Stages of Political Development* (New York: Knopf, 1965). In *Interpretations of Fascism,* Gregor has attacked several aspects of Organski's analysis. See pp. 169, 191, and 195, for example. Gregor is unwilling to consider the Italian regime as anything but modernizing, while Organski sees it as split between traditionalism and modernization. Nonetheless, there are many areas of commonality between the two works.

142 Organski, p. 22. For similar statements from Gregor, see *Italian Fascism,* pp. 134 and 162, and *Interpretations of Fascism,* p. 124.

143 Gregor, *Ideology,* p. 81. See also pp. 147, 149, 161, 354, 365 and *Italian Fascism,* p. 140.

144 Gregor, *Interpretations of Fascism,* pp. 172–173. See also Nolte, pp. 221–222 and 238–239. This was also true to some extent in France. See Sternhell, *Neither Right nor Left,* p. 108.

145 Gregor, "Fascism and Modernization," p. 373.

146 Nolte, p. 222. Sternhell makes a similar point about France. See *Neither Right nor Left,* pp. 201 and 211.

147 See Alfred Schmidt, *History and Structure,* tr. Jeffrey Herf (Cambridge: MIT Press, 1981), p. 17.

148 Alan Cassels, "Janus: The Two Faces of Fascism," *Historical Papers* (1969): 174. See the very similar comment in Organski, who discusses "the attempt to permit the nation to be both modern and non-modern, to modernize economically without the socio-political consequences of such modernization . . . ." (p. 33). Gregor discusses other similar theories in *Interpretations of Fascism,* p. 202.

149 For an analysis of the class background of fascism, see Poulantzas. For the contradictory Fascist approach to the small producers, see Sarti, *Fascism and the Industrial Leadership,* p. 84.

150 See, for example, JM, p. 100 and EPS p. 101. Gregor discusses the "Battle for Grain" in *Italian Fascism,* pp. 144–145. He says in "Fascism and Modernization" that feats like making the trains run on time were often taken as evidence of "Fascism's modernizing dispositions" (p. 377).

151 For comments praising Hitler for "putting men over machines," see EPS, p. 49. For praise of the homestead, see EPS, pp. 31 and 176. On this issue, see also Casillo, pp. 27–28. Mussolini's own inconsistency on this score is discussed by Nolte, who notes his eugenic suspicion of industrialism and a corresponding desire to "ruralize" Italy (p. 224). Mussolini began to use conventionally anti-modern language as the war turned against him, even decrying materialism and "the skyscraper, vast factories, and mass production." See Sarti, "Fascist Modernization," p. 1045.

152 See also SP, p. 300.

153 Gregor, *Interpretations of Fascism,* p. 197, and *Italian Fascism,* p. 155.

154 Such is Pound's faith in the industrial plant of the West that he worries more about overproduction than scarcity. See SP, p. 222 and EPS, p. 81.

155 For another discussion of the idea that a concern with distribution is characteristic of stable societies, see Hans Blumenberg, *The Legitimacy of the Modern Age,* tr. Robert M. Wallace (Cambridge: MIT Press, 1983), pp. 138–139.

156   One irony is that industrial production of the kind Pound celebrated was achieved in Italy only by severely limiting consumption. See Gregor, *Interpreting Fascism,* p. 199.

157   For a discussion of the tension between modernity and tradition in Pound, see Craig, p. 260.

158   See also JM, pp. 80 and 112 and SP, pp. 316 and 347.

159   Thus speed came to have first an economic and then a moral value in Pound's thinking. See the excellent discussion in Rabaté, pp. 41–42. Obstruction, the opposite of speed, came to represent all that was disgusting to Pound. Of many discussions, see Murray's, p. 181.

160   See SP, pp. 346–348. For denunciations of the "Black Myth" of money see SP, p. 307 and EPS, p. 271. There is a particularly interesting discussion of this point in Sieburth, where it is argued that Pound wants to see money as in fact motivated *because* it decays as natural values decay. But Sieburth finally decides that there is a conflict between Pound's monetary theories and his poetic ones on this issue, the former undermining the motivated sign established in the latter. See pp. 154 and 156–157.

161   See the interesting discussion of this possibility in Nicholls, p. 152.

162   See Sieburth, p. 161.

163   Lukács, *History and Class Consciousness,* p. 89.

164   Nicholls, p. 74.

165   Quoted in Heymann, p. 327. See also Sieburth, p. 161.

166   Rabaté, pp. 191–198. The best discussion of the implications of this double meaning is Marc Shell, *The Economy of Literature* (Baltimore: Johns Hopkins University Press, 1978).

167   Maccoby, p. 63. This is, of course, the general argument of Casillo's book.

168   As Nolte says, this association of Bolshevism with Jewry was a commonplace of Hitler's propaganda. See p. 10. See also Daniel Pearlman, "Ezra Pound: America's Wandering Jew," *Paideuma* 9 (Winter 1980): 467 and Charles Berezin, "Poetry and Politics in Ezra Pound," *Partisan Review* 48 (1981): 274.

169   Nolte, p. 181. See also p. 189. Yeats had also seen capitalism and communism as essentially the same. See Donald T. Torchiana, *W.B. Yeats and Georgian Ireland* (Evanston: Northwestern University Press, 1966), p. 255.

170   Casillo, p. 71.

171   Gregor, *Ideology,* p. 266. See the entire discussion, pp. 266–268.

172   Gregor, *Ideology,* p. 277. For a number of similar comments, see Nolte, pp. 225–226. But see Nolte's account of Italian discrimination against foreign ethnic groups in the North (p. 223) and the account of the later race laws (pp. 230–231).

173   See the account of a June 1934 meeting between Hitler and Mussolini in Smith, p. 185.

174   Gregor, *Ideology,* p. 260.

175   See Craig, pp. 274–275.

176   Pound was not the only fascist to make this accusation. See Sternhell, *Neither Right nor Left,* p. 263.

177   "Race," *The New English Weekly,* 15 October, 1936, p. 12. See also "Totalitarian Scholarship," p. 95.

178   Nicholls, p. 155.

179   See Casillo's very thorough discussion of these metaphors, especially pp. 44 and 52.

180   Rabaté, p. 219. See also Casillo's discussion of this point.

181   Weber, p. 78.

182   Brooker, p. 24.

183   Sieburth, p. 171.

184   Ezra Pound, *Selected Letters 1907–1941,* ed. D.D. Paige (1950; rpt., New York: New Directions, 1971), p. 180.

185   Quoted in Donald Hall, *Remembering Poets* (New York: Harper & Row, 1978), p. 241. To Hall, Pound confessed that he was "stuck."

186   See the excellent discussion in Rabaté of the relationship of speed and stasis in *The Cantos,* pp. 43 and 64. Previous such discussions, such as that in Daniel Pearlman's *The Barb of Time* (New York: Oxford University Press, 1969), have tended to resolve this relationship in favor of one of the constituents, in favor of stasis in Pearlman's case. See later in this chapter for a discussion of similar resolutions in the work of Kenner and Davie.

187   Rabaté, p. 120. For another very useful discussion of the role of the unexpected in Pound's personal history, see Jerome J. McGann, "The *Cantos* of Ezra Pound: The Truth in Contradiction," *Critical Inquiry* 15 (Autumn 1988): 1–25.

188   Chace, p. 93.

189   Theodor Adorno, *Aesthetic Theory,* tr. C. Lenhardt (London: Routledge & Kegan Paul, 1984), p. 251.

190   The nature of this relation is of great controversy in Pound criticism. See, for example, the discussion of this passage in Christine Brooke-Rose, *A ZBC of Ezra Pound* (Berkeley: University of California Press, 1971), pp. 113–116.

191   Rodolphe Gasché, "Edges of Understanding," in *Responses: On Paul de Man's Wartime Journalism,* ed. Werner Hamacher, Neil Hertz, and Thomas Keenan (Lincoln: University of Nebraska Press, 1989), p. 213.

192   See, for example, Nicholls, p. 172.

193   Kenner, p. 475.

194   See Kenner, pp. 483–484 and Donald Davie, *Ezra Pound* (New York: Viking, 1975), pp. 74–76.

195   Paul de Man, *Allegories of Reading* (New Haven: Yale University Press, 1979), p. 68.

196   Carroll F. Terrell, *A Companion to the Cantos of Ezra Pound* (Berkeley: University of California Press, 1984), 2:365.

197   See LE, p. 245.

198   Rabaté, p. 162.

199   Rabaté, p. 180.

200   Noel Stock, *The Life of Ezra Pound* (1970; rpt., New York: Avon, 1974), p. 534.

201   De Man, *Allegories of Reading,* p. 14.

Conclusion

1   G.W.F. Hegel, *The Difference between Fichte's and Schelling's System of Philosophy,* tr. H.S. Harris and Walter Cerf (Albany: State University of New York

Press, 1977), p. 91. See the discussion by Jürgen Habermas in *The Philosophical Discourse of Modernity,* tr. Frederick Lawrence (Cambridge: MIT Press, 1987), pp. 19–20.

2 Raymond Williams, *Culture and Society: 1780–1950* (1958; rpt., New York: Columbia University Press, 1983).

3 John Crowe Ransom, *The New Criticism* (Norfolk: New Directions, 1941), pp. 144–145. For a good discussion of the ways in which New Criticism applied a "simplifying image of modernism's ironic essence," see Daniel O'Hara, "'The Unsummoned Image': T.S. Eliot's Unclassic Criticism," *Boundary* 29 (Fall 1980): 91–124.

4 Paul de Man, *Blindness and Insight: Essays in the Rhetoric of Contemporary Criticism,* 2nd ed. (Minneapolis: University of Minnesota Press, 1983), pp. 245 and 240. In *Allegories of Reading* (New Haven: Yale University Press, 1979), de Man calls reconciliation "a highly respectable moral imperative," but he then goes on to show that it is also "the elective breeding-ground of false models and metaphors," the falsehood of which it will be his purpose to expose (pp. 3 and 5). *The Aesthetic Ideology,* de Man's still forthcoming final work, is described by Ian Balfour in "'Difficult Readings': De Man's Itineraries," in *Responses: On De Man's Wartime Journalism,* ed. Werner Hamacher, Neil Hertz, and Thomas Keenan (Lincoln: University of Nebraska Press, 1989), pp. 9–10. This volume will be referred to in the text as R.

5 Thus Miller quarrels even with works of deconstruction, such as Joseph N. Riddel's *The Inverted Bell: Modernism and the Counterpoetics of Williams Carlos Williams,* that retain a notion of the historical character of modernism. See J. Hillis Miller, "Deconstructing the Deconstructers," *Diacritics* 5 (1975): 24–31, and, for Miller's own most recent ideas about some of the canonical modernist writers, *The Linguistic Moment: From Wordsworth to Stevens* (Princeton: Princeton University Press, 1985). Meisel divides modernism into "weak" and "strong" variants, divided according to the rigor with which they resist the temptation to misrepresent the modern situation as historically determined. See Perry Meisel, *The Myth of the Modern: A Study in British Literature and Criticism after 1850* (New Haven: Yale University Press, 1987).

6 De Man, *Blindness and Insight,* p. 161.

7 De Man had slightly different attitudes to the three subjects of this book. Of Pound, he had nothing to say, of Eliot only a bit in the dismissive mode. Yeats he reinterpreted instead of dismissing. See *The Rhetoric of Romanticism* (New York: Columbia University Press, 1984), pp. 145–238. For discussions of the resemblances between de Man and the modernists, see Ronald Bush "Paul de Man, Modernist," in *Theoretical Issues in Literary History,* ed. David Perkins, (Cambridge: Harvard University Press, 1991), pp. 35–59 and Reed Way Dasenbrock, "Paul de Man, the Modernist as Fascist," *South Central Review* 6 (Summer 1989): 6–18.

8 See Paul de Man, *Wartime Journalism: 1939–1943,* ed. Werner Hamacher et al (Lincoln: University of Nebraska Press, 1988), p. 209 (referred to hereafter as WJ) and Jacques Derrida, "Like the Sound of the Deep Sea within a Shell: Paul de Man's War," *Critical Inquiry* 14 (Summer 1988): 599. Derrida's article is reprinted in R, pp. 127–164.

9 For the earlier articles, see WJ, pp. 13 and 19. Derrida's analysis of this early work is most valuable. See p. 601.

10 See also similar judgments in R, pp. 195 and 428. This is also the explanation suggested by Zeev Sternhell in his review of the controversy, "The Making of a Propagandist," *New Republic,* March 6, 1989, pp. 30–34.

11 For comments on this passage, see John Brenkman, R, p. 22 and Ortwin de Graef, R, p. 107. Derrida discusses similar passages and also shows that de Man sometimes praises French individualism (pp. 617–619).

12 For a similar discussion, see WJ, pp. 313–314.

13 De Man, *The Rhetoric of Romanticism,* p. 122. Goodhart quotes this passage and comments on it in a perceptive discussion of the issue of relation in the controversy (R, p. 227). It is interesting that the word "singular" should figure so largely in the defenses of de Man. Derrida uses it in a number of seemingly innocuous contexts, but Rodolphe Gasché makes a specific, and highly useful, defense based on an explicit argument for singularity. See Derrida 594, 595, 596 and Rodolphe Gasché, "Edges of Understanding," R, pp. 208–220. Despite this reliance on the notion of singularity to quell arguments that would link de Man to his early work, Derrida, Gasché, and others involved in the controversy also demand that their opponents interpret the wartime articles "in context" or in their "totality." See Derrida, pp. 591, 598–599, and 623; Gasché, p. 217; and elsewhere in R, pp. 210, 305, 335 and 338. One might have thought that Derrida had sufficiently debunked these notions.

14 De Man, *Blindness and Insight,* p. 151.

15 De Man, *Allegories of Reading,* p. 255.

16 Peter Dews, "Adorno, Poststructuralism and the Critique of Identity," in *The Problems of Modernity: Adorno and Benjamin,* ed. Andrew Benjamin (London and New York: Routledge, 1989), p. 13.

17 Dews, p. 18.

18 Theodor Adorno, *Aesthetic Theory,* tr. C. Lenhardt (London and New York: Routledge & Kegan Paul, 1984), p. 143.

19 Adorno, p. 48.

Index

235